SAMUEL BECKETT AND MUSIC

Samuel Beckett and Music

EDITED BY

MARY BRYDEN

CLARENDON PRESS · OXFORD
1998

Oxford University Press, Great Clarendon Street, Oxford OX2 6DP

Oxford New York

Athens Auckland Bangkok Bogota Bombay
Buenos Aires Calcutta Cape Town Dar es Salaam
Delhi Florence Hong Kong Istanbul Karachi
Kuala Lumpur Madras Madrid Melbourne
Mexico City Nairobi Paris Singapore
Taipei Tokyo Toronto Warsaw
and associated companies in
Berlin Ibadan

Oxford is a trade mark of Oxford University Press

Published in the United States by
Oxford University Press Inc., New York

British Library Cataloguing in Publication Data
Data available

Library of Congress Cataloging-in-Publication Data
Samuel Beckett and music / edited by Mary Bryden.
Includes bibliographical references and index.
1. Beckett, Samuel, 1906– —Knowledge—Music. 2. Music and
literature—History—20th century. I. Bryden, Mary, 1953– .
PR6003.E282Z817 1997
848'.91409—dc21 97-33497
ISBN 0-19-818427-1

1 3 5 7 9 10 8 6 4 2

Typeset by Best-set Typesetter Ltd., Hong Kong
Printed in Great Britain by
Biddles Ltd, Guildford and King's Lynn

Foreword

BY EDWARD BECKETT

This volume of essays is a welcome addition to the ever-growing commentary on Samuel Beckett's work. There has been much said about the influence of music on his writing, but little has appeared in print. Here at last, we have a wide range of views from both the 'Words' and 'Music' sides, as well as two personal pieces, one by a member of Beckett's family.

I am often asked about Samuel Beckett's musical background, and it might interest readers to know a little about it.

Samuel Beckett came from a musical family. His grandfather's wife, Frances Beckett (née Crothers), had at least one musical composition published, a setting of Tennyson's poem 'Crossing the Bar'—a sentimental drawing-room ballad. His uncle Gerald was an accomplished pianist, and two cousins, John and Walter, are established and gifted musicians.

Neither of Samuel Beckett's parents played instruments or sang, but he was given piano lessons, and practised on the piano at home. He became quite a proficient pianist, favouring Beethoven and Haydn sonatas, which he continued to play throughout his life, as well as works by Chopin and Schubert; he had a piano in his flat in Paris and also in his house in the country. He was a regular concert-goer, either alone or with his wife, who was an excellent pianist and teacher. Many of his friends were musicians; indeed, he collaborated with one, Marcel Mihalovici, and with his cousin, John Beckett.

It is an enigma that, although he loved music, my uncle never had anything that could remotely be called hi-fi. 'Lo-fi' would more accurately describe the audio equipment he owned during his lifetime: small transistor radios and portable cassette players for listening to the voice recordings that he was sent. Any LP discs that he was given were passed on to me, for, although he did not have one himself, he had bought me a record player! He did, however, listen to music at friends' houses, and, as well as the old favourites, he became interested in the music of Berg, Dallapiccola, and Webern.

Perhaps his love of words and music coincided most in Schubert's settings of Heine and Goethe. He loved these songs, and used to sing some of them to his own accompaniment in a most moving way.

I am sure that this book will be of great interest to all lovers of Beckett's texts, and help perhaps to throw some light on this hitherto relatively unexplored area of 'Beckett and Music'.

Acknowledgements

I am indebted to many people who have helped and advised me in the course of what has been a fascinating but often very complex project. These include Edward Beckett and John Beckett, whose warm encouragement I greatly appreciate. James Knowlson, as always, furnished much useful information, especially concerning little-known musical settings. Ruby Cohn, Everett Frost, Bill McCormack, and Robert Robertson all provided crucial suggestions for contacts at an early stage of the project. Philippe Albèra and Roger Hinsley both shared with me their musical expertise, and in this respect I am particularly grateful to Henrietta Brougham, Ian Pace, and Paul Rhys, who went far beyond the call of duty in their repeated helpfulness. I enjoyed fruitful conversations with Frans Haverkamp and Erick Aufderheyde. Erick was also extremely kind in providing bibliographical information. The composers Richard Barrett, Gerald Barry, Gyula Csapó, and William Kraft all supplied assistance, as did the percussionist James Wood. Pam Kay's secretarial assistance was much appreciated. Ron Knowles, Ray Loveridge, and Yoshiki Tajiri all passed on to me information which might not otherwise have come my way. In addition to translating from Italian one of the essays in the volume, my colleague Walter Redfern has been constant in his encouragement of the project; I am fortunate in having been able to draw upon his reserves of expertise, practicality, and humour. The artist Avigdor Arikha was kind enough to allow me to use a reproduction of his *Cello in its Box* (1985) on the front jacket. I acknowledge kind copyright permissions from Jérôme Lindon (for one page from Beckett's 'Whoroscope' notebook), Theodore Presser Company (for one page from Earl Kim's *Dead Calm*), Schott (for excerpts from the score of Wolfgang Fortner's *That Time*), Universal Editions (for excerpts from the score of Morton Feldman's *Neither*), and Éditions Jean Michel Place (for permission to translate and adapt two essays—by Jean-Yves Bosseur and Edith Fournier—which had appeared in French in the special Beckett issue of *Revue d'esthétique* in 1986). Finally, I recall with pleasure stimulating conversations with my final-year undergraduate students upon the subject of the musicality of Beckett. One of them, Dominic Gregr, produced a recorder in class one day and gave a breathtaking performance of *Music for a Bird*, by the Swiss composer Hans-Martin Linde. He alleged that it bore a keen resemblance to the musical dynamic of Samuel Beckett. He was absolutely right.

M.B.

Contents

Notes on Contributors

Philippe Albèra studied music at the Conservatoire of Geneva, and at Paris VIII. He established the Contrechamps concerts in 1976, and the Contrechamps Ensemble in 1980. He founded the journal *Contrechamps* in 1983, and has edited it ever since. In 1991 he established Éditions Contrechamps. He has been Artistic Director of the Salle Patiño in Geneva since 1983, is a music-programming consultant for France-Culture, and an Adviser for the Festival d'Automne in Paris. As well as editing texts by composers, he has written extensively on twentieth-century composers, including Schoenberg, Berio, Zimmermann, Ives, Ferneyhough, Nono, Holliger, and Kurtág.

Clarence Barlow was born in 1945 into the English-speaking minority of Calcutta. He began composing in 1957, writing twelve-tone music by 1965. Moving to Cologne in 1968, he regularly attended the composition classes of Zimmermann and Stockhausen, as well as studying electronic music at the Cologne Music Academy and at the Institute of Sonology in Utrecht. He began to use computers as compositional tools in 1971, his interests centring upon the use of tonality and metricism as number-generated phenomena. After periods of work at the electronic studios at EMS (Stockholm) and IRCAM (Paris), Barlow began composing from a home-based computer. He now intersperses this with teaching and organizational work, including the International Summer Courses for New Music at Darmstadt, the Cologne Music Academy, and the Institute of Sonology at the Royal Conservatory in The Hague. He continues to pursue the development of his real-time pitch and rhythm composition programme AUTOBUSK, and of the manipulation of sound-waves as the source of musical timbre.

Walter Beckett was born in Dublin in 1914. His father was first cousin to Samuel Beckett's father. Like Samuel Beckett, Walter Beckett attended Portora Royal School and then Trinity College Dublin. He took his IRAM in 1934, his B.Mus. and ARCO in 1936, and obtained his doctorate in 1947. He was music critic to the *Irish Times* from 1946 to 1952, and studied conducting in Rome. His work includes compositions for symphony orchestra (including *Dublin Symphony; Symphonic Suite in Three Movements; The Falaingin Dances*), chamber music, song cycles (including *Golden Hair*, for mezzo soprano or baritone, to words by James Joyce), piano and organ pieces. Many of his arrangements and orchestral suites based upon Irish airs were written for RTE Radio. In 1956, Walter Beckett's biography of Liszt appeared (since translated into several languages), and in 1958 he collaborated with Humphrey Searle in *Ballet Music*. He was for many years Professor of Harmony and Composition at the Royal Irish Academy of Music, and in 1975 his *First Harmony Course* was published. Walter Beckett died in April 1996.

Luciano Berio was born in 1925 in Oneglia, Italy. He studied at the Milan Conservatoire, where he obtained his composition diploma in 1950. Berio's distinguished international career as composer, conductor, and teacher has included periods of teaching at Darmstadt, Dartington, Cologne, and Harvard. From 1965 to 1972 he taught at the Juilliard School of Music, where he also conducted the Juilliard Ensemble, founded by him. He has worked at Italian Radio, and at IRCAM in Paris, where he worked in close association with Pierre Boulez. Berio has been awarded many prizes for his contributions to contemporary music, including the Italia Prize, the Sibelius Prize, and, in 1989, the Siemens Prize. In the summer of 1995, his seventieth birthday was commemorated in concerts at the London Proms, where his *Shofar* received its première. Berio's extensive *œuvre* includes stage, orchestral, vocal, chamber, and instrumental works.

Jean-Yves Bosseur was born in Paris in 1947. He studied composition in Cologne with Stockhausen and Pousseur, and obtained his doctorate from the University of Paris I. He is co-founder of the group 'Intervalles', and has won prizes from the Royaumont Foundation (France) and the Gaudeamus Foundation (Netherlands). His compositions include ballet music, film music (for Arrabal's *Viva la muerte*), and music for television, radio, and stage (including plays by Arrabal, Ionesco, Beckett, Shakespeare, and Achternbusch). He has written several books on contemporary music.

Mary Bryden is a Senior Lecturer in the Department of French Studies at the University of Reading. Her undergraduate and doctoral degrees were undertaken at the University of Reading, and her Master's degree is from Salford University. She is Joint Director (with John Pilling) of the Beckett International Foundation at Reading University. Her book on *Women in the Prose and Drama of Samuel Beckett: Her Own Other* was published in 1993, and in 1992 she co-edited with John Pilling a collection of essays on unpublished manuscripts held in the Beckett Collection at Reading. She is completing a monograph on *Beckett and the Idea of God*, and she also has research interests in French feminism and modern drama.

Melanie Daiken was born in London of a Canadian mother and a Dublin-born father. She studied at the Royal Academy of Music. In 1965, she was awarded a French Government Scholarship to study composition with Olivier Messiaen, and piano with Yvonne Loriod. She is now a Lecturer in Composition and Academic Studies at the Royal Academy of Music. As well as *Quatre poèmes*, her works include orchestral, vocal, and chamber works.

Edith Fournier is a scholar and distinguished translator who has translated a number of Beckett's texts. These include (into French) *Proust*, *Cap au pire* [*Worstward Ho*], *Quad, et autres pièces pour la télévision* [*Quad, and other television plays*], and *Bande et Sarabande* [*More Pricks Than Kicks*] (all published by Éditions de Minuit, Paris). She has also translated [into English] *L'Image* [*The Image*] and *La Falaise* [*The Cliff*].

Everett Frost is a Professor at the Institute of Film and Television at New York University, specializing in contemporary media and drama. His radio productions include *The Beckett Festival of Radio Plays*, the Brecht/Weill radio cantata, *The Flight of Lindbergh*, *Stories from the Spirit World: The Myths and Legends of Native Americans*, and the *SoundPlay* and *SoundPlay/Hörspiel* radio drama series.

Julian Garforth was born in 1964 in Sheffield, South Yorkshire. He studied French and German at Birmingham University, where he also completed a doctorate (in 1992) entitled 'Samuel Beckett in Germany: His Work in the German Theatre'. He has published articles on Beckett, and is currently working on a book (based upon his Ph.D. thesis) examining Beckett's position in the German Theatre.

Philip Glass was born in 1937. He studied at the Peabody Conservatory in Baltimore, the University of Chicago, and the Juilliard School of Music. He studied with Nadia Boulanger in Paris (1964–6), and was Musical Director of the Mabou Mines Company from 1965 to 1974. He founded the Philip Glass Ensemble in 1968. His works include operas, film scores, theatre music, and instrumental works, and his numerous awards include the Benjamin Award (1961).

Miron Grindea was born in Moldavia in 1909. Educated at Bucharest University and the Sorbonne, he moved permanently to England (from Romania) in 1939. In 1941, he founded the *ADAM International Review*, of which he remained Editor until his death. During the war, he was a founder member (with Benjamin Britten, Stephen Spender, and Henry Moore) of the International Arts Guild, and undertook work with the BBC European Service and Ministry of Information. A Chevalier de la Légion d'Honneur (1974), a Commander of the Order of Arts and Letters, France (1985), and a recipient of the Prix de l'Académie Française (1955) and of the Lundquist Literary Prize, Sweden (1965), he not only gave coast-to-coast lecture tours in the USA, but was also a Visiting Lecturer in many universities, including Paris, Aix-en-Provence, Athens, Karachi, Kyoto, Montreal, Toronto, Reykjavik, and Jerusalem. Miron Grindea was awarded the MBE in 1977 and the OBE in 1986. A regular contributor to national newspapers and literary journals, his published books included *Malta Calling* (1943), *Jerusalem: A Literary Chronicle of 3000 Years* (1968) (second edition: *Jerusalem, the Holy City in Literature*, with preface by Graham Greene, 1982), and *Natalie Clifford Barney* (1963). Miron Grindea died in November 1995.

Veronica Heath was born in 1962, in Birmingham. She has taught part-time since 1988 at Reading University, where she obtained both her BA (1985) and her Ph.D. (1989). Her specialisms are nineteenth- and twentieth-century French and English literature.

Heinz Holliger, oboist and composer, was born in Switzerland in 1939. Having studied oboe with Cassagnaud and composition with Veress at the Bern Conservatory, he studied oboe and piano at the Paris Conservatory. He won first prize in the Geneva competition in 1959, and thereafter played in the Basle Symphony Orchestra. In his subsequent international career, he has toured widely as a soloist, and given master classes, and his compositions include stage, orchestral, vocal, and chamber works, as well as pieces for piano and organ. His outstanding mastery of the oboe has elicited works written for him by composers such as Berio, Henze, and Stockhausen.

Earl Kim, an American composer of Korean descent, was born in Dinuba, California, in 1920. He studied composition and theory at the University of California, Los Angeles, with Schoenberg, and then became a student of Bloch at the University of California at Berkeley. He took his MA at Berkeley in 1952. He has taught at Berkeley, Princeton, and Harvard Universities, and has also made appearances as a pianist and conductor. His compositions include opera, orchestral music, chamber and vocal pieces, and among his awards have been the Prix de Paris, and the Brandeis University Creative Arts Award.

Catherine Laws is a pianist and a Lecturer in Music at De Montfort University, Leicester. She is currently completing a doctorate examining the musicality of Beckett's language.

Giacomo Manzoni was born in Milan in 1932. He studied composition at Messina and at the Milan Conservatory, and began his career as an orchestral player and choral director. As well as being music critic of *L'Unità*, he has taught extensively, at the Conservatory of Milan and of Bologna, as well as in Berlin and Fiesole. He has given seminars and courses in many parts of the world. Giacomo Manzoni has written prolifically, undertaking translations of Adorno and Schoenberg, and contributing essays on early and modern composers (including Monteverdi, Brahms, and Dallapiccola) to a variety of publications. He has won several international prizes for his compositions, which include theatre, vocal, orchestral, and chamber works. In 1991 he was awarded the 'Omaggio a M. Mila' prize for his pedagogical activity.

John Pilling is Professor of English and European Literature and Joint Director of the Beckett International Foundation at Reading University. He edited the *Journal of Beckett Studies* from 1979 to 1985. His books include: *Samuel Beckett* (Routledge & Kegan Paul, 1976), *Frescoes of the Skull: the Later Prose and Drama of Samuel Beckett* (with James Knowlson), (John Calder, 1979), and *Fifty Modern European Poets* (Heinemann, 1982). He edited *The Cambridge Companion to Beckett* (Cambridge University Press, 1994), and co-edited (with Mary Bryden) *The Ideal Core of the Onion: Reading Beckett Archives* (Beckett International Foundation, 1992).

Walter Redfern is a Professor of French at Reading University. He has translated into French his own study, *Puns*, and the novel written in English by Georges Darien: *Gottlieb Krumm*. His books include studies of: Giono, Nizan, Queneau, Darien, Vallès, Tournier, Sartre, and clichès and coinages. He has also written BBC scripts on parts of speech.

Roger Reynolds lives in Del Mar, California, where he composes and writes. He is Professor of Music at the University of California, San Diego, and won the prestigious Pulitzer Prize in Music in 1989 for a string orchestra composition, *Whispers out of Time*, based on a poem by John Ashbery.

Peter Szendy was born in Paris in 1966. A musicologist, and principal editor of *Cahiers de l'Ircam*, he is the author of numerous articles on contemporary music and musicians, including György Kurtág and Emmanuel Nunes. He is a committee member of the Paris Festival d'Automne, of the Ensemble Inter-Contemporain, and of the journal *Contrechamps*.

Brigitta Weber was born in 1963 in Melle, Lower Saxony. Her Ph.D., awarded in 1992, was entitled 'Die Opernkompositionen von Wolfgang Fortner'. She has worked (1992–5) as head of the Theatre Museum and Archive of the Lower Saxony State Theatre, in Hanover, and, more recently, as a musical director with the Lower Saxony Opera in Hanover. The legal assignee of Wolfgang Fortner, Dr Weber has published on contemporary music and theatre history.

Harry White is Professor of Music at University College Dublin. A graduate of the University of Dublin (Trinity College) and the University of Toronto, he holds degrees in Music, in Modern English and American Literature, and in Musicology. His research interests include music at the imperial court in Vienna (1680–1740), the history of music in Ireland, and the history of musicology since 1945. He has published widely on these topics and is a contributor to many journals of musicological research. His books include *Musicology in Ireland*, *Music and the Church* (co-edited with Gerard Gillen), and *Johann Joseph Fux and the Music of the Austro-Italian Baroque*, and he has also published on the relationship between music and drama in the *Irish University Review* and in *Modern Drama*.

Katharine Worth is Emeritus Professor of Drama and Theatre Studies in the University of London, Honorary Research Fellow at Royal Holloway, and Visiting Professor at King's College London. She is the author of *The Irish Drama of Europe from Yeats to Beckett* and many other books and articles on English and Irish drama. She edited *Beckett the Shape Changer* and adapted Beckett's novella, *Company*, for the stage. In collaboration with David Clark, she produced *Eh Joe* and three of Beckett's radio plays: for two of these, new music was written by Humphrey Searle.

Introduction

'A book could be written on the significance of music in the work of Proust', wrote Samuel Beckett in his 1931 study of Proust.[1] Over sixty years later, it seemed to me that Beckett's writing had supplied a similar proposition: namely that a book could—indeed should—be written on the significance of music in the work of Beckett.

That the experience of music was profoundly important to Beckett was clear to those who knew him, including several amongst the contributors to this volume. The artist Avigdor Arikha spent many hours listening to music with Beckett and asserts that 'Listening to music was essential to him.'[2] Although Beethoven, Schubert, Haydn, and Brahms featured prominently, they also listened, during the 1950s, to twentieth-century serialist music. Indeed, although Beckett's interest in dodecaphonic music is not generally recognized, his correspondence with Thomas MacGreevy reveals a positive response to Schoenberg, Berg, and Webern as early as 1949.[3]

Moreover, Beckett's sensitivity to a broad range of music was part of a much wider attunement to the aural medium, to ambient sounds, and to silence. The implications of this are multiple. Perhaps the musicality of Beckett's writing finds its clearest manifestation within the dynamics of theatre or live reading, such that many actors, when directed by Beckett, have reported feeling like musical instruments or channels of resonance. Very often, the precarious negotiations between lightness and weight, humour and desperation, regret and bravado, surface most surely when Beckett's texts are read aloud.

Nevertheless, all of Beckett's texts, whether they be prose, poetry, or drama, are the product of one who, by his own account, *heard* them in advance of writing them.[4] They abound with evocations of aural memories, sounds and their withdrawal, acoustic qualities, rhythms and melodies. If Beckett heard them in advance, however, he was not merely a passive receptor or conduit for them. On the contrary, the achievement of a satisfactory auditory balance was a matter—as his many draft

---

[1] Samuel Beckett, *Proust, and Three Dialogues with Georges Duthuit* (London: John Calder, 1965), 91.
[2] See James Knowlson, *Damned to Fame: The Life of Samuel Beckett* (London: Bloomsbury, 1996), 495.
[3] See, for example, Letter No. 178 (27 Mar. 1949) in Trinity College Dublin MS 10402.
[4] See, for example, Beckett's remark to André Bernold: 'J'ai toujours écrit pour une voix' [I've always written for a voice], in André Bernold, *L'Amitié de Beckett* (Paris: Hermann, 1992), 107.

manuscripts demonstrate—of multiple refinements, cancellations, retunings. Patrick Bowles quickly discovered this infinitely painstaking method of composition when working with Beckett on the translation of *Molloy*: 'Occasionally Beckett would throw the cat among the chickens by saying, "Give it a bit of rhythm". That could mean re-casting an entire paragraph. One could not just inject a drumbeat into one phrase alone. It had to play its part in the paragraph.'[5]

Whether read aloud or silently, Beckett's careful words resemble elements of a musical score, coordinated by and for the ear, to sound and resound. They are lean and muscular, never lush. They play a discrete and discreet part in the text(ure) which they form. As well as being endowed with an intense and immediate musicality, however, they frequently create and evoke sound-scapes within the narrative itself. Here are to be found sounds to remember with, as in that uncharacter-istically peaceful segment in *Molloy*: 'None but tranquil sounds, the clicking of mallet and ball, a rake on pebbles, a distant lawn-mower, the bell of my beloved church. And birds of course, blackbird and thrush, their song sadly dying'.[6] Yet there is also a musical grammar of pain in Beckett's work, as with the narrator in *Malone Dies*: 'I feel, deep down in my trunk, I cannot be more explicit, pains that seem new to me. I think they are chiefly in my back. They have a kind of rhythm, they even have a kind of little tune.'[7]

These two examples illustrate the protean functions of music in Beckett's writing. The first example is a finely ironized sound-painting: the picturesque orchestra of a summer's afternoon, recruited to manu-facture a moment of nostalgic stillness. Music here fulfils its common-place role as mood-bearer. The second example proceeds in inverse direction. Here, the mood or language of discomfort is *translated* into music. The music is embodied. It both plays upon the nerves, and forms a vector for the pain-waves.

Beckett's music, then, makes demands upon its listeners. It will never be elevator-music. It will not necessarily give the auditor a lift. But neither is it depressor-music. Above all, his compositions—like those of all great artists—are potentially dangerous, polyvalent. They may pipe followers down unaccustomed alleyways. They may peter out altogether on the path to extinction. In her autobiography, the actress Billie Whitelaw describes how acting under Beckett's direction in *Footfalls* seemed to impel her towards a spiralling process of evaporation in sound and rhythm: 'As the play progressed, I began to feel more and

---

[5] Patrick Bowles, 'How to Fail: Notes on Talks with Samuel Beckett', *PN Review*, 20/4 (Mar.–Apr. 1994), 24–38 (p. 24).
[6] Samuel Beckett, *Molloy*, in *The Beckett Trilogy* (London: Picador, 1979), 85.
[7] Id., *Malone Dies*, ibid. 182.

more like a "thing" of the spirit, something that was vaporising as we went on. Smoke has a tone and a rhythm. Sometimes it whirls around, sometimes it almost disappears, only to start whirling again in a gush, before disappearing in a diminuendo of nothingness.'[8]

Given the almost palpable musicality of Beckett's writing, it is perhaps not surprising, then, that the number of composers who have felt drawn to affiliate their compositions with Beckett texts is considerable. Moreover, it is noticeable that the most successful of these Beckett-inspired works are those which have respected that very dynamic of diminution of which Whitelaw speaks. Once the reader/listener becomes committed to that uncompromising sparseness, Beckett's texts often deliver a through-route, or a route to a space which is not as threatening as it might first appear.

Such was the experience of the Hungarian singer, Ildikó Monyók. Badly injured in a road accident in 1982, she lost the power of speech, and could no longer write or count. Only after seven years of complete dumbness did she slowly begin to recover the ability to speak. On hearing her hesitant attempts to sing again, the composer György Kurtág recognized in her the same struggle to find a voice which he discerned in Beckett's last text, 'What is the Word'.[9]

Using the Hungarian translation of the work, since Monyók knows neither French nor English, Kurtág wrote a first setting of the text (Op. 30a). This preliminary version was written when Monyók, still finding speech difficult, was beginning to experiment with singing. The piece, for reciter and piano only, constituted vocal therapy for the singer, with its carefully prescribed pitches of speaking, screaming, and shouting. The second version (Op. 30b), for reciter, singers, and instrumental ensemble, adds extra complexity to the impassioned search—of Beckett, and of the newly voiced woman—for the unnamed or unnamable word. In Kurtág's setting of the longest line of the Beckett text, the reciter joins with the other singers in a slow-swelling unison melody, beginning on Middle C, which seems to be reaching out to a (possibly conceivable) word. Kurtág's *What is the Word?*[10]—dedicated to Monyók—was performed as part of the London Promenade Concerts on 30 August 1996. Monyók gave full vent to her now strong and flexible vocal capability. The reaction of the audience left one in no doubt that Beckett's fading but struggling text, conceived musically by Kurtág, had been perceived as a most remarkable channel for the rebirth of a singer.

---

[8] Billie Whitelaw, *Billie Whitelaw ... Who He?* (London: Hodder and Stoughton, 1995), 146.

[9] See Samuel Beckett, *As the Story was Told* (London: John Calder, 1990), 131–4.

[10] Kurtág's title inserts a final question mark which is not there in Beckett's original.

Kurtág's *What is the Word?* demonstrates an extraordinarily close alignment between text and music. Similarly, it seemed to me essential in preparing this book to bring together the perceptions of both composers and scholars. Yet composers primarily write music, rather than *about* music. One or two wrote to me regretfully to say that, while supportive of the project, they had found it impossible to set out in words what they were about when engaging musically with Beckett's texts. Scholars, on the other hand, produce textual analysis, but may not feel equipped to broach the technicalities of describing musical composition and performance. Accordingly, the book's contents are divided into two main sections. Rather than designating these 'Theory' and 'Practice', I have opted to gather them under the respective headings of 'Words' and 'Music'. Although these sections are osmotic, rather than hermetic, they nevertheless denote two differing, if complementary, spheres of creativity.

It also became clear at an early stage that, since musical responses to Beckett's work have occurred in many different cultural contexts, the collection should be as international as possible. Thus, the book brings together contributors from England, France, Germany, Ireland, Italy, the Netherlands, Switzerland, and the United States. Most of the essays have been written specially for this volume; the remaining few have been adapted and translated, in collaboration with the authors, and are appearing for the first time in English.

The first part, 'Words', consists of ten chapters. Seven of them focus upon particular composers, all of whom have distinguished themselves in their Beckett-inspired compositions. Thus, Katharine Worth writes of Humphrey Searle; Philippe Albèra and Peter Szendy of Heinz Holliger; Edith Fournier of Marcel Mihalovici; Everett Frost and Catherine Laws of Morton Feldman; Brigitta Weber of Wolfgang Fortner. Of the remaining three essays, John Pilling examines Beckett's treatment of music and of Schopenhauer within his early work *Proust*; Harry White draws a range of Beckett texts into affiliation with techniques of serialism in modern music; my own chapter considers the musicality of Beckett under the headings of listening, composing, and conducting.

The second part, 'Music', consists of eight chapters by contemporary composers. They include interviews with two composers—Luciano Berio and Philip Glass—who speak of the influence of Beckett upon their work. Roger Reynolds describes working with several Beckett texts; Giacomo Manzoni sets the context for the collage of Beckett texts which constitute his *Parole da Beckett*; Clarence Barlow outlines a piano setting of *Ping*, while Jean-Yves Bosseur writes of his setting of *Ping*'s French version, *Bing*; Melanie Daiken recalls her compositions based upon Beckett's poetry, and Earl Kim provides a musical example from his *Watt*-prompted piece, *Dead Calm*.

In between these two sections are two shorter and more personal pieces. One is by Walter Beckett. A second cousin of Beckett, Dr Beckett was a fine musician in his own right, as well as a gifted writer and teacher. The other is by Miron Grindea, for so long a prominent figure in literary circles, and the founder of the *Adam International Review*. In correspondence and/or conversations during 1995, both Dr Beckett and Dr Grindea expressed to me their warm support and encouragement for this volume. Sadly, both have died during the past year. I had already decided to bracket their careful and committed pieces together under the heading of 'Memories'. These memories of Beckett—among the last written pieces which they undertook—have now taken on an added poignancy of memory. Their authors are remembered here with affection and respect.

Finally, it should be added that this is a volume which has both unifying and disparate elements. On one level, composers and scholars who 'spark' to Beckett's writing speak the same language. On another level—that of their professional expertise—they may not. Inevitably, some of the deep-structure musical analysis contained here may appear demanding to the non-specialist. Nevertheless, I trust that, just as a piece of music may contain movements of varying complexity and intensity, this collection may engage variously and multiformly.

Part I

Words

Words for Music Perhaps

KATHARINE WORTH

My title is borrowed from Yeats, who used it for a collection of his poems admired by Beckett and possibly in his mind at the time of writing *Words and Music* (Words's 'Arise then and go now' makes sly allusion to 'The Lake Isle of Innisfree'). The tentative, exploratory ring of Yeats's 'Perhaps' seemed rather apt for Beckett's dramatic uses of music in *Words and Music* (1962) and *Cascando* (1964). I offer a few reflections on the role of music in these plays, arising from the experience of producing new versions of them (in 1973 and 1984 respectively), with music by Humphrey Searle. I cannot speak of the music in musical terms, only from the viewpoint of someone seeking to understand better the thrust of the plays and how music enters into this. It is the account of a personal response, though I hope it may have some general interest.

The music for the two plays first became a question for me in the early 1970s when I was presenting a series of public lectures in London on Samuel Beckett's *œuvre*. I had hoped to illustrate my lecture on the radio plays with illustrations from the BBC productions but discovered that recordings were not to be had. The BBC would arrange for individual listening *in situ* but had no loan system; private off-air recordings were not routinely kept in those days, and in any case the plays had not been re-broadcast since the transmission of the first productions of the BBC's Third Programme a decade earlier.[1]

It was *Words and Music* and *Cascando* which raised the hardest questions to answer without the aid of sound recordings. The plays seemed to suggest: might music be combined with words to tap springs of imagination inaccessible to words alone? 'Perhaps' was as far as the answer went on the printed page: each play contained a measure of achievement but appeared at the end to sound a note of frustration or incompleteness. *Words and Music* ends with Croak shuffling off and Words uttering a deep sigh; *Cascando* with Voice cut off in mid-

---

[1] *Words and Music* was first broadcast on the BBC Third Programme, 13 Nov. 1962, with repeats on 7 Dec. 1962 and on 7 May 1963. *Cascando* was first broadcast on the BBC Third Programme, on 6 Oct. 1964, with a repeat on 28 Oct. 1964. *Cascando* in its original French was broadcast by RTF, Paris, in 1963.

sentence, as far away as ever from the 'rest . . . sleep' he imagines he would achieve if he could finish his story.

Wherever one looked in the texts there was a sense of enigma. Music in *Words and Music* had been given a remarkably vivid dramatic presence, even without aid of sound, but the effect was, paradoxically, to make it more mysterious. It was a being at once independent (no one else in the plays had its powers of expression) and—like Music in *Cascando*—totally dependent on a controlling force to allow it full voice.

To what extent this controlling force really was in control of the process he conducted was another teasing question, within the plays as for the reader. Croak and Opener are formally in command, each of his particular 'text-music tandem' (Beckett's phrase). Yet whether they drive or are driven is uncertain. If they have a ruling purpose, it is wrapped round in clouds of doubt and unknowing. They have apparently no creative ability as musicians yet are compelled to create through music as well as words. Croak hands out themes—'Love', 'Age'— unaccompanied by instructions on how to realize them: his 'servants' have to stumble by roundabout ways to reach the desired epiphany. Opener is still more in the dark about his connection with Music: 'And that . . . is that mine too?'

Of course there was plenty to discuss with an audience, even without benefit of music and voices. There were the parallels, drolly hinted at in the text, between the struggles of Croak and Opener to produce a work of art and those engaged in by their author. Beckett had said of *Cascando*: 'It does I suppose in a way show what passes for my mind and what passes for its work.'[2] A wry joke, but it was true that the central fact of his life—his commitment to composition—was made his subject in these two plays as never before in his theatre. The pains of artistic creation, an esoteric topic, became living and real, dramatized through such odd, poignant, and drily humorous relationships as that of Croak with 'Joe' and 'Bob'.

But what would the sound of music add to these expressive texts? The idea of music's dramatic role was already vivid on the page. In *Words and Music* a highly coloured personality came through textual directions of almost novelistic fullness. It was possible to think one knew him to the full, or at least in all his sportiveness: the 'humble muted adsum' he returns to Croak's call; the 'soft music worthy of foregoing, great expression' which he supplies as a follow-up to rhetorical waffling from Words. But the music was really a great unknown quantity. How its sensuous impact on a listener might affect interpretation was something

---

[2] Letter of 21 Sept. 1962, in Harvard Collection.

no reading could tell. 'Opera' was a term that had been applied (though not by Beckett) to these fusions of words and music.[3] If it had any relevance (as I guessed it had), music must affect the emotional imagination of the listener in some way. It could well tip the balance of feeling in those equivocal endings.

For future use, I knew I must have musical illustrations and wondered about the possibility of making recordings, given the difficulty of buying or borrowing them. The University of London at that time had an Audio-Visual Centre, one of whose chief functions was to provide audio-visual materials requested by teachers of the University. The director, Michael Clarke, generously supported my proposal for a programme of productions, and a talented senior producer at the Centre, David Clark, then chiefly engaged in work for scientists, seized with relish the opportunity to direct the more adventurous and subtle technical operation required for the Beckett plays.

Beckett kindly gave me permission, the first of several, to make a new production with the Audio-Visual Centre (for non-commercial, limited educational use). We began boldly with *Eh Joe*, having had the good fortune to engage the interest of Patrick Magee in playing Joe. Then in 1973 we turned to *Words and Music*, expecting at that stage simply to make a new production of an existing text, using the music written for it by John Beckett. But when I requested the composer's permission to use his music, he told me, courteously but without explanation, that he had withdrawn it. (I later learned that he had become diffident about it, despite its having pleased Beckett.) We were thus faced with a more formidable proposition—of commissioning new music—should Beckett agree to our doing so.

I had no idea whether this was likely. It might be that he would think of the play with its music as a 'seamless coat', like the first radio play, *All That Fall*, which had Schubert's music delicately woven into its dramatic fabric. In the stage plays too, I recalled that music was carefully specified by the author. Krapp sang 'Now the day is over', a neatly appropriate hymn (later cut by Beckett as being rather too neat); Winnie's tune from *The Merry Widow* was exactly right for her. When a tune wasn't specified, it was because it didn't matter, as with Vladimir's dog song which called only for a droning impression of words going round and round.

Music in *Words and Music* was in a different category, of course, being written for the occasion and initially an unknown quantity to the author. But John Beckett was Beckett's cousin, they had collaborated

---

[3] 'This play is the closest thing there is in the Beckett canon to an opera.' Said of *Words and Music* by Clas Zilliacus in his *Beckett and Broadcasting* (Abo: Abo Akademi, 1976), 103.

before and had no doubt worked closely together on *Words and Music*. I wondered if Beckett would be willing to have a character so well established as his Music unstitched and remade.

He was prepared to allow it, however, and when I asked if there were any composer he would care to recommend, he suggested Humphrey Searle. This reduced much of the apprehension that had accompanied the idea of changing the music. Only later did I realize how exactly judged that recommendation was, and why Searle's musical style might have struck Beckett as having possibilities for this play.

The production at last began to form when Humphrey Searle accepted the invitation to write new music. He told me he was pleased that Beckett had suggested him, also that he had been invited to compose music for a new radio play Beckett was writing for the BBC.[4] He gave me the impression when we met of being, though a shy man, temperamentally in tune with the drily humorous, idiosyncratic world of *Words and Music*, with its fantastical twists and turns of feeling. I knew he had set to music a number of virtuoso modernist pieces, notably by Edith Sitwell (*Gold Coast Customs*, 1949) and James Joyce (*The Riverrun*, 1951) and I gathered that he had recently completed a song cycle, *Les Fleurs du mal*, a Baudelaire-inspired work that might well have had a special appeal for Beckett, who had once translated Rimbaud's *Le Bateau ivre*. The self-awareness of *Words and Music*, its fondness for parody and dissonance, its leaps of style, seemed bound to attract the interest of a composer who had been so closely associated with modern movements, had studied with Webern, and was adept in producing music for a wide range of media, including radio and film. How he would react to the romantic and mystical aspects of the play I was curious to discover.

Humphrey wanted me to hear John Beckett's music before we started and arranged for it to be played for us at Broadcasting House. I liked its austerity, and touches such as a faint suggestion of plainsong which picked up the quasi-medieval notes in the text. It was hard to see why the composer had withdrawn it. But of course the play was so many-sided that it must offer other ways in, to other composers. Humphrey would bring a different style, but he was anxious for it to tune with Beckett's concept, as John Beckett's had done in his. He had met Beckett in Paris some time before[5] and thought of going again now to discuss his approach to the play, but Beckett thought this unnecessary. Having proposed a composer, he was ready to leave him full scope to be himself.

---

[4] Letter to the writer, 14 Sept. 1973. This project did not develop.
[5] Mrs Searle told me that they had met through Barbara Bray, but she could not recall the date of the meeting in Paris.

This seemed interestingly different from the degree of control he had been known to exert over directors and designers.

First priority for Humphrey was the timing of each piece of music: it had to be done early because of the close interaction between actors and music (twice culminating in near-operatic sequences) and the fact that we had very limited time with the actors. They were accepting modest fees for this non-commercial production, and had to fit us into cracks in busy schedules. We obtained a rough timing which brought out the very different speech rhythms: Patrick's Words expansive and florid, Denys Hawthorne's Croak lighter and more hurried. A timing for the music was then arrived at.

What was the music to express? Our discussions were concerned chiefly with shades of mood and specific points of mood-change. The general drift was clear from the text: I summarize here the way it looked at that stage, with Music's role especially in mind.

In the opening sequence, quarrelling with Words or idling on vague themes, Music's tendency was evidently to be histrionic and emotional (its weak point, as Words's was pedantry). It wasn't certain whether there should be an element of self-mockery in this, though it seemed likely. There was surely a touch of irony in its 'humble muted adsum' and obvious scope for it in the 'love and soul music' offered on the 'Love' theme. Beckett's recommendation of Humphrey Searle as composer suggested that such ironic nuances would not come amiss.

The high points of mood-change came with the two lyrics which Music persuades Words to sing. The movement from the first of these to the last was one of stops and starts, impeded by Words's reluctance to commit himself to feeling and Music's over-indulgence in it. Under Croak's direction, they could never take a direct route to a desired end but had to go 'roundabout'. Croak hands out an abstract theme 'Love' (getting only clichés back) when what he really wants is a particular image, the ardently remembered 'face', on which he is brooding when he enters the soundscape.

The play suggested that the romantic vision could only be approached by way of a hard look at life in its unromantic aspect. Music and Words alike shrink from the disagreeable theme, 'Age'. Croak has to force them to collaborate on it: 'Together, dogs!' Once they do, they succeed in creating a lyric. Words hits on the first line—'Age is when to a man'—without aid of music but is hesitant, stumbling. Music has to prompt him, lead him on with 'improvements', help him to transform the wry image of the old man in the ingle, waiting for the 'hag' to see to his creature comforts, into the vision of memory: 'The face in the ashes | That old starlight | On the earth again'.

Conflict seemed to be an essential element in the creative process that was being dramatized. The lengthy narrative in which Words expands the image of the 'face' was a battle between 'cold' and 'warm' approaches. Music would become increasingly impatient with Words's quasi-clinical tone in his account of the beautiful girl in the starlight, returning to normal consciousness after what has clearly been (though this is never made explicit) an ecstatic sexual experience. Words is too expert a narrator not to evoke the scene vividly: the starry sky, the colour returning to the girl's face. But it is left to Music to supply the feeling. When the narrative arrives at the girl's lovely breasts, its 'warm' suggestions culminate in an 'irrepressible burst of spreading and subsiding music'.

This looked like a turning point. Music's outburst could be seen as finally shaking Words out of self-consciousness. As he describes the slow opening of the girl's eyes, he moves hesitantly into deep feeling. 'Then down a little way', he begins, as if still anatomizing the physical beauty, but then, repeating the line, he changes (without irony in Patrick's reading) to: 'Poetic tone. Low'. A lyric begins to shape. Again it needs the confidence of Music, who seems to know from the start that there is a mystical dimension to the ecstasy revealed in the narrative. It is Music who must guide a reformed Words to 'try' and sing of a region beyond words—'All dark no begging | No giving no words | No sense no need'—and of the reward for going 'down': 'one glimpse | Of that wellhead'.

How complete the fulfilment was for the characters at the end of the play still seemed uncertain. Croak, for whom the lyrics were composed, lets fall his club and stumps off, possibly displeased. Words is left longing for more sustenance. 'Music', he begs (changing hastily from the familiar 'Bob' when Music makes a 'brief rude retort'). He is granted a reprise: (of the 'elements already used or wellhead alone', the text says). But he is refused an encore and the play ends with his 'deep sigh'.

There were several questions about tone and mood that couldn't be pursued far from discussion of the text alone; those, for instance, to do with the degree of sentimentality Music's various 'warm' responses should have. Music was instructed by the text at one such point to be 'warmly sentimental'; not likely to be a term of praise from Beckett. But where did sentimentality end? These fine changes of musical tone were left to Humphrey. Music had its own logic, as he remarked. It was now in his hands, he completed his score, and we met with actors and musicians for final rehearsal and recording in the BBC sound studio Michael Clarke had arranged for the event. The music was played by the Sinfonia of London, a small group of strings, woodwinds and percussion, which Humphrey conducted.

The process of performance drew us dangerously far into the process of composition embodied in the play. We listened to the sounds of the 'small orchestra softly tuning up', as in the text, precariously unsure how the 'arias' would register, not yet having heard voices and music together. The outcome seemed at one time about as uncertain for us as for Croak. The actors too were feeling their way. Patrick had played Voice in the original production but this music was new to him and we had not the resources of the BBC: the time for assimilating it had been minimal. He joked that the textual direction, 'Trying to sing', was likely to be only too convincing in performance.

That could not be said of the music. It had the confidence in itself required by the text, both for teaching Words to sing 'true' and for indulging in histrionics. Touches of mockery abounded: the orchestral 'timidity' was mimicry. An ironic sense of enjoyment in the acrimonious exchanges with Words came through the sharp discordancies of violin and cello, flute, oboe, and percussion (pointed up by the mischievous incursions of the glockenspiel). The same ironic dissonances marked the mercurial changes of mood and the showy 'love and soul music'.

It was less easy for a non-musician to distinguish the moments where the music moved in and out of sentimentality: a trained ear was probably needed here. But there was no doubt about the electric contrast with the earlier 'idling' which came about with the lyrics. Orchestral discordancies fell away on the two occasions when a single instrument— first bassoon, then viola—emerged to lead Words into song. It was oddly satisfying in the first lyric, 'Age is when to a man', that the 'Age music', as Beckett had called it, contrived to keep a partly playful note until the moment of transcendence. The bassoon seemed to enjoy a joke by applying its deep-toned resonance to the humdrum detail of the opening: the old man waiting for the hag to put the pan in the bed. 'And bring the toddy', the bassoon reminded, mischievously. But it had already struck out the pure, strong line of melody which would draw Words on to the painfully recovered memory: 'The face in the ashes | That old starlight | On the earth again'.

Humphrey's music appeared to be following its own logic from this point, building up swiftly to a crescendo from the whole orchestra for the 'irrepressible burst of spreading and subsiding' which we had seen as the turning point. The triumphant brio of the music at this point would have been hard for Words to resist. The two 'servants' were really working together now. Patrick's Words, after a last effort to mimic detachment, moved into poetic tone without irony as he dwelt on the vision of the eyes opening. He offered the first line of the lyric, 'Then down a little way', as if to a collaborator, the music. The invitation was taken up by a viola, and a dark, strong melody given back, for the words to cling to. There was a curious impression of the complete 'poem with music' having been there all the time, in some unknown space, waiting for the collaboration to achieve it.

This calm, deep-toned music had no difficulty in suggesting the region beyond words at which Words was aiming. Its sombre downward movement ended with a dramatically upward thrust for the closing image of the 'wellhead'. It compelled Words to raise his voice upward too, aspiring to the same lofty harmony. Words could speak of this image, the wellhead, but he was only 'trying' to sing. The grave melody of the viola gave the impression of being already there. It dwelt on 'wellhead' in a long sustained note, assuring Words that they had reached the transcendent climax of their lyric.

The sensous impact of music and words, in their conflicts and their agreements, had brought about this dark harmony. It was clear by the end that neither could have done without the other. Everything needed its opposite. The austere perceptions of the lyric had only been made possible by the delight in physical beauty which the music had felt freer than the words to celebrate wholeheartedly. I found Humphrey's 'wellhead' melody haunting, so much so that in thinking of the words now, I hear the music playing quietly behind them.

Effects such as these made it harder to envisage the play ending on a note of frustration. Croak's shuffling, non-committal exit seemed to suggest not so much dissatisfaction as the extent to which he had been shaken by the intensity of the achieved vision. He could drop his club; it was no longer needed. So too with Words. His deep sigh, the last sound of the play, now clearly expressed longing to 'sing' again, his sadness as the melody died away. Music emerged as the dominant partner. The tap of Humphrey's baton drew from the orchestra one last tiny reprise, in response to Words's appeal (the emphasis on the wellhead motif). No more would be offered: the work was complete.

The experience of 'hearing' the text suggested that it could be taken as an oblique statement about the shaping power of music in poetic composition. The words of a poem had their own source and force but stumbled till they followed the shape music dictated. Melody and rhythm were in the end what made them 'right' and released the meanings they were seeking. Only Beckett could have made a whole play out of this notion.

'Music always wins', Beckett said, when I played him our recording. He asked me to convey his congratulations to Humphrey and commented that the 'little poem' at the close had come up well.

There was encouragement here for the idea we had been contemplating of going on to the other 'text-music tandem'. It was not for some time that we arrived there: we used to joke that it looked like being a

'Woburn' journey, never finishing. Financial problems, one cause for going slowly, were solved when the Consortium for Drama and Media in Higher Education undertook co-funding. Beckett generously gave permission again, and in 1978 we invited Humphrey formally to write new music for *Cascando*. The further delay (of six years) before the production was completed was due chiefly to Patrick's difficulty in finding spare time in an increasingly heavy programme, and then, sadly, to his illness and death, a very great loss.

Before then, Humphrey had set about composing, with timing as usual the immediate need. In this play there was no interaction between Music and the verbal partner, now known as Voice. Each existed in his own space, not 'cooped up together' in Words's phrase: they sometimes performed separately, sometimes together. What sort of music would be right for Voice's strange story of Woburn, the elusive traveller: always on the move, across dunes, into a boat, out on the open sea, forever being 'changed', never arriving anywhere?

Cascando had been seen by critics as a particularly enigmatic text, one reason being that Music's role was represented only by a dotted line and the directions for performance were minimal. Apart from the silences (in both plays, a crucial feature of the timing) there were only indications of length and volume here and there ('Brief', 'Weakening') and a direction from Opener: 'Full strength'. Beckett had completed his text (in its original French) before Mihalovici produced the music; the two streams of creativity, as in the play, had been separate but collaborative. Different ideas on how this collaboration might work had been noted by Clas Zilliacus, whose comprehensive study of Beckett and broadcasting appeared in 1976.[6] Some critics had imagined Music telling the same story as Voice, others as correcting, changing, or even contradicting it. Another idea, of some gradual convergence between the two, drew support from Opener's line: 'As though they had linked their arms'.

Our circumstances made any of the more complicated approaches impractical. In any case, I felt that the emphasis should fall not so much on adjustments between words and music as on the central mystery: Opener's agony of puzzlement over his obligation to call up both. Lacking directions on tone and mood such as we had had for *Words and Music*, Humphrey would draw them out from Voice's narrative. The two versions of the story would flow together, Music always entering at the point reached by Voice, though free to look forward and backward and to emphasize key themes, in ways the internal structures of the music might suggest.

The chief recurring motif, 'Woburn', would, Humphrey thought, be

---

[6] Zilliacus's book (see n. 3) remains the most detailed and searching study of the topic.

associated with the flute. Other motifs would be the 'island' and 'the journey', one linked with ethereal light and space, the other with restlessness and images of falling, getting up again, walking with a stick and so on. Some of these were homely and humorous—'same old stick [. . .] same old broadbrim'—some darkly agitated.

From a provisional timing based on read-throughs, Humphrey was able to move to the exact timing he required: he then completed the music. It was recorded, with David directing the recording process as before, in the same BBC studio used for *Words and Music*. Humphrey conducted a similar 'small orchestra' of strings, woodwinds, and percussion, the Sinfonietta of London. The effect of this music on first hearing I found exhilarating. It seemed to have captured the high-running tide of feeling in the play, its ups and downs, its restless, sometimes whimsical return to a few haunting, obsessive themes. The theme of 'change' ('he's changed . . . not enough') came through the musical variations with great spirit and naturalness. Underlying dissonances reflected the play's desperate drives and questionings—and there was something less easy to hear from the text alone: its piercing harmonies.

Alas, Humphrey did not live to hear his fine music integrated with the voices of Opener and Voice. He died in 1982, leaving us stricken and keenly missing him. The other severe blow, the death of Patrick Magee, much mourned by us, meant that we had to search for an actor to play Voice in his place, and find an Opener to match him. In 1984, we had the good fortune to interest David Warrilow and Sean Barrett in the roles.

The meticulous exactitude of Humphrey's timing—1′30″, 80″, and so on at the very start of the proceedings—had always impressed our production team, unused to working with a professional musician. Now they stood us in good stead indeed. The final recording was made[7] in a studio of the Audio-Visual Centre, where David was now director, following Michael Clarke's retirement. The actors had not met before and we had wondered if the two days planned for rehearsing, playing back to the music, and recording would be adequate. But they accomplished this with ease within a day. Humphrey's music led the way, issuing from the recording space, as if from some empyrean where it lived on, making his presence in the studio almost palpable.

The effect of the music in its full setting, it seemed to me, was magically to expand the play. A story was being told in a dimension which curiously transformed it. Intricate waves of sound carried Woburn's bark in directions the music had no doubt about. A sharply

---

[7] Our production of *Cascando* was recorded on 8 Sept. 1984; of *Words and Music*, on 12 Dec. 1973.

playful note sounded through some of the discordancies among the strings and woodwinds, inviting the listener to recognize an element of comic battle going on between breathless Voice and would-be olympian Opener. There were some similarities here to the tug-of-war between 'cold' Words and 'warm' Music in *Words and Music*.

The pleasures as well as the pains of composition were brought out by the music through piquant blendings of instruments and changes of rhythm. It had a brio which pointed up the relish for evocative detail in Voice's narrative—as much part of it as the anxiety to finish. The element of anxiety was not missing from the music. Plaintive tones of viola and cello suggested the tension, even fear, in the Opener's sombre declarations ('I'm afraid to open. But I must open'). The thumping thrust of the journey motif, sometimes paced by a measured kettledrum, had a half-playful, half-ominous quality.

But other instruments, including at one point what sounded like a tin whistle, came in to lighten the mood. Bells introduced a silvery tremolo as the journey moved into a more ethereal atmosphere. The high notes of the flute provided a unifying effect: soaring upwards, they seemed to be arriving at some distant haven—or consummation—such as Woburn might arrive at, if only he could 'see'.

One of the puzzling moments in the text for Sean Barrett as Opener, before he heard the music, had been the exclamation, 'God', twice repeated. What tone was called for here? 'Despairing', perhaps? Opener seemed for much of the time to be on the verge of despair. Perhaps the exclamation responded to the feeling of frustration in Voice's narrative, as he describes Woburn just missing the 'lights' which are tantalizingly close: 'he need only . . . turn over . . . he'd see them . . . shine on him . . . but no . . . he clings on . . .'. Immediately comes in the music (after one of the silences into which words and music continually ran). The Opener's exclamation occurred in that context, the first 'God' interrupting the music, the repeat occurring at its close. In such a context, I thought the Opener's cry must surely suggest not despair so much as awe and wonder. Dark tones were part of the musical sound, but the total effect was many-coloured, lightened by high, silvery notes and lightsome percussion. It brought to the fore the beauty of lights, clouds, sky, and distant island which hovers over the action. The desired 'ending' might, after all, exist: the music had arrived at it.

In the final sequence, when Opener had abandoned his mask of detachment and was urging Voice and Music onward 'fervently', the music mounted to a climax which drew all its scattered, vividly contrasting threads together. The flute maintained its unifying, skylark role; the drum, no longer ominous, struck a note of calm finality. Voice had no sense of arriving—he is calling 'come on . . . come on—' as the play ends—but the music hinted that the story of Woburn had been realized. Voice's 'come on' might mean not so much anxiety to end as eagerness to continue, a reaction close to the 'Again' of Words in the earlier play. Music, Voice, and Opener, separately but mysteriously in collaboration, had composed a work of art that Music knew to be 'finished'. The play could almost be seen as a demonstration of how Beckett's whole theatre works: failure the theme, the drama itself perfectly complete.

Interpretations of two such subtle, teasing plays as *Words and Music* and *Cascando* are bound to vary according to individual temperament. But they will all need to take into account the sensuous impact of the music, as I have tried to do. I hope our productions, made essentially as teaching material, have contributed usefully to the stock of recordings on which students of the plays can draw.[8] Humphrey Searle's music will surely always have a respected place there.

---

[8] These recordings are now, through the kindness of Katharine Worth, available for consultation at the Beckett Collection in Reading University Library [*Ed.*].

2

Beckett and the Sound of Silence

MARY BRYDEN

> *Question*: I have noticed that you write durations that are beyond
> the possibility of performance.
> *Answer*: Composing's one thing, performing's another, listening's a
> third. What can they have to do with one another?
>
> (John Cage, 'Experimental Music: Doctrine', in *Silence*, 15.)

The composer John Cage was adept at asking questions. In his spoken
and written dialogues he often presents them in the guise of answers.
Thus the reader is rendered recruit, co-respondent, neophyte. This is, I
think, consonant with an art—that of music—which Samuel Beckett
once described as 'perfectly intelligible and perfectly inexplicable'.[1]

Those three activities cited by Cage—composing, performing, listening—are all implicated within the phenomenon we call music. Conven-
tionally, and most simply, they are executed, in linear fashion, by three
separate functionaries:

composer composes . . . performer performs . . . listener listens.

The auditory transfer is a snapshot in a historical process, for all parties
have rehearsed the moment. The composer has practised composing
(on paper, in his or her mind), the performer has practised decoding
musical notation and relaying it to third parties, and the listener has
heard other sounds and has practised listening to, and perhaps reflecting
upon, these sounds. There is an apparent complicity here which promises
hermeticism. Within this cooperative field, the composer, his or her work
completed, listens to listeners listening to a performer who is reconstitut-
ing the sound to which the composer first imaginatively listened.

However, music is not a solidaristic, closed system: it is a profoundly
and famously unpredictable one. It does not necessarily, as St Augustine
hoped,[2] attune the human person to the divine rhythm, or turn the

---

[1] Samuel Beckett, *Proust*, in *Proust, and Three Dialogues with Georges Duthuit* (London:
John Calder, 1987), 92.
[2] See, for example, *St Augustine's* De Musica, ed. W. F. Jackson Knight (Westport, Conn.:
Hyperion Press, 1979). See Book IV in particular.

listener, as Hindemith hoped, 'towards everything noble, superhuman, and ideal'.[3] All parties may be in earnest, but yet disaffection results. However measured the input, the output or result remains mysterious. Composers may profess disdain for, or indifference to, their putative listeners; they may feel betrayed by interpreters of their work (as Stravinsky could feel about Nijinsky); listeners may feel affronted by a musical work which does not meet their expectations, whether they be early seventeenth-century listeners startled by the novel diminished seventh chord of Monteverdi, or early twentieth-century listeners startled by a twelve-tone composition of Schoenberg.

Yet, given an altered assemblage of variables, an altogether different outcome might obtain. This time, it is performed on a national holiday; these ticket-buyers are different from the last; the artiste has been substituted; the concert hall is more comfortable, or more imaginatively arranged. The music itself has not changed, and yet now all is different.

I am, of course, using the word 'music' here in two quite different senses. One—which 'has not changed'—is the music whose skeleton lies in a written score. The second is that which is played and performed. These two categories are sometimes referred to as 'virtual', or 'potential' music on the one hand, and 'real', or 'actual' music on the other.

There is an undoubted parallel here between music and drama. These two activities share the characteristic that (unless wholly improvised), they have a dual identity: the written and the performative. It is not surprising, then, that many composers should have been especially responsive to playwrights: thus, Philip Glass speaks of his enthusiasm for Brecht, Genet, and Beckett,[4] while Luciano Berio states: 'I am interested in all aspects of theatre. I grew up with Brecht, Pirandello, Shakespeare and Beckett.'[5] In both music and theatre, there is a whole dimension of risk and dynamism which attends upon performance. John Cage's conception of music contains this privileging of the experimental: 'Music is simply trying things out in school fashion to see what happens. Etudes. Making it easier but not real. Theatre is the only thing that comes near what it is.'[6]

Despite these affiliations between music and theatre, we do not refer to play-texts as being 'virtual plays', or 'potential drama'. *Waiting for Godot* is drama on page and stage. Similarly, it seems to me a diminish-

[3] Paul Hindemith, *A Composer's World: Horizons and Limitations* (Cambridge, Mass.: Harvard University Press, 1952), 5.

[4] See Philip Glass, *Music by Philip Glass*, ed. Robert T. Jones (New York: Dunvagen Music Publishers, 1987), 4.

[5] See *Luciano Berio: Two Interviews*, trans. and ed. David Osmond-Smith (New York: Marion Boyars, 1985), 159.

[6] John Cage, '45' for a Speaker', in *Silence* (London: Calder & Boyars, 1968), 146–93 (p. 189).

ment of unperformed music to call it 'virtual', as if it were somehow still hovering on the brink of existence. A score represents in one sense a culminatory point in the creative process: it is a completed piece of music. Perhaps a move from the ontological to the temporal is indicated. A text (musical, dramatic) is not embryonic matter, awaiting the fullness of life. It may speak in past, present, and future tenses: 'I played' (in the auditory imagination of the writer); 'I play' (in the auditory imagination of all who read me now, or remember having read me); 'I will play' (in minds, memories, or performance). A performance, on the other hand, can only exist in the present (although it may secure a partial continuance within the selective memory of individual witnesses).

Thus, rather than having the status of preliminary and event, text and performance are, respectively, two realizations along an ideational continuum. Gordon Epperson expresses it aptly: 'Music is [. . .] in and out of time. Whatever its order of abstraction, it can never have the stillness of a Chinese jar, because we can conceive it only as moving. We use up physical time even as we imagine the course of a melody. We can have it both ways.'[7] In Beckett's *Dream of Fair to Middling Women*, Belacqua indeed has it both ways when, standing on the Frica's doorstep, he both remembers a tritone Beethoven bass-clef melody (C♯; C natural; B)[8] and manipulates it in time: 'It was with this phrase, the ut sharpened, quantified and sustained to a degree that had never been intended by the Swan of Bonn, moaning in his memory, that he rang hell out of the Frica's door.'[9] In this instance, music recalled and adapted in the auditory imagination does not merely accompany a physical action: it has a part in prompting or determining its nature. One might compare Victor Zuckerkandl's description of the middle C held for some three seconds at the beginning of Beethoven's Coriolanus Overture: 'Our hearing of the tone gives us not only the feeling of something stationary but, together with it, the feeling of a growth, of an inner swell, of a dynamic phenomenon [. . .]. It is like a tugging and pulling in the tone, a rapidly increasing pressure, clamoring, as it were, for something to happen.'[10] Belacqua's inwardly heard music is not being performed, but it is fully achieved, efficacious, and not in any meaningful sense 'virtual'.

[7] Gordon Epperson, *The Musical Symbol: A Study of the Philosophic Theory of Music* (Ames: Iowa State University Press, 1967), 305.

[8] This fragment may be found in the cello part of the first movement of Beethoven's Seventh Symphony, across bars 128–9. (I am indebted to Japanese Beckett scholar Yoshiki Tajiri for pinpointing its location and for kindly passing the information on to me.) The duration of the first C♯ is indeed doubled within Beckett's note transcription, as his reference to quantification and sustaining suggests.

[9] Samuel Beckett, *Dream of Fair to Middling Women* (Dublin: Black Cat Press, 1992), 229.

[10] Victor Zuckerkandl, *Sound and Symbol: Music and the External World*, trans. Willard R. Trask (London: Routledge & Kegan Paul, 1956), 249.

The above example, it will have been realized, is taken not from a theatre text but from Beckett's first novel. While not denying the linkage which is appropriately established between music and drama—(indeed, I shall return to it later when considering Beckett as a director of his own plays)—I want to assert the importance of music in other genres of Beckett's writing, and, in particular, of that ability of the Beckettian mind to think, play, and hear music at multiple levels within the inner and outer realms of experience. In so doing, I shall return in what follows to the categories invoked at the outset of this chapter, although in a different order. Listening, it seems to me, is primary, and will therefore be considered first. Composing will follow, to give way to a final brief section on playing.

LISTENING

A listener must be presupposed in every act of music. To compose, one must first have listened. To play or sing well, one must have, or develop, an 'ear'. Beckett was undoubtedly a gifted pianist; moreover, his interlocutors speak unfailingly of his qualities as an attentive and courteous listener. Such a quality is rare. That he was an equally attentive listener to music is apparent on the evidence of his texts alone.

Yet why should one choose to focus on music in Beckett's writing? George Bernard Shaw—to take a random example—was similarly gifted in musical knowledge and sensitivity, and yet his texts themselves do not readily elicit musical comparisons. Luciano Berio asserts that: 'Music is everything that one listens to with the intention of listening to music' (*Two Interviews*, 19), but one still needs an explanation of what predisposes to that intention in specific contexts. There are, I would suggest, two main reasons. The first is that Beckett's texts exhibit an extraordinarily acute attunement to sound: not just to noise, but to intimate, ambient sound. The second is that there is a peculiarly rich role allocated to silence in Beckett's writing.

These two observations might at first seem paradoxical, for ambient sound, noise, and silence are sometimes viewed as being at variance with music. It was a distinction quite clear to Beckett's contemporary, Jean-Paul Sartre, who professed to speak for a whole generation when he stated in an interview in 1978:

On conçoit aujourd'hui la musique comme *l'art des bruits*, *le son* étant un bruit comme un autre qui vient à un certain moment mais pourrait être remplacé par des bruits, alors que les gens de ma génération considèrent la musique comme *l'art des sons*, ce qui fait une différence. Nous ne sommes pas hostiles aux formes nouvelles, mais nous comprenons mal ce passage du son au bruit. . . . Et je me demande ce que devient *la beauté,* dans les formes nouvelles d'art. [Music is viewed today as *the art of noise, sound* being a noise like any other, which arises now and then but could be replaced by noises, whereas my generation thinks of music as *the art of sounds,* which is not the same. We aren't hostile to new music, but we can't really understand this transition from sound to noise. . . . And I wonder what becomes of *beauty,* in these new art forms.][11]

It is not clear from Sartre's statement whether his definition of a sound is a (subjectively appointed) *beautiful* noise, or one which is decorative rather than merely functional, or both. For John Cage, the responsibility rests with the listener: 'Wherever we are, what we hear is mostly noise. When we ignore it, it disturbs us. When we listen to it, we find it fascinating. The sound of a truck at fifty miles per hour. Static between the stations. Rain. We want to capture and control these sounds, to use them not as sound effects but as musical instruments' ('The Future of Music: Credo', in *Silence,* 3).

Such a conception of the status of ambient sound, of 'musique concrète' is now much more familiar than it was when John Cage delivered his manifesto in 1937. Moreover, it seems to me essential to consider music in this broad sense when approaching Beckett's voicers, so keenly attuned to the sounds of their environment. Thus, the narrator in *Texts for Nothing IV* conjectures: 'What am I doing, talking, having my figments talk, it can only be me. Spells of silence too, when I listen, and hear the local sounds, the world sounds, see what an effort I make.'[12]

This intensity of listening is to be found everywhere in Beckett's writing. He himself underlined its importance in 1973, in a conversation reported by Charles Juliet: 'Il me répète que l'ouïe prend de plus en plus d'importance par rapport à l'œil' [He tells me again that the sense of hearing is increasingly becoming more important than that of sight].[13] (Interestingly, it was in that same year—1973—that Beckett wrote his short prose text, *Sounds,* in which the subject is seen 'head in hand as shown listening trying listening for a sound').[14] Yoked within the acoustic domain, the twin functions of listening and speaking are in Beckett's writing often given more weight as attestors of presence than is the function of seeing. In *The Unnamable,* for example, it is 'this blind voice, and these moments of held breath when all listen wildly, and the

[11] Jean-Paul Sartre, 'Sur la musique moderne', interview with Michel Sicard and Jean-Yves Bosseur, in Michel Sicard, *Essais sur Sartre: entretiens avec Sartre 1975–1979* (Paris: Éditions Galilée, 1989), 297–328 (p. 307). (This and all other translations within this essay are my own.) This interview was drawn to my attention by my colleague, Walter Redfern, to whom I am also indebted for his suggestions of further Sartrean parallels.

[12] Samuel Beckett, *Collected Shorter Prose 1945–1980* (London: John Calder, 1986), 83.

[13] Charles Juliet, *Rencontre avec Samuel Beckett* (Paris: Éditions Fata Morgana, 1986), 31.

[14] Samuel Beckett, *Sounds,* in *Essays in Criticism,* 28/2 (Apr. 1978), 155–6 (p. 156).

voice that begins to fumble again, without knowing what it's looking for, and again the tiny silence, and the listening again' which is affiliated to the 'sign of life'.[15]

Accordingly, the faculty of hearing is often prized in Beckett's work when other functions of the body are ailing, as with the halt narrator in *Molloy*: 'Not that I was hard of hearing, for I had quite a sensitive ear, and sounds unencumbered with precise meaning were registered perhaps better by me than by most.'[16] Frequent too is an often painful or problematic accommodation to the alternation between sound and its cessation. Yet that cessation is never complete. The voice in *Texts for Nothing XIII* wonders whether silence might ever ensue: 'Is it possible, is that the possible thing at last, the extinction of this black nothing and its impossible shades, the end of the farce of making and the silencing of silence, it wonders, that voice which is silence, or it's me, there's no telling' (*Collected Shorter Prose*, 114). John Cage was prone to recalling frequently his 1951 experience of entering a supposedly anechoic or soundless chamber:

Try as we may to make a silence, we cannot. [. . .] Such a room is called an anechoic chamber, its six walls made of special material, a room without echoes. I entered one at Harvard University several years ago and heard two sounds, one high and one low. When I described them to the engineer in charge, he informed me that the high one was my nervous system in operation, the low one my blood circulation. Until I die there will be sounds. And they will continue following my death. One need not fear about the future of music. ('Experimental Music', in *Silence*, 8).

Such music is to be found frequently in Beckett's writing. It may impinge upon the listener precisely because of its otherness or remoteness, as with 'the far unchanging noise the earth makes and which other noises cover, but not for long' (*Molloy*, 46). On the other hand, it may impinge because of its very familiarity: 'I seem to have again the hearing of my boyhood. Then in my bed, in the dark, on stormy nights, I could tell from one another, in the outcry without, the leaves, the boughs, the groaning trunks, even the grasses and the house that sheltered me.'[17] Or the music may be neither of these. It may constitute, as in the short French poem, a 'musique de l'indifférence | cœur temps air feu sable | du silence . . .' [music of indifference | heart time air fire sand | silence . . .'].[18] Yet, in every case, its listener is straining to hear, always implicated, never indifferent:

---

[15] Samuel Beckett, *The Unnamable*, in *The Beckett Trilogy* (London: Picador, 1979), 342.
[16] Id., *Molloy*, ibid. 47.
[17] Id., *Malone Dies*, ibid. 189.
[18] Id., *Collected Poems 1930–1978* (London: John Calder, 1986), 46.

The only sounds, apart from those of the body on its way, are of fall, a great drop dropping at last from a great height and bursting, a solid mass that leaves its place and crashes down, lighter particles collapsing slowly. Then the echo is heard, as loud at first as the sound that woke it and repeated sometimes a good score of times, each time a little weaker, no, sometimes louder than the time before, till finally it dies away. Then silence again, broken only by the sound, intricate and faint, of the body on its way.[19]

Silence, then, is part of a continuum of sound. On one level, human life in Beckett's writing is discerned as a brief flicker between two great silences, from cradle to grave, as Pozzo describes in *Waiting for Godot*: 'They give birth astride of a grave, the light gleams an instant, then it's night once more.'[20] Yet this streamlined account must be set against the evidence of a multitude of Beckettian organisms, living long and dolorously, and holding on like grim life to their capacity to speak or to fall silent. In this, Beckett's writing is like the music of a composer he admired—Debussy—within Vladimir Jankélévitch's account:

Le double silence baigne la musique de Claude Debussy, qui flotte ainsi toute entière dans l'océan pacifique du silence... E *silentio, ad silentium, per silentium*! du silence au silence, à travers le silence: telle pourrait être la devise d'une musique que le silence pénètre de toutes parts. [A dual silence bathes Claude Debussy's music, sailing along wholly thus, in the pacific ocean of silence... From silence to silence, through silence: such might be the watchword of a silence everywhere penetrated by silence.][21]

Jankélévitch's extended and beautiful exposition of the dependence of music upon silence—'car la musique ne respire que dans l'oxygène du silence' [for music can only breathe in the oxygen of silence] (p. 168)—is wholly applicable to the dynamic of Beckett's writing:

Le silence musical [...] n'est pas le vide; et en effet il n'est pas seulement 'cessation', mais 'atténuation'. Comme réticence ou développement interrompu, il exprime une volonté de rentrer dans le silence le plus tôt possible; comme intensité atténuée il est, sur le seuil de l'inaudible, un jeu avec le presque-rien. [Musical silence [...] is not nothingness; and indeed it is not only 'cessation', but 'attenuation'. As with reticence or interrupted exposition, it expresses a will to return as soon as possible to silence; as an attenuated intensity it toys with near-nothingness, on the threshold of inaudibility.] (p. 175)

In this respect one might draw together the resonant silence which ensues after the bell-sound at the conclusion of Stravinsky's *Les Noces* and the 'chime even a little fainter still. Pause for echoes' which

---

[19] Id., *He Is Barehead*, in *Collected Shorter Prose 1945–1980* (London: John Calder, 1986), 189.

[20] Id., *Waiting for Godot* (London: Faber, 1965), 89.

[21] Vladimir Jankélévitch, *La Musique et l'ineffable* (Paris: Éditions du Seuil, 1983), 164.

concludes Beckett's play *Footfalls*.[22] As Pierre Boulez describes in his tribute to Roger Désormière: 'No passing-bell could have been more apt than the last page of *Les Noces* as he had once conducted it, giving an extraordinary reality to the "paralysis" of the final chord, where sound melts into silence.'[23] These moments—the closure of *Les Noces*, the closure of *Footfalls*—are not so much withdrawals of sound as intensifications of the surrounding silence; they are perfect examples of the elasticity of acoustic presence and absence.

Pre-eminent among the sounds in Beckett's writing is that of the voice. Few of those present will forget the intensity of the opening moments of the stage adaptation of *Company*, rendered by the late David Warrilow: 'A voice comes to one in the dark. Imagine.' In Beckett's drama, voices are often frail but tenacious, threatened with extinction and yet committed to utterance. As they proceed, they command attention by virtue of the multiple auditory layers which emanate from them. As if in a hall of mirrors, these are voices listening to and reflecting upon themselves, or upon another version of themselves. Projected to without, they refer within. Such is the third-person speaker of *A Piece of Monologue*, who 'stands staring beyond half hearing what he's saying',[24] or the blind man of *Rough for Theatre I*, who seeks to render present his musical past: 'I once had a little harp. Be still and let me listen.'[25] Other plays foreground moments of intense listening to others, as is the case with the three women of *Come and Go*. Moreover, the Auditor in the stage version of *Not I*, and the Listener in *That Time*, are present expressly and exclusively to listen.

Within these sound fields, singing is sometimes seized upon as a means of quelling other, more unwelcome auditory intrusions: the ever-reeling soundtrack of conjecture, memory, or regret. As Jankélévitch points out: 'Chanter dispense de dire . . . Chanter est une façon de se taire!' [Singing dispenses you from speaking . . . Singing is a way of being silent!] (*La Musique et l'ineffable*, 173). After evoking 'all the dead voices' which return inexhaustibly to their consciousness, the two wayfarers of *Waiting for Godot* (Act II) consider having recourse to song as a means of eluding these insistent echoes. Winnie in *Happy Days* is ever-aware of the same expedient: '(*Long pause.*) I hear cries. (*Pause.*) Sing. (*Pause.*) Sing your old song, Winnie.'[26]

There is, however, an important caveat to be mentioned here. My

[22] Samuel Beckett, *Footfalls*, in *Collected Shorter Plays* (London: Faber, 1984), 243.

[23] Pierre Boulez, 'Roger Désormière: "I Hate Remembering!"', in *Orientations*, ed. Jean-Jacques Nattiez, trans. Martin Cooper (London: Faber, 1990), 500–12 (p. 512).

[24] Samuel Beckett, *A Piece of Monologue*, in *Collected Shorter Plays*, 268.

[25] Id., *Rough for Theatre I*, ibid. 73.

[26] Samuel Beckett, *Happy Days/Oh les beaux jours*, bilingual edition ed. James Knowlson (London: Faber, 1978), 78.

exposition thus far has dwelt upon the notion of sound not only as continuum, but also as part of the texture of Beckettian music as I have defined it. How, then, may music be recruited to *silence* sound? The reason is that, in the cases cited above, internal sound is demoted by external sound or execution. The performance entered upon is that of singing a song whose expression is already determined and whose form is effortlessly retained in the memory. Self-aware though the participants may be, they may nevertheless, for the space of a song, allow prescription to replace dilemma or travail, as do Dante's purgatorial shades (*Purgatorio*, Canto II), when they gather to listen to Casella's song instead of proceeding on their way. Singing thus provides a respite for the Beckettian organism whose inner ear is all too often a straining, buckling receiver for a stream of sound-scars. It is, thus, appropriate that the song which has come to be a kind of emblem for all of Schubert's *lieder*—'An die Musik'—should have been so evocative for Beckett. A setting of two stanzas of Schober's poem of the same name, it celebrates the power of music to relieve and enhance existence: 'du holde Kunst, ich danke dir' [Thou lovely art, I thank thee]. Not only does Beckett painstakingly copy out the words and melody of 'An die Musik', by hand, in the 'Whoroscope' notebook he kept in the 1930s (Reading University Library MS 3000/1: See Figure 2.1), but he also paraphrases the song's aspiration towards 'better times' in the closing lines of the short story 'Walking Out', in *More Pricks Than Kicks*: 'They sit up to all hours playing the gramophone, An die Musik is a great favourite with them both, he finds in her big eyes better worlds than this'.[27]

Significantly, this joy in listening to recorded music, shared by Belacqua and Lucy, has ensued from a dreadful accident which has prevented any possibility of their sharing the joys of sexual union. The exchange may seem disproportionate. Yet Anthony Storr points out that: 'Music can penetrate the core of our physical being. It can make us weep, or give us intense pleasure. Music, like being in love, can temporarily transform our whole existence.'[28] It is as if the power of music wholly to absorb the listener's attention occludes or circumvents the circuitry of the body. More earthily, one might cite for comparison the man seated at the piano in the 'Addenda' of *Watt*, 'naked save for stave-paper resting on lap', who, in his attitude of 'anguish, concentration, strain, transport and self-abandon', is quite oblivious to the sweat and dirt caked all over his body.[29]

One cannot proceed too far, however, along the route of considering

[27] Id., *More Pricks Than Kicks* (London: Calder & Boyars, 1970), 121.
[28] Anthony Storr, *Music and the Mind* (London: HarperCollins, 1992), 4.
[29] Samuel Beckett, *Watt* (London: John Calder, 1976), 251.

Fig. 2.1

music as a consolatory option. This is not to preclude that property. Indeed, Beckett would probably have endorsed Berio's assertion that: 'My hackles rise when I hear young Italian would-be-Adornos passing summary and disdainful judgement on those large portions of humanity who dare to acknowledge a consolatory dimension in music' (*Two Interviews*, 29).

Further, the motor force of the play *Words and Music* derives from Croak's desire for his 'comforts' and 'balms',[30] by means of the hard-won accommodation of words to music. More often, however, the identity of music in Beckett's work—I refer here to the use of instrumental musical fragments—is that of an autonomous, mysterious presence. It is never a rapturous or transformatory force. It may even be a source of suffering or melancholia in itself, for, in its associative power, it affords a means of reliving a lost moment. Such seems to be the effect, for example, of the fragment of Schubert's song 'Nacht und Träume' upon the solitary male listener in Beckett's play of the same name.

On the whole, then, Beckett leaves private and inexplicit the matter of any emotive relationship between music and listener. This is entirely in keeping with his conception of music, as expressed to Lawrence

[30] Samuel Beckett, *Words and Music*, in *Collected Shorter Plays*, 128, 129.

Shainberg, as 'the highest art form', since 'it's never condemned to explicitness'.[31] By refusing to anatomize or domesticate it, Beckett allows music to retain for the listener its full force of ambiguity.

Part of that ambiguity lies within a domain which was briefly referred to earlier: that of the temporal. For the listener, sound and music are perceived in the present, often intensely so. As Stravinsky asserts: 'Music is the sole domain in which man realizes the present.'[32]

Attunement to sound in Beckett's writing is symptomatic of a concentrated focus upon all elements of the speaker/narrator's immediate environment. One might instance the experience of Macmann in *Malone Dies*: 'The rain pelted down on his back with the sound first of a drum, but in a short time of washing, [. . .] and he distinguished clearly and with interest the difference in noise of the rain falling on him and falling on the earth' (*The Beckett Trilogy*, 220).

There is thus a sense in which sound—'urgent, unique, uninformed about history and theory' (Cage, 'Experimental Music: Doctrine', *Silence*, 14)—can dissolve all before and after it. This capacity is particularly pronounced in ambient or improvised sound. Speaking of the jazz improvisation of Charlie Parker, Sartre observes: 'Ce n'était pas un autre, avec une musique déjà jouée, déjà marquée' [It wasn't another, with music which had already been played and marked out'] (*Essais sur Sartre*, 321). Like the jazz melody in Sartre's novel *La Nausée*, music retains an autonomy which cuts adrift from the past in order to colonize the present, or to inaugurate an alternative present of its own. Theodor Adorno assents with this view: 'Late Schoenberg shares with jazz—and moreover with Stravinsky—the dissociation of musical time. Music formulates a design of the world, which—for better or for worse—no longer recognizes history.'[33]

In Proust's *A la recherche du temps perdu*, the listening Swann is arrested by a phrase in a Vinteuil sonata. As the music showers, fragments, and reforms around him, he feels a strange rejuvenation: a peeling back of time which is nevertheless a promise of a hitherto unlived future. Beckett's own personal copy of *Du côté de chez Swann* (kept in Reading University Library) bears testimony to his fascination with this capacity of music to defer (though not indefinitely) the dictates of time and space, for the pages bearing this passage are carefully annotated in his hand. Later, the brief Vinteuil phrase will come to be indelibly associated for Swann with his love for Odette, but, for the

[31] Lawrence Shainberg, 'Exorcising Beckett', *Paris Review*, 29/104 (Fall 1987), 100–36 (p. 116).

[32] Igor Stravinsky, *An Autobiography* (London: Calder & Boyars, 1975), 54.

[33] Theodor Adorno, *Philosophy of Modern Music*, trans. Anne G. Mitchell and Wesley V. Bloomster (London: Sheed & Ward, 1973), 60.

moment, it constitutes what the narrator calls 'pure music'. In the words of Beckett, it 'synthesises the moments of privilege and runs parallel to them' (*Proust*, 92–3).

Yet music can never be purely, merely, moored in the present, for time passes during the listening process. Moreover, during that present continuous, both past and future may be implied within the consciousness of the listener. Mention has already been made of the association of music, within Beckett's work, with past (and present) loss. This association may be more readily established when the perceived sound is already registered in the listener's memory, or mental repertoire. As the narrator observes in *The Unnamable*: 'The sounds I do not yet know have not yet made themselves heard' (*The Beckett Trilogy*, 272). Once heard, and known, such a sound may reach both forwards and backwards in time.

Music, then, is not a paralysing agent in Beckett's work, locked into an eternal present, but is a nomadic, mobile force. As such, it can supply an impetus for movement, and illustrates Zuckerkandl's contention that 'Musical contexts are *motion* contexts, kinetic contexts' (*Sound and Symbol*, 76). In *Happy Days*, Winnie uses the ritual of her song from *The Merry Widow* not only as a means of temporary reassurance, but also as a means of accelerating the present towards a (possibly happier) future. Such a dynamic might be summed up by a telling passage by Sartre:

Si tant de gens se sont avisés de chercher des consolations dans la musique, c'est, il me semble, parce qu'elle leur parle de leurs peines avec la voix dont ils en parleront eux-mêmes quand ils seront consolés et parce qu'elle les leur fait voir avec leurs yeux d'après-demain. [If so many people have seen fit to look for consolation in music, I think it's because music speaks to them of their woes in the same voice they will use to speak of them when they are consoled, and because it makes them see things the way they will see them the day after tomorrow.][34]

The Beckettian listener can never feel convinced that tomorrow will be in any way preferable to today, but, *en attendant*, an attunement to sound, silence, and music may provide a bridge (occasionally a privileged one) to the next moment.

COMPOSING

In 1982, Beckett told André Bernold: 'J'ai toujours écrit pour une voix' [I have always written for a voice].[35] Moreover, this speaking, faltering,

---

[34] Jean-Paul Sartre, 'L'Artiste et sa conscience', *Situations: IV* (Paris: Éditions Gallimard, 1964), 17–37 (pp. 35–6).
[35] André Bernold, *L'Amitié de Beckett* (Paris: Hermann, 1992), 107.

persisting voice is to be heard not only in Beckett's drama, but also in his prose. Unsurprisingly, some of Beckett's prose texts (*Company*, for example) have adapted strikingly to the context of staged monologues. Anthony Storr goes so far as to assert that a prose writer's sensitivity to the auditory medium renders his or her work qualitatively 'better': 'Writers who "hear" their sentences as if read aloud tend to write better prose than those who merely see them' (*Music and the Mind*, 41).

Whether or not this is the case, Beckett's sensitivity to voice, pitch, resonance, and duration often makes his manuscript drafts resemble musical scores. Others, like the manuscript and typescript drafts of *Quad* (RUL MSS 2198/2199) bear some similarity to orchestrated ballets. Does this mean that Beckett was aiming towards some kind of miniaturized *Gesamtkunstwerk*: a total artwork, complete in its own terms? I believe not. Beckett is reported as having denounced such enterprises, in a conversation with Georges Duthuit in the early 1950s: 'C'est du wagnérisme. Moi je ne crois pas à la collaboration des arts, je veux un théâtre réduit à ses propres moyens' [That's Wagnerism. I don't believe in art synthesis: I want a theatre thrown back on its own resources].[36]

On this point, Beckett concurs with Gabriele d'Annunzio, whose novel *Il Fuoco* he cites in *Proust*. It would be difficult to find two more dissimilar writers; indeed, although he praises d'Annunzio's description of Giorgione's 'Concerto', his approval drains inexorably away when subsequently appraising d'Annunzio's florid style. Nevertheless, although Beckett's analysis of *Il Fuoco* does not touch upon d'Annunzio's writing on opera, the young poet Stelio Effrena speaks memorably and persuasively in that work of his distrust of the Wagnerian synthesis. When distinct art forms are viewed merely as components, he argues, they lose their essential autonomy and particularity: 'Concorrendo a un effetto comune e totale, esse rinunziano al loro effetto particolare e supremo: esse, insomma, appaiono diminuite' [By converging on a communal, total effect, they sacrifice their particular and supreme effect; that is to say, they appear diminished].[37]

Just as Stelio (and no doubt d'Annunzio) fears the subordination of the Word to the alternative rhythms of music, Beckett fears the enforced materialization of music which opera effects. In a passage following hard upon the heels of the d'Annunzian reference, Beckett writes in *Proust* with revulsion of the art of opera, which, in his view, seeks to subject the inexplicable to a spatialized account: 'Thus, by definition, opera is a hideous corruption of this most immaterial of all the arts: the

---

[36] Rémi Labrusse, 'Beckett et la peinture', *Critique*, 46/519–20 (Aug./Sept. 1990), 670–80 (p. 676).
[37] Gabriele d'Annunzio, *Il Fuoco* (Milan: Fratelli Treves, 1904), 280.

words of a libretto are to the musical phrase that they particularize what
the Vendôme Column, for example, is to the ideal perpendicular'
(*Proust*, 92). Stravinsky shares this distaste, seeing in Wagnerian opera
an attempt to mask disorder with the semblance of order, the cumber-
some paraphernalia of mastery: 'From the moment song assumes as its
calling the expression of the meaning of discourse, it leaves the realm of
music and has nothing more in common with it.'[38] This reluctance to
claim the power of expression is in fact an even deeper-rooted instinct
within both artists. While Stravinsky states: 'I consider that music is, by
its very nature, essentially powerless to *express* anything at all, whether
a feeling, an attitude of mind, a psychological mood, a phenomenon of
nature' (*An Autobiography*, 53), Beckett writes of 'the expression that
there is nothing to express, nothing with which to express, nothing from
which to express, no power to express, no desire to express, together
with the obligation to express'.[39]

These insights are not, perhaps, particularly original ones, even for
their time. Moreover, both statements have had to bear the weight of
considerable academic scrutiny since. They are, nevertheless, important
for the fact that they achieve in self-commentary what both artists
profess to be unattainable in their art: namely, an *expression* revelatory
of their own personal writing credo. And while Beckett carries the
statement further than does Stravinsky with regard to the ever-renewed
obligation to express, the sentiment that a work of art can do no more
than embody its composer's endeavours and integrity is one that is
common to both.

Paul Hindemith renders the thesis a little more explicit when he
asserts: 'Music cannot express the composer's feelings' (*A Composer's
World*, 35). This is not to say that feeling does not attend the act of
composition: merely that music can never be a straight and transparent
conduit for the transfer of ideas. In the end, the composition must lie
naked in the air. Just as John Cage compares contemporary music to
contemporary milk—'at room temperature it is changing, goes sour etc,
and then a new bottle' ('Composition as Process', *Silence*, 44)—a composition is organic and must bear the risk of decomposition. Beckett, for
one, could face this: 'At the end of my work there's nothing but dust—
the namable.'[40]

In championing the 'intimate and ineffable nature' (*Proust*, 92) of

[38] Igor Stravinsky, *The Poetics of Music*, trans. Arthur Knodel and Ingolf Dahl (London:
Geoffrey Cumberlege/Oxford University Press, 1947), 42–3.

[39] Samuel Beckett, *Three Dialogues with Georges Duthuit* [with *Proust*] (London: John
Calder, 1987), 103.

[40] Israel Shenker, 'An Interview with Beckett [1956]', in Lawrence Graver and Raymond
Federman (eds.), *Samuel Beckett: The Critical Heritage* (London: Routledge and Kegan Paul,
1979), 146–9 (p. 148).

music, Beckett is implicitly aligning his own compositional art with that same dynamic of inexplicability. By permeating his writing with his own sensitivity to sound and music, he is not seeking to add an extra dimension of 'meaning', but rather to enhance its ambiguity. This is noticeable on many levels.

In the case of the voice, Beckett's work resists any notion of a unified vocal identity. This is so even in his theatre, where the use of recorded, disembodied voices (as, for instance, in *Footfalls, Rockaby, Krapp's Last Tape*) imparts complexity to the vocal event. Sartre speaks admiringly of the work of Berio for precisely this quality: 'Ses voix se doublent ou se triplent: [. . .] c'est *la même* voix qui se multiplie; c'est ainsi qu'il faut l'écouter, à la fois comme plusieurs et comme une seule' [His voices double or triple: [. . .] it's *the same* voice multiplying; that is the way it must be heard, as both one and several] (*Essais sur Sartre*, 317). Beckett even toyed at one time, according to Bernold, with the idea of a play dedicated to the deaf Beethoven, which, paradoxically, 'consistait simplement à faire entendre l'absence d'une voix' [simply consisted of making audible the absence of a voice] (*L'Amitié de Beckett*, 53). In a play such as *Play*, on the other hand, the staccato rhythm of utterances, high and low but purged of inflection and coloration, brings the vocal delivery very close to a kind of litany or *Sprechgesang*, as described by Jean-Yves Bosseur with reference to Schoenberg's *Pierrot lunaire*:

Schönberg joue sur l'équivoque d'un état vocal intermédiaire entre la voix parlée et chantée, nous en fait profondément ressentir la matérialité, la sensualité propres à des modes d'émission rejoignant le rire, le cri. [Schoenberg plays with the ambiguity of a vocalization midway between speech and song, bringing home to us the materiality and sensuality involved in modes of utterance inclusive of both laughter and shouting] (*Essais sur Sartre*, 298–9).

The same ambiguity remains on the level of movement, with which, as the previous section explored, music in Beckett has important linkages. This was a dynamic which Morton Feldman profoundly respected in his setting of Beckett's text 'Neither' (one line of which presented him with the challenging task of rendering 'then no sound'). Noting the first line of the text—'To and fro in shadow from inner to outer shadow'—Feldman evolved a shifting, alternating musical texture, to reflect the structuring principle he had discerned. He describes this in an interview as: 'You're back and forth, back and forth'.[41]

This back-and-forth movement may be between two poles, or it may be between movement and immobility. In the case of the television play *Quad*, with its interplay of pure movement, light and percussion, all

[41] Howard Skempton, 'Beckett as Librettist', *Music and Musicians*, 25/9 (May 1977), 5–6 (p. 6).

three elements contain the threat, or possibility, of their own extinction. Thus, when each cowled figure is no longer scurrying across the lighted square, his or her individual percussive instrument ceases, and he or she disappears into the unfathomable darkness beyond, before re-emerging again. If movement, light, and percussion continue when the figure is beyond the square, such events are invisible or inaudible to the spectator. Moreover, the jerky veering away from the midway point on each figure's diagonal route (accompanied by a slight crescendo of percussion in the Süddeutscher Rundfunk production from Stuttgart) hints at a further source of immobility within that still, untrodden central zone.

Beckett speaks (with musical applicability) of *Quad* as 'une fugue statique' (*L'Amitié de Beckett*, 108). Not only does the central deviation represent a potential disruption of the pattern, but also *Quad II*, in the Stuttgart production, was played at a much more dragging pace. The tempo of this 'static fugue' might be thought of as tempo rubato, for which Gordon Epperson offers the best definition he has come across: 'Hold back; but go ahead' (*The Musical Symbol*, 307). Indeed one might be tempted to think of *Quad* as a kind of 'hesitation waltz', were it not for the headlong nature of the hurtling movement, and the self-absorbed attitude of the participants. In view of its pattern—(one of action/ completion/resumption on a prescribed number of occasions)—it might be more aptly described as a perpetual or infinite canon. The philosopher Gilles Deleuze does in fact use the term 'canon' in describing *Quad*, although the more fascinating part of his discussion centres around the principle of repetition and refrain in the play, which he characterizes as 'une ritournelle essentiellement motrice, avec pour musique le frottement des chaussons' [an essentially motor refrain, with the friction of slippers for music].[42]

That friction of feet is important, for it provides a constant reminder of the cost or effort of that movement, thus endowing an aerial play with a solidly earth-bound resonance. In this respect it might be compared with the radio play *All That Fall*, where 'dragging feet' is a constantly recurring stage direction, as Mrs Rooney pursues her way to and from the station: a journey beset with setbacks and always threatened with stasis. Nevertheless, it is the orchestra of sounds which she hears en route which seem to sustain her in movement, marking and punctuating her progress. (Interestingly, in his 1968 work *Sinfonia*, Luciano Berio chooses, among his quotations from Beckett's *The Unnamable*, to use directional or automotive phrases such as 'where now?' and, in particu-

---

[42] Gilles Deleuze, *L'Épuisé*, with *Quad* (Paris: Éditions de Minuit, 1992), 57–106 (p. 81).

lar, 'keep going', as prompts or preludes for his allusions to the scherzo of Mahler's Second Symphony).[43]

On the return journey from the station, Mrs Rooney and her collected husband pass a house in which a 'very old woman', living all alone, is playing a record. 'All day the same old record', observes Mrs Rooney.[44] The music is Schubert's 'Death and the Maiden'. On the face of it, there is a feasible connection to be made between the title of the song and the image of an old woman living alone, particularly since the directions indicate that the 'music dies'. Yet, even that analogic journey is interrupted by ambiguity, since the maiden of Schubert's song is still young when Death comes to claim her. This old woman, on the other hand, has had the leisure to play the music over and over again. She is not so much dying as reliving (and thus suspending) the experience of proximate death. The final word may be (for the moment) not with Death, as in Schubert's song, but with the woman's exclamation from the earlier part of the song: 'geh', Lieber! und rühre mich nicht an' [in Pinkerton's rendering, 'Go! leave me now alone!']. Mr and Mrs Rooney do indeed trudge on, disconsolate but persevering. Music, tempo rubato, has again provided both pause and spur.

This uneasy balance in his work between movement and stasis, fragility and tenacity, is an important characteristic of Beckett as composer. On the one hand, the musicality of his work is to be found, as the previous section has explored, in an intensity of attunement to voice and sound. This runs deeper than a passive sensibility or responsiveness: Beckett, as a gifted musician, also took a keen interest in more technical aspects of sound production and acoustics. In the 'Whoroscope' notebook referred to earlier, he devotes attention to the difference between a decibel and a phon—the former, he notes, relating to energy, the latter to pitch or frequency. Beckett also gives evidence of some interest in the profession of piano tuning: that wondrously difficult art of accommodating a series of keys to the compromised pitches of the modern scale. In addition to the Galls, father and son, in *Watt*, there is a reference in *The Unnamable* to 'piano-tuners up our sleeve, they strike A and hear G, two minutes later' (*The Unnamable*, 343).

In addition to overt citations of composers—(Beethoven, Schubert, Haydn, etc., not forgetting a charming reference to the 'wary elegance' of Brahms in the 'Whoroscope' notebook)—there is to be found in Beckett's work a wealth of explicit allusion to the codes and conventions of the musical world, particularly in the early writing. *Murphy* is a rich

[43] For a full description of this work, see David Osmond-Smith, *Playing on Words: A Guide to Luciano Berio's 'Sinfonia'* (London: Royal Musical Association Monographs, 1985), 56.

[44] Samuel Beckett, *All That Fall*, in *Collected Shorter Plays*, 37.

picking-ground for such testimonies of expertise, music often being associated here with sexual enjoyment. One might cite, for instance, the description of Murphy's joyfully protracted nights with Celia as 'serenade, nocturne and albada',[45] these terms denoting, respectively, music for evening, night, and (in the more common designations of 'aubade' or 'alborada') morning. The episode of Murphy kissing Celia 'in Lydian mode' (p. 82) is similarly robust (the Lydian mode representing the modern major scale), as is Miss Counihan's lingering kiss from Wylie, which is 'like a breve tied, [. . .] over bars' times its equivalent in demi-semiquavers' (p. 69).

To embark on an inventory of such allusions, however, is not within the brief of this essay. The radio plays *Words and Music* and *Cascando* deservedly receive quite considerable attention within this volume, from musicians more gifted than I, to which I shall not add. Neither do I intend to undertake an analysis of the multiplicity of musical forms to which Beckett's writing might be compared. This has already been competently covered by a small but impressive company of analysts, of whom a selective listing is given in the Bibliography. See, for example, Mary Catanzaro's comparison of *Lessness* with forms of statistical composition;[46] William Grim's exploration of the 'developing variation' of *Molloy*;[47] Kenneth Gaburo's account of vocal texture in *Play*;[48] Eric Park's wide-ranging survey of music in *Murphy* and *Watt*;[49] and some excellent musical engagements with *Watt*.[50]

To be aware of Beckett as a composer, however, also involves being aware of the fragility, the 'almost-not-thereness' of his textual music. Beckett described to Bernold in 1981 his desire to find 'une *ombre vocale*, [. . .] une voix qui soit une ombre. Une voix blanche' [a *vocal shadow*, [. . .] a voice which is a shadow. A white voice' (*L'Amitié de Beckett*, 108). He had used in his writing a similar metaphor many decades previously. In *Dream of Fair to Middling Women* can be found a short and exquisite passage which refers to the 'plane of white music,

---

[45] Samuel Beckett, *Murphy* (London: Picador, 1973), 46.

[46] Mary Catanzaro, 'Musical Form and Beckett's *Lessness*', *Notes on Modern Irish Literature*, 4 (1992), 45–51.

[47] William Grim, 'The Developing Variation in Samuel Beckett's *Molloy*', *Romance Studies*, 11 (Winter 1987), 47–52.

[48] Kenneth Gaburo, 'The Music in Samuel Beckett's *Play*', *Review of Contemporary Fiction*, 7/2 (Summer 1987), 76–84.

[49] Eric Park, 'Fundamental Sounds: Music in Samuel Beckett's *Murphy* and *Watt*', *Modern Fiction Studies*, 21/2 (Summer 1975), 157–71.

[50] See, for example, Heath Lees, '*Watt*: Music, Tuning, and Tonality', in S. E. Gontarski (ed.), *The Beckett Studies Reader* (Gainesville, Fla.: University Press of Florida, 1993), 167–85; Susan Field Senneff, 'Song and Music in Samuel Beckett's *Watt*', *Modern Fiction Studies*, 10 (Summer 1964), 137–50; Bernard Vouilloux, 'Tentative de description d'une écriture sérielle: sur une séquence de *Watt*', *Poétique*, 91 (Sept. 1992), 259–72. (I am grateful to Brigitte Rièra for drawing the last article to my attention.)

[. . .] still flat white music, alb of timeless light. [. . .] It is the dawn-foil and the gift of blindness' (*Dream*, 181–2). The conjunction of 'white' music/voice with shadow occurs in both these instances. It seems to correspond to the second, 'half light' zone of Murphy's mind, as described in Chapter 6 of *Murphy*. This is the zone in which 'the pleasure was contemplation' (*Murphy*, 65). The 1981 statement is, however, differentiated in an important way. The privileging of spaces of light and colourlessness is retained; now, however, receptor cedes to enunciator as Beckett ponders how to render perceptible a voice which is scarcely there. Bernold describes adroitly the complexity of this search for the 'white voice' in which 'l'ombre dans la voix se lève comme une clarté quand le noir se fait sur la scène, souffle pâle et glacé, presque inaudible, proche, trop proche, aube inflexiblement étrangère' [the shadow in the voice emerges like light when the stage grows dark, a pale and frozen breath, almost inaudible, near, too near, the unyielding strangeness of dawn]' (*L'Amitié de Beckett*, 108). Aideen O'Kelly faced the search for the 'voix blanche' when playing Winnie in *Happy Days*, and finally 'got it through the music of the language. [. . .] I realized that the "voix blanche" was something like the Queen of Night in *The Magic Flute*— a pure, cold voice'.[51]

Indeed, throughout Beckett's long writing career, one can trace an extended preoccupation with compositional boundaries: between light and dark, audible and inaudible, perceptible and imperceptible—and, above all, between sound and silence. Jankélévitch's beautiful exposition of the music of Satie and Mompou might also be a description of Beckett:

Le silence de la musique est lui-même un élément constitutif de la musique audible. [. . .] Le laconisme, la réticence et le pianissimo sont ainsi comme des silences dans le silence. [. . .] Dans la concision habile comme un désir de troubler le silence le moins longtemps possible. Sans doute la *réticence* doit-elle être considérée comme un silence privilégié [. . .]. Ainsi *ne pas dire* est souvent plus persuasif que *tout dire*. [Silence in music itself constitutes an element of audible music. [. . .] Terseness, reticence and pianissimo are therefore like silences within silence. [. . .] It is as if concision harbours a desire to disturb silence as briefly as possible. No doubt *reticence* must be considered as a kind of privileged silence [. . .]. Accordingly, *not saying* is often more persuasive than *saying everything*] (*La Musique et l'ineffable*, 173–4).

Once again Beckett and Wagner can be placed at opposite extremes, for, as Storr aptly points out: 'A concise Wagner is inconceivable: the effect

---

[51] Aideen O'Kelly, interviewed by Rosette Lamont, in Linda Ben-Zvi (ed.), *Women in Beckett: Performance and Critical Perspectives* (Urbana: University of Illinois Press, 1990), 35–40 (p. 37).

of his music is inseparable from its opulent duration' (*Music and the Mind*, 179).

For artists who specialize in that 'opulent duration', the practice of reduction might seem dangerously close to that of dehumanization, cancellation, or effacement. Reduction is not, in fact, the same as scantiness: it is the result of intense labour. It is the renunciation not of notation *per se*, but of its excessive elaboration or ornamentation in writing. Its *effect*, however, may be linked with notions of lightness, improvisation, or ephemerality, like the 'petit air de jazz-hot, unique et éphémère' [little hot-jazz melody, unique and ephemeral] with which Sartre describes the sculptural mobiles of Alexander Calder.[52]

Beckett's manuscript drafts, with their careful rhythms of statement, erasure, restoration, modification, or variation, indeed demonstrate his commitment to the erasure of superfluity. In this connection, John Cage reports the remark of Schoenberg to him that, in an erasing pencil, the erasing end 'is just as important as the other end' ('Composition as Process', *Silence*, 34). For Adorno, 'music, compressed into a moment, is valid as an eruptive revelation of negative experience' (*Philosophy of Modern Music*, 37). He cites, accordingly, Hölderlin's poem 'Brevity', in Michael Hamburger's translation: 'Why so brief now, so curt?' Significantly, in Beckett's own personal copy of Hölderlin's complete works, held in Reading University Library, this poem ('Die Kürze') is one of the few to receive Beckett's pencilled markings. This attraction to a dynamic of brevity may perhaps be likened to that of Stravinsky, in whose music, according to Adorno, 'the concept of renunciation is basic' (*Philosophy of Modern Music*, 148). Beckett's late plays and prose works are, on one level, works of compression: on another, however, these pause-filled pieces are works of infinite space.

In this respect, it is apposite to draw together briefly the domains of music and mathematics: both spheres in which Beckett took a deep and abiding interest. The 'Whoroscope' notebook, for instance, contains evidence of Beckett's reading of the French mathematician and philosopher Henri Poincaré, for a long passage from the chapter entitled 'L'Histoire de la physique mathématique' in *La Valeur de la science* is there copied out. As Hindemith points out, music was at the time of the Roman Empire one of the 'quadrivium': the four sciences (music, geometry, astronomy, arithmetic) dealing with measurement (*A Composer's World*, 7–8). Music and mathematics have obvious differences. Nevertheless, they share a grounding in mensuration, an adherence to an abstract domain, a preoccupation with patterning and interconnection. Enoch Brater has already explored fruitfully this allegiance of music and

---

[52] Jean-Paul Sartre, 'Les Mobiles de Calder', *Situations: III* (Paris: Éditions Gallimard, 1949), 307–11 (p. 309).

mathematics in his analysis of *Lessness*.[53] So, too, has Edith Fournier, in her article on *Sans*, the French original of *Lessness*.[54]

Mathematical models are not, of course, merely logical, sequential ones: they can also be characterized by those principles of elegance and economy which we might deem 'aesthetic'. As Storr observes of music and mathematics: 'Aesthetic appreciation of this kind is not simply a cold, cerebral, intellectual exercise; it touches human feelings. We delight in perceiving coherence where there was none before; we take pleasure in contemplating perfect form' (*Music and the Mind*, 182). Beckett's love of form and permutation is clear both from his manuscript drafts and from his completed works, and I shall not add to the volume of writing on that subject, except perhaps to posit a potentially interesting parallel between the famous 'sucking stones' episode in *Molloy* and techniques of serialism and twelve-tone composition in music. Just as a composer such as Schoenberg eschewed the adherence to beginnings and endings, in favour of a logic of continuation which accords an equal importance to all twelve notes of the octave, Molloy is tormented by the problem of how to ensure that his 'sixteen stones will have been sucked once at least in impeccable succession, not one sucked twice, not one left unsucked' (*The Beckett Trilogy*, 67). One must, however, not extend this comparison too far. Molloy, at length, tires of the permutational cycle and restricts his mineral hoard to one stone alone. His creator, too, both converges upon and distances himself from serialist techniques, for Beckett remarked in an interview with John Gruen: 'Perhaps, like the composer Schönberg or the painter Kandinsky, I have turned toward an abstract language. Unlike them, however, I have tried not to concretise the abstraction—not to give it yet another formal context.'[55]

In so far as form encroaches upon music in a more general sense, one might observe that Walter Pater's dictum that: 'All art constantly aspires towards the condition of music',[56] finds its echo in Beckett's conception of his own compositional art. In music, asserts Pater, 'the end is not distinct from the means, the form from the matter, the subject from the expression; they inhere in and completely saturate each other' (p. 109). This is not the same as asserting that identity of form and content which was so prized by Beckett, although it testifies to a similar unificatory

[53] See Enoch Brater, *The Drama in the Text* (New York: Oxford University Press, 1994), 93–7.

[54] Edith Fournier, 'Samuel Beckett mathématicien et poète', *Critique*, 46/519–20 (Aug./Sept. 1990), 660–9.

[55] John Gruen, 'Samuel Beckett talks about Beckett', *Vogue*, 127/2 (Feb. 1970), 108.

[56] Walter Pater, *The Renaissance: Studies in Art and Poetry* (1893 version), ed. Donald L. Hill (Berkeley and Los Angeles: University of California Press, 1980), 106. (The applicability of Pater's analysis was suggested to me by Walter Redfern.)

goal. Beckett concurs with Pater in regarding the art of music as being 'unique' in inhabiting a zone of abstraction and immateriality. Thus, in *Proust*, he presents music in Schopenhauerian terms as 'the Idea itself, unaware of the world of phenomena, existing ideally outside the universe' (*Proust*, 92). The composer of music, like the composer of mathematics, can work in a self-referential world, a world of virtuality and abstraction. In the case of music, that world might also be termed 'spirit', and in that respect I am grateful to John Beckett, Samuel Beckett's cousin, for giving me permission to quote a remark made to him by Beckett: 'I think that the opening of Schubert's String Quartet in A minor (Deutsch 804) is more nearly pure spirit than any other music'. 'Pure spirit' is here pure praise.

PLAYING

Playing the piano was for Beckett not a schoolboy occupation later abandoned, but a lifelong enthusiasm. André Bernold reports of Beckett that: 'Vers ses quatre-vingts ans, il s'était remis au piano, demandant à ses mains de déchiffrer quelques sonates de Haydn' [Towards the age of eighty, he had taken up the piano again, putting his hands to the task of sight-reading some Haydn sonatas] (*L'Amitié de Beckett*, 74). This represented a significant achievement on the part of a man whose fingers were by then beginning to stiffen. This brief section will, however, focus not upon that essentially private activity of playing the piano, but upon the playing of Beckett's work in public: the performative domain.

It was only comparatively late in life that Beckett started to fulfil the role of conductor of his own music, when he began to direct his own plays. Prior to that, however, he had been for a long time immersed in the absorbing art of self-translation. There is, of course, no unproblematic, correspondingly nuanced transference from one language to another. As the Italian proverb has it: 'Traduttore traditore' [to translate is to betray]. Stravinsky had in mind this association of crossover with double-crossing when he wrote of performance: 'To speak of an interpreter means to speak of a translator. And it is not without reason that a well-known Italian proverb, which takes the form of a play on words, equates translation with betrayal' (*The Poetics of Music*, 127). Given the fact that music or theatre, unlike other art forms, requires the intermediary of performers, 'the composer runs a perilous risk every time his music is played, since the competent presentation of his work each time depends on the unforeseeable and imponderable factors that go to make up the virtues of fidelity and sympathy' (p. 123). This mention of 'fidelity' is central, for it puts under the spotlight not only the notion of a consistent 'intention' on the part of the writer/composer, but also the ever-renewed dynamic of the theatrical space. Is it advisable for a composer to direct his or her own work? And, if so, should that direction remain invariable, or should performers be permitted to modify the delivery in accordance with perceived performative need?

Vociferous supporters may be found on either side of the 'fidelity' debate. Aaron Copland, in Epperson's account, 'concedes that an interpreter may even discover in a score nuances which the composer had not consciously intended' (*The Musical Symbol*, 265). Pierre Boulez is firmly on the side of the artwork finding its own identity in the interpretative space, 'for it must surely be obvious that it is just the ability to escape from its own contingent character that constitutes the greatness of a work' ('A Short Postscript on Fidelity', in 'Lulu', *Orientations*, 400). Luciano Berio is an interesting case, since, although he professes to enjoy the interaction of the rehearsal room, he also retains a deeply personal attitude towards the interpretation of his own work: 'I prefer to direct my own works because I think I know them better than anyone else, and am able to give the clearest and most legible account of them' (*Two Interviews*, 132).

Stravinsky is quite trenchant upon the subject: 'I have always been sincerely opposed to the rearrangement by anyone other than the author himself of work already created' (*An Autobiography*, 46). In order to reduce further the interpretative risk attendant upon performance, Stravinsky—whom Storr terms 'one of the most meticulous, orderly, and obsessionally neat composers in the history of music' (*Music and the Mind*, 6)—took extraordinary pains with his score directions to ensure, as Epperson puts it, 'as faithful an adherence as possible to his intentions. Once the image is crystallized in his imagination he hardly dares entrust it to the world' (*The Musical Symbol*, 266).

Beckett never closed his mind to the possibility of modifying some aspects of his original conceptual work when it was being transferred to the medium of the stage, provided that he was convinced of the desirability of such modification. Nevertheless, as previous sections have explored, the aural nuances of Beckett's work are of paramount importance. For a writer immersed in the infinite gradations of tonality within his internal attunement to the text, questions of pitch, tone, duration, rhythm, and audibility were not optional extras, or embellishments available to the vocal event. Rather they *were* that meaning, that vocal event. They were, to return to Pater's analysis, both 'form and matter, in their union or identity' (*The Renaissance*, 109).

Thus, for Beckett, exactitude of tone, sound, and silence were crucial, for, when music leaves the realm of the mind, it becomes an auditory body vulnerable to violation. In Stravinsky's congruent insight: 'Music does not move in the abstract. Its translation into plastic terms requires exactitude and beauty' (*The Poetics of Music*, 128). Hence, it is fascinating to note that, when Beckett had lunch with Stravinsky in Paris in 1962, these were precisely the matters discussed. Noting Beckett's 'light, very musical voice', Robert Craft reports that 'Beckett is interested in the possibility of notating the *tempo* of performance in a play, and of timing the pauses in *Godot*, and I.S. [Stravinsky] likes the idea of such controls, of course, but thinks that circumstances are too variable.'[57]

For Beckett's trusted actors, the notion of such meticulousness in tone and tempo was familiar. Indeed, such actors recurrently use musical analogies when describing the experience of being directed by Beckett. Aideen O'Kelly says of *Happy Days* that: 'The whole play is like a musical score' (Ben-Zvi, *Women in Beckett*, 40). In an interview with Jonathan Kalb, David Warrilow describes how, in rehearsing *Ohio Impromptu*, 'the issue was tone and tempo, because the way the author hears that piece is somewhat different from the way it lies in my being'.[58] In her autobiography, Billie Whitelaw observes that: 'Working on *Play* was not unlike conducting music or having a music lesson.'[59] Thus, gradations in the timing of pauses could be infinitesimal, so that Whitelaw came to understand the rhythmic import of such requests as: 'Will you make those three dots, two dots' (p. 77). For actors such as Whitelaw and Warrilow, the voice became not so much an interpreter of a Beckett text, as a musical instrument. They were, one might say, being played or sung by Beckett. Likening the parts she played to 'Chopin's etudes', Irena Jun could maintain in an interview with Antoni Libera that: 'Rehearsing and playing Beckett gives an actor the opportunity to master his own body and to turn it into a perfect instrument' (Ben-Zvi, *Women in Beckett*, 48). This clearly cannot be achieved without concentrated practice, and thus Warrilow observes: 'If I get it right, if I sing it "on key", "in tune", it's going to vibrate properly for somebody else' (Kalb, *Beckett in Performance*, 224).

It should be emphasized that attending to the fine detail of tonal and temporal delivery is not the same as prescribing the outcome or semantic reception of that delivery. In matters of critical commentary or verbal analysis of his own work, Beckett remained famously reticent. In this, his instincts accord with those of Pierre Boulez: 'If [the composer] persists in such descriptions after the actual act of creation—when the

---

[57] Robert Craft, *Stravinsky: Chronicle of a Friendship 1948–1971* (London: Victor Gollancz, 1972), 153, 154.

[58] Jonathan Kalb, *Beckett in Performance* (Cambridge: Cambridge University Press, 1989), 224.

[59] Billie Whitelaw, *Billie Whitelaw . . . Who He?* (London: Hodder & Stoughton, 1995), 78.

work is finished, that is to say—this is an absolute proof that he has failed to realize his idea' ('Putting the Phantoms to Flight', *Orientations*, 67). Sartre is similarly minded:

Or l'artiste *ne doit pas être* pour le public le commentaire de son œuvre: si la musique est engagée, c'est dans l'objet sonore tel qu'il se présente immédiatement à l'oreille, sans référence à l'artiste ni aux traditions antérieures, qu'on trouvera l'engagement dans sa réalité intuitive. [Now the artist *must not be* for the public the commentator upon his/her own work: if the music is committed, it is in the immediacy of the auditory event as it presents itself to the listener, without reference to the artist or to previous traditions, that the reality of that commitment will be intuited] ('L'Artiste et sa conscience', *Situations: IV*, 28–9).

Beckett thus saw his responsibility as ending at the last rehearsal. Accommodation to the sound, and therapy after it, were not his concern. He could therefore state (in musical terms) in a much-quoted letter to Alan Schneider, with reference to *Endgame*:

My work is a matter of fundamental sounds (no joke intended) made as fully as possible, and I accept responsibility for nothing else. If people want to have headaches among the overtones, let them. And provide their own aspirin. Hamm as stated, and Clov as stated, together as stated, nec tecum nec sine te, in such a place, and in such a world, that's all I can manage, more than I could.[60]

Indeed, all that can be managed or provided for is an aural and visual event which must stand or fall in the immediacy of its theatrical performance, and it was to that enterprise that Beckett directed his energy and integrity. This is not to say that questions must not be asked, that words are precluded vectors for engagement with a performance phenomenon. As Boulez points out, there will be those who, expectations challenged, feel the need to dream up 'snatches of conversation between these two empty (and stinking) shoes the sight of which opens the second act of *Waiting for Godot*' ('Experiment, Ostriches and Music', *Orientations*, 431). Similarly, there may well be those who will react with hostility or boredom to Beckett's extensive use of pause and silence. When Billie Whitelaw suggested this, during rehearsals for *Footfalls*, Beckett replied: 'Bore them to death [. . .]. Bore the pants off them' (*Billie Whitelaw . . . Who He?*, 145). One person's eloquent silence may indeed be diagnosed by another as absence, or *longueur*, just as Rousseau reacted adversely to the careful silence inserted by Rameau at a climactic point in his opera *Armide*: '[Rameau] a fait un silence qu'il n'a rempli de rien dans un moment où Armide avoit tant de choses à sentir, et par conséquent l'orchestre à exprimer' [Rameau created a

---

[60] Letter of 29 Dec. 1957, quoted in Ruby Cohn (ed.), *Disjecta* (London: John Calder, 1983), 109.

silence filled with nothing at a moment when Armide had so much to feel, and the orchestra thus to express].[61]

The reverse reaction may, however, obtain. Thus, though Lawrence Shainberg could conceive of the full weight of *Endgame* in rehearsal as 'nothing but theatre, repetition, a series of ritualized games that the actors are doomed to play forever' ('Exorcising Beckett', 121), he could relate the play's quips and responses in performance to the lightness and mutability of jazz, so that the exchanges between Nagg and Nell could be described thus: 'Each was a measure, clearly defined, like a jazz riff, subordinated to the rhythm of the whole' (p. 119).

Beckett's 'all I can manage' is not an abdication of responsibility. As listener, composer, and conductor, 'all he could manage' was not the least he could manage, but the best. In view of Beckett's own admiration of Beethoven, it is appropriate that, immersed in rehearsals of his first complete cycle of Beethoven symphonies, the conductor Simon Rattle should conclude a 1995 interview with a quotation from Beckett's *Worstward Ho*:[62] 'That word struggle again. Rattle leaves with a quotation from Samuel Beckett, which he has adopted as a pertinent motto for his Beethoven: "Ever tried. Ever failed. No matter. Try again. Fail again. Fail better"'.[63]

---

[61] Jean-Jacques Rousseau, 'Lettre sur la musique françoise', in *Écrits sur la musique* (Paris: Éditions Stock, 1979), 257–323 (p. 316).

[62] Samuel Beckett, *Worstward Ho* (London: John Calder, 1983), 7.

[63] 'Rattle and Brum', Interview with Stephen Pettit, *The Sunday Times*, 20 Aug. 1995, Part 10, pp. 4–5 (p. 5).

3

The Note Man on the Word Man:
Morton Feldman on Composing the Music for Samuel Beckett's *Words and Music* in *The Beckett Festival of Radio Plays*

EVERETT FROST

In undertaking new American radio productions of all of Samuel Beckett's extant radio plays, *Words and Music* presented a singular difficulty. The music composed by John Beckett, the author's cousin, at the time of the play's conception, was withdrawn soon after the production's première on the BBC in November 1962 (and its subsequent French production, as *Paroles et musique*), and remains unavailable. But the play cannot be produced without music, since it appears as 'Bob', an actual character in the play. As we formulated our plans for *The Beckett Festival of Radio Plays*, Samuel Beckett reconfirmed to me, as apparently he had to Katharine Worth[1] and other enquirers, that it would be 'impossible' for us to use the John Beckett score and that we would therefore have to provide our own. Yet it seemed to me that Beckett had a special fondness for the play and was pleased that it might be revived with what he called a 'fresh go'. He suggested Morton Feldman as the composer.[2] They had met previously: Mr Feldman had set Mr Beckett's very short text, 'Neither', into a very long work for the Rome opera in the 1970s, and Beckett had been pleased by the result. Beckett apologized that, now at an advanced age and increasingly in poor health, he felt unable to enter once again into the kind of collaborative or consultative effort that he had once given his cousin, John. Aside from what help he had provided in his conversations with me, we would have to proceed on our own.

As I came to learn in our work together, Mr Feldman was well versed in Beckett's work, and he accepted my offer with a mixture of enthusiasm and genuine, almost awkward, humility. It would be difficult, he

---

[1] See Katharine Worth's own essay within this volume [*Ed.*].

[2] I have speculated on why *Words and Music* has a special place in the Beckett canon in 'Fundamental Sounds: Recording Samuel Beckett's Radio Plays', *Theatre Journal*, 43/3 (Oct. 1991), 361–76.

said: the radical concisions required by the text worked against the current direction of his music, which was elaborating in the direction of longer and longer forms. It would take time. It risked altering the direction of his work—a risk he would take, owing to his profound respect for Samuel Beckett.

Mr Feldman worked at it for over a year, in and out of his other commitments, which were prodigious at that time. From time to time we would meet when he was in New York, or discuss it on the phone. There was little to say: 'I can't *describe* music to you, Everett, I can only write it. [. . .] I've got to find the metaphor, the way in to it. Until I do that, there's no point in talking. The trouble is, that it's not a metaphoric piece.' What seemed to help was to read passages from the play aloud and to time them. I am not a good imitator, but I tried as best I could to convey what I had learned from hearing Beckett recite from the play in his exquisitely French-accented Irish brogue. (As I had expected, Beckett was unwilling to allow me to record him.) For reasons having to do with the alignment of impossible schedules, by mid-November of 1986, the recording dates were fixed for 9 and 10 March 1987 in the (tragically, now no longer existent) RCA studios in New York, with the distinguished Beckett actor David Warrilow as Joe (Words) and his equally distinguished colleague Alvin Epstein as Croak. It was only a week before the recording sessions that the conductor (and close friend and former student of Mr Feldman's), Nils Vigeland, received the score to distribute to his Bowery Ensemble musicians: Bunita Marcus (piano); Michael Pugliese (percussion); Barbara Held and Rachel Rudich (flutes); Laura Seaton and Tim Pelikan (violins); Sarah Carter (cello).

Mr Feldman supervised the rehearsal, recording, and mixdown of his music, with tremendous wit and energy, and an exacting ear. A remarkable rapport developed among us that made it possible for everyone involved to do their best work, and to take great pleasure in it. The two and a half days of rehearsal, recording, and production went so well that I persuaded Mr Feldman to record a short interview for inclusion in the documentary that would accompany the broadcast. The interview went on for an hour, and when the studio time was gone, and the tape had run out, we were still talking. Throughout all this, if he was ill, he gave no sign of it; it seems clear to me that he did not know. I did not see him again. When I called in August to convey the news that we had secured the funding for *Cascando* and could go ahead—we had agreed that he would compose the score—he was too ill to come to the phone. He died that September. (The music for *Cascando* was written by William Kraft, a composer Mr Feldman admired and, indeed, suggested. William Kraft, who knew the circumstances, in no sense 'replaced' Mr Feldman, but rather gave it a 'fresh go'—and a remarkable one—of his own.)[3]

Words and Music proved to be the next-to-last work Mr Feldman would complete. It had changed the direction of his music: the last work, an orchestral composition, was inscribed simply 'For Samuel Beckett' and premièred in the composer's presence in Holland in June 1987.[4] The impromptu interview we did (on 10 March 1987) at the end of our session proved to be, as far as I know, the last interview to be recorded with him. Those who knew him will hear his love of conversation and his deliberately pungent New York accent in the words transcribed below.[5]

INTERVIEW WITH MORTON FELDMAN

EVERETT FROST. What I want to ask you first is, just generally, what strikes you about Beckett, why you find him interesting.

MORTON FELDMAN. I'd like to start with an interesting remark I heard last night. I had dinner with Francesco Clemente and his wife and we were talking about Beckett. As you know, Clemente is very submerged in literary metaphors. I didn't see the collaboration that Mr Beckett did with Jasper Johns. Clemente did. And his comment was that it seemed obvious that Jasper Johns would be a very good choice for Beckett, because he was closed to the world. He wasn't closed to *his* world. But he was closed to *the* world. And I thought that was a very interesting point because, when you get a world, either like Jasper Johns' (especially in his new paintings) or like Beckett's, the reference to some degree is closed to any other experience but his own. Now, to me, the exciting thing is that neither Jasper Johns nor Beckett are narcissistic: you don't feel the sense of an egoism there. But at the same time you feel

[3] William Kraft (born in 1923 in Chicago) has had a long and active career as composer, conductor, percussionist, and teacher. Writing to me of the exquisitely beautiful music he composed for *Cascando*, Professor Kraft states: '*Cascando*, like *Works and Music*, deals with frustration—the latter with the limitations of words, the former with the creative process itself. The character Woburn is trying to reach a destination—"the island"—which might be either the completion of the story or, more likely, of the process of creation, for which *Cascando* might be seen as an analogy' [Ed.].

[4] The UK première of Feldman's *For Samuel Beckett* was on 10 Nov. 1995, in a London Sinfonietta performance at the Queen Elizabeth Hall, London [Ed.].

[5] The production of *Words and Music*, accompanied by a documentary (produced by Charles Potter) containing portions of the interview, was distributed as part of *The Beckett Festival of Radio Plays* in April 1989. *Words and Music* was funded by grants from the National Endowment for the Arts and the National Endowment for the Humanities, with additional funds from New York University, and is a co-production of Voices International and Westdeutscher Runkfunk (WDR), Cologne, Germany.

a complete and closed artistic experience. That is the contradiction. And that's the contradiction that I identify with. I feel that I, too, am not open to musical experiences other than my own. And yet this project is the happiest of all the things I've done: more so than some things in which I was more in control of how I would want to do it, in terms of its structure.

When I first met Beckett and told him that I'd like to do something—at that time it was for the Rome Opera—the first thing he said to me was that he hated opera. And so did I. I mean, I hardly ever go to the opera. I just don't experience what exactly is meant theatrically by opera. If I had to talk about it, I wouldn't want to use a term like prosaic or clichéd, but it's something to some degree related. But with *Words and Music* you could see why Beckett won the Nobel Prize. That is, he's in the tradition.

EF. The tradition of?

MF. He's in the tradition of a great communicator. He's involved with the subject that haunts most of us.

EF. That makes me want to go back to something that you said earlier: you said that Beckett writes in a self-contained world. That's true. That's one of the experiences that all of those who work with him have. The other is that it's so universal—that so many people find things in Beckett to relate to, on a very personal and emotional level. That's one of the wonderful contradictions in him. One of my subtexts in the series is that lots of ordinary people will listen to this who are not scholars or academics, but who will find things to move them even in *Words and Music*, which is not an easy text.

MF. You know, I had a memorable conversation with Mr Beckett. He was directing a Beckett Festival in Berlin. This was about 1975 or 1976, I believe. And he asked me: if he did write something for me, what would he write? Just like I ask people who are close to me: 'What is it exactly, and what do you think it conveys?' People think that you have this subject and then you superimpose the whole compositional or structural process. That might be true for someone who's doing a cartoon strip. But for most artists the structural concerns are uppermost, and out of it comes the content, which you yourself are to some degree ambiguous about. And in this conversation with Beckett he was a little bit ambiguous about exactly what his subject was. I had to tell him. [Laughs].

EF. What did you tell him?

MF. Well, I don't know if this is proper for a radio interview. But at the same time in Berlin, a very close friend of mine was having breast surgery, and she was in a very bad situation. And I said to Beckett: 'Well, of course, compared to Sarah, you're comic relief'. And by 'comic relief' I mean that there's really no way out. It's beyond existentialism. If you feel that God is dead, then long live humanity. But Beckett isn't involved in that, because there's nothing saving him. For example, the subject essentially of my opera, *Neither*, is to do with whether you're in the shadows of understanding or non-understanding. Finally you're in the shadows. You're not going to arrive at any understanding at all; you're just left there holding this hot potato which is life.

I never liked anyone else's approach to Beckett. I felt it was a little too easy; they were treating him as if he were an existentialist hero, rather than a tragic hero. And he's a word man, a fantastic word man. And I always felt that I was a note man. I think that's what brought me to him. A kind of shared longing: this saturated, unending longing that he has, and that I have.

EF. In *Words and Music*, the word man, Beckett, has provided the text and a series of instructions for the note man. What did you do with them?

MF. I can tell you now, although if I'd said this to you earlier you'd have been very upset. [Laughs.] I hardly read it. Oh, of course, I read it. But I started at the end; I started in different places. That was my way to get to know Beckett. Because I couldn't read it without the music, and there was no music. And so I couldn't get the total experience. I could never have written the last two minutes that I did unless I'd started like that. I didn't ask where I was going to start to swim in the middle of the Atlantic Ocean. The whole idea of a beginning, middle, and end, which was very apparent, would not help as an emotional structure. And so I dipped into it all the time. I learned a lot about Beckett by reading his very early study on Proust. It told me a lot about him. It told me about the way he thinks. It's a kind of clinical understanding. And I'm a very clinical composer at the same time that I'm a note man. The swing, luckily, is going back, from something where the feeling is revealed to something where the feeling is less revealed. The varying degrees of feeling or meaning can be either brought up or brought down, like lighting. That's why a monologue of his is the whole world for me; it's like Homer. There's everything there because of these graduated nuances. I don't know how he does it, but I'm quite sure that, many times, his way of arriving at something must be much more clinical, almost pedantically so, than one would think. But process isn't the main concern: the end-results are what we're involved with here. It's in that context that I understand him to some degree as an artist. I know that there is a clinical approach and that he's learned how to lose it, or to work with it, or to change it. He did tell me that he says things over to himself, over and over. I work the same way. I play things or look at things over and over and over. Not consciously looking for something. Just trying to get the content a little less evasive.

EF. You mean the content of his words?

MF. The contents of his work, or contents of my own work in relation to his work. I could never have written it using his terminology, because I wouldn't know what his terminology meant. I know what it means in terms of Puccini. If Beckett says he wants something sentimental, I have no idea what that means. It's like saying 'a thump'. I mean, what kind of 'thump'? With Beckett, you realize that you don't understand the simplest word, like 'thump'. So I don't try. It's as if you're with someone you love dearly. You're listening to them, and you don't want to be patronizing, but at the same time, language is not telling you. So you're looking in the eyes, you're looking at the body language. In Beckett, you're looking for everything except his directions. If I were to follow his direction 'sentimental', for example, it would have turned out like a John Ford movie or something. [Laughs.]

EF. So what was the way in to *Words and Music*? What began to unlock it for you?

MF. I went to the quintessence of it. The fact that, in very prosaic terms, there was a situation in which two people were having some problems. As prosaic as that. And music essentially had to bend. At the same time the music is always there and has terrific power, even though it's incongruous to some degree. And it's always incongruous when it gets away from clichéd responses. Literature can be universal, but when music is universal it never gets beyond the level of, say, a Shostakovitch. We have a lot of problems in music. Our 'universal' themes come from a different kind of history.

EF. Your character, 'Music', in *Words and Music* is given some universal concepts and invited—in fact, coerced—to create musical structures around them. There's Love, Age, and then finally, the Face. He's handing you universals.

MF. Yes, but it was a technical thing. It wasn't a universal. I didn't pick up, you see, on Age. He wrote this when he was younger than I am now. He was in his mid-fifties. But it was the fact that the language was halting that created for me that pizzicato section, which was not really focused on one place, which gave me an aspect of age. So I tried to carry through the focus of the material and then present it in a more fragmentary way. I was finding my balance, but the balance was a technical thing. I can't disentangle the subject from the technical way of arriving at it. It's a technical metaphor which brings forth the psychological, emotional, or dramatic situation.

EF. I remember that in one of our early conversations when we were first initiating the project, we were talking about musical styles, and I was nudging you in the direction of trying to give me some sense of the musical style, the instrumentation, and so on . . .

MF. [Pause.] I had an emotional vested interest in this. Beckett had been very much a part of my life since the 1950s. He was for my generation a Fifties writer, when Barney Rosset and Grove Press brought him to New York for us. I feel he's a contemporary, although he's twenty years older than me. So I was very excited about doing the project; it meant a lot to me. It was a labour of love. But I approached it the same way I approach everything I do. I don't try to articulate what I'm looking for. I don't give it a name. There is no style. All the musicians said, if you noticed: 'It's you and it's not you'.

EF. What of it is you and what of it is not you?

MF. [Pause.] What's like me is the technical devices or the construction, just the way I would layer something. What's not like me is that I tried to meet Beckett half-way in the sentiment. I don't write in terms of literary images, though 95, 98 per cent of the world's music is in literary images.

EF. And you found that awfully difficult?

MF. I didn't find it difficult because I know what it is. It's as if I had this glass which I could look out from but no one could look in. My music has arrived at a certain degree of abstraction that has a mood and is identifiable. But the mood has to do with instrumental images. I know when he wants something whirling; I understand how to make it whirl, technically, you see. And I think it happened. I'm very happy with the project. I think it's like *Zen and the Art of Archery*. Remember where the German went to study Zen and he practised with the lights on and they broke his bow? He got the bull's eye with the lights on and he was supposed to practise in the dark! [Laughs.] That's the approach, where you develop a certain type of skill and precision to hit the bull's eye. But the objective is not just to practise to hit the bull's eye.

EF. One of the things that put me at ease was the extent to which the score was so carefully structured against exactly what the actors had to do. The score was structured around the various beats that David Warrilow has to do as Words, in a way that was absolutely comprehensible, and suggests to me an awful lot of reading the text. And fitting into it.

MF. I didn't measure it to the text, but I created a composite line of the first line to my scale, which was essentially my air. And then, musically, I tried to work within it. It was the first line that gave me his rhythm and pacing. And I hoped that I would have a sense of the same proportion that he does. Again, it was like working in the dark, and I got there. You couldn't structure. I had no idea what was going to happen in terms of David's pacing. I said to myself: 'I hope he doesn't fight my pacing'. I felt it was Beckett's pacing. I felt it was my pacing also, as well as not being my pacing; it was faster. David is fabulous. But I was just worried about how the actor would want to handle the poem. You can't work it exactly; you just have to feel an overall proportion. I didn't count; I didn't use numbers. I just felt that if I had the first line I'd be able to go through. I read the poem over and over again. It was word painting. It's not Wagnerian in terms of the layering of the word into the structure and body of the music. It's more distant. It's going along. I wanted its presence and its remoteness, its unattainableness. An unattainableness and yet a marvellous presence which is music. It doesn't have to be Beckett. This mystery that the emotion of music has for so many people. That helped me to write it. To be close and distant at the same time. And the closer you get, the more tragic it becomes, and the more compelling it becomes. And the more distant you get, the more tragic it becomes, and the more compelling it becomes. You see. Those were the images. How to arrive at it, I don't know. You can't just write a few measures of music and create something like his final poem in a few lines.

EF. So you found the time restraints difficult, then?

MF. I had to think faster; I had to write faster. I had to compress it faster. Usually I give myself a lot of time, because I'm involved with the experience and want to make it more comprehensible. You see, I grew up in a tradition where technical facility was the metaphor of comprehensibility. The Schoenberg School. Here, I needed time; and yet, I didn't have it. So I had to choose metaphors that would put me into Beckett's world in five seconds flat. No set-up, no preparation, no room for development. It was very difficult to write under those constraints. And the most important thing was the instrumental balance. There are very few places—and they're usually in a kind of soft edge (the vibraphone and the piano)—where I can get onto another high layer without disturbing the surface, so to speak, rather than using a high flute. I'm not talking about the more agitated responses where I use a doubling of the piccolo and the flute: I'm talking about the more gentle sections. The problem with a lot of composers who use Beckett is that they get very histrionic. They can't take that tragic state; they're fighting it all the time. Notice how, in a lot of sections, the two flutes are low. I would say to myself, 'Oh, my God, I'm famous for getting out there and stratifying this instrument and using these things'. I couldn't do it here, couldn't do it at all. I had to begin to do things that were appropriate.

EF. Describing music is difficult, but there are parts of the music that to me are simply beautiful, in a very conventional sense. And I think that's one of the strengths of the piece. Were you, then, willing to . . .

MF. Oh, yes, of course! I would use the term 'very beautiful'. It was not just one type of beauty. It was different levels, because the tune, so to speak, goes through different metamorphoses all the time. It appears in different ways. Sometimes distant and laid back: other times, a little warmer. And what happens at the end is that I just burst out with a little more sensual harmony. There's nothing to interrupt the flute line, and then the modulation takes it away from just the repetition of the thing in different ways over and over again. It adds to the emotional leap. I modulate three times in just a minute, which is unheard of. It sounds great, so you take it for granted, but you don't know the difficulty, technically, of doing it. It's very, very difficult. And what's marvellous about music is that you get it and you accept it, but a lot of people really don't know what the composer has done in order for somebody to respond to it.

EF. Well, I think you've done it. There is a remarkable new score for *Words and Music*.

MF. I'm very happy. It doesn't happen this way very often. I'm finishing something now for the Holland Festival, and I said: 'Gee, I hope I'm not influenced by the seduction of my music being a little faster.' I think I will be. But maybe, in somewhat more abstract terms, I know that this production's going to enter into my life.

4

Morton Feldman's *Neither*: A Musical Translation of Beckett's Text

CATHERINE LAWS

Many composers have been attracted to Beckett's work. Traditionally, there have always been two alternatives for word-setting: either the composer aims to serve the words' own meaning and construction, in the belief that the music may underline particular dimensions of the text, or else the composer asserts the right to create an entirely different work, recasting the textual rhythms in line with the new context and respecting the original solely from the point of view of its relevance to the composition. From either of these perspectives, however, the choice of a Beckett text seems strange; the increasing concentration of Beckett's work is such that no individual aspect of meaning or expression can be separated from another. To highlight a chosen dimension can only be detrimental to the piece as a whole, and the rhythmic precision is such that an additional layer of musical rhythm will destroy rather than enhance the text. Thus the first method is invalidated, and yet to choose a Beckett text for the second approach seems merely perverse: if the words are to be set in such a way as to create an entirely new work, then why choose a text that is already so complete?

Despite these objections, there have been many attempts to set Beckett's words to music. More interestingly, however, certain composers have been drawn to Beckett's work, but have sought different ways of responding to it. Bernard Rands' solo trombone piece *Memo 2*, for example, is derived from the structure of *Not I*, but uses none of the words, while Roger Marsh's *Bits and Scraps* takes fragments from *How It Is*. More recently, Mark-Anthony Turnage's orchestral piece *Your Rockaby* uses rhythmic elements from *Rockaby*, and Richard Barrett has composed a whole series of pieces which imply an aesthetic correspondence by having Beckett quotations written into the scores.[1]

---

[1] Rands wrote his solo trombone piece *Memo 2* for performance by Miles Anderson. Bernard Rands, *Memo 2* (London: Alfred A. Kalmus (Universal Edition), 1973). Marsh composed *Bits and Scraps* for the vocal ensemble Electric Phoenix, who gave the first performance in May 1979 at the Roundhouse, London. Roger Marsh, *Bits and Scraps* (London: Novello, 1979). Turnage's *Your Rockaby* was premièred in 1993 by saxophonist Andrew Robertson, with the BBC Symphony Orchestra (conducted by Andrew Davis). Mark-Anthony Turnage,

One of the most interesting and successful attempts to set a Beckett text is Morton Feldman's one-act opera for a single soprano and orchestra, *Neither*. This work, first performed in May 1977 by Rome Opera, was composed upon a text specifically requested for the purpose and supplied to Feldman by Beckett in 1976. A mutual friend had told Beckett of Feldman's wish to set some of his work to music and Beckett had suggested several already existent possibilities. Feldman, however, felt that none of these pieces needed music. At an initially rather awkward meeting, the author embarrassedly explained that he liked neither opera nor his words being set to music, only to find that Feldman was in complete agreement with him: ' "In fact it's very seldom that I've used words. I've written a lot of pieces with voice, and they're wordless". Then he looked at me and said, "But what do you want?" And I said, "I have no idea!" '[2] Given Beckett's well-known pronouncements on his sense of working with 'impotence' and 'ignorance',[3] Feldman's attitude might well have seemed attractive, leading to the subsequent agreement to send Feldman a libretto.

Ironically, considering his earlier rejection of other Beckett texts on account of their not needing music—and especially considering his stated wish 'slavishly to adhere to *his* feelings as well as mine' (Skempton, 'Beckett as Librettist', 5)—Feldman began writing the music before receiving the libretto: hence the absence of the soprano in the opening.[4] This fact, however, seems less strange when one considers how the words are set; Feldman neither sets the text so as to allow the words to be clear to the audience, nor gives the sense of commenting on the words through the highlighting of a certain dimension or of particular textual relationships. Instead, he remains stubbornly indifferent to

Your Rockaby (London: Schott, 1993). Several of Richard Barrett's pieces take their titles from Beckett: *I open and close* (1983–8) for string quartet and optional amplification, and *another heavenly day* (1989–90) for E♭ clarinet, electric guitar, and contrabass, for example. Other works are prefaced by quotations from Beckett, or else have quotations written into the scores, alongside the music. Examples are *ne songe plus à fuir* (1985–6) for amplified solo cello, *Anatomy* (1985–6) for eleven instruments, and *Tract, part one* (1984–9) for solo piano. The works are all published by United Music Publishers, London.

[2] Howard Skempton, 'Beckett as Librettist', *Music and Musicians*, 25/9 (May 1977), 5–6 (p. 5).

[3] See, for example, Israel Shenker's interview with Beckett (1956), reprinted in Lawrence Graver and Raymond Federman (eds.), *Samuel Beckett: The Critical Heritage* (London: Routledge & Kegan Paul, 1979), 146–9 (p. 148).

[4] It seems that Feldman often prefers to approach his texts in an unconventional manner; in an interview following a recording of Beckett's *Words and Music* (for which Feldman composed the music), Feldman said that he hardly read the play before starting to compose, and that what reading he did 'dipped in and out' of the play, starting in various different places. *Samuel Beckett, Words and Music: A Radio Play and a Documentary about the Production* (New York: Voices International (The Beckett Festival of Radio Plays), 1988) (Audiotape); and see p. 51 above.

any expected need to present the text sympathetically in terms of audibility or clarity of meaning. The textual rhythms are obscured by the setting of individual words or even syllables in isolation, often intoned on repeated notes, or spread across a group of two or three notes without indication of the precise rhythm in which they are to be sung.[5] For much of the opera, the soprano remains in the top register of the voice, and this again ignores any perceived need for clarity. The combined effect suggests that the listener either must know the text in advance, or else must trust that the music corresponds so closely to the text that the simultaneous apprehension of the two would be rendered tautologous.

Given Feldman's general concern to avoid symbolism through the presenting of sonorities 'objectively without the complexities and superfluities of process or "message"',[6] this approach to word-setting begins to seem appropriate. As with Beckett (if we are to believe his early statements concerning the communicative impossibilities of art[7]), with Feldman's work we are, as John Cage observed, 'in the presence not of a work of art which is a thing, but of an action which is implicitly nothing. Nothing has been said. Nothing is communicated.'[8] Beyond this, however, Feldman's statement that he agrees 'with Kafka. We already know everything. So there's no need for me to finish the piece in terms of anyone's expectations'[9] allows the extension of such an interpretation, suggesting that the libretto is not merely being treated as known in the sense of it having been read before the performance, but rather in terms of some vague, pre-existent, perhaps even pre-conscious knowledge, however inexpressible. This in turn seems to correspond to Feldman's statement that, in looking for a text, he was 'looking for the quintessence, something that just hovered' (Skempton, 'Beckett as Librettist', 5).

Beckett's 'Neither'[10] is free from the specifics of name, place, or event, evoking nothing more substantial than oscillatory motion. The sense is

---

[5] In the setting of the phrase 'away from gently part again', each word is spread across three notes, with no indications as to how the three-syllable words should be divided. Morton Feldman, *Neither* (London: Universal Edition, 1977), 19.

[6] Robert Ashley, 'Morton Feldman: An Interview with Robert Ashley', in Elliott Schwartz and Barney Childs (eds.), *Contemporary Composers on Contemporary Music* (New York: Holt, Rinehart & Winston, 1967), 362–6, (p. 362).

[7] 'Art is the apotheosis of solitude. There is no communication because there are no vehicles of communication.' Samuel Beckett, *Proust, and Three Dialogues with Georges Duthuit* (London: John Calder, 1965), 64.

[8] John Cage, *Silence* (Cambridge, Mass.: MIT Press, 1966), 136.

[9] Cole Gagne and Tarcy Caras, *Soundpieces: Interview with American Composers* (Metuchen, NJ: Scarecrow Press, 1982), 172.

[10] Samuel Beckett, 'Neither', in *As the Story Was Told* (London: John Calder, 1990), 108–9.

of a dislocated 'between-ness', a ghostly movement coming and going between different gradations of shadow, between self and unself equally impenetrable, achieving stasis only through the abandonment of such distinctions and even then located by the negative, inexpressible terms of 'unspeakable home'. The movement seems evocative of the unceasing search for an essential 'I', but such absolute presence remains beyond the reach of the shadows, denied by the inability to find a central locus from which true self-knowledge (knowledge of both self and other) would be apprehendable: the saying of 'I' requires the location within that self, but the objective existence of this subjectivity cannot be verified other than from without.

Feldman's initial reaction was to be struck by the visual punctuation of the work—the spaces on the page between each of the ten 'sentences'. As he read and reread the lines, Feldman gradually became aware of the relationship between the separated sentences: 'I'm reading it. There's something peculiar. I can't catch it. Finally I see that every line is really the same thought said in another way. And yet the continuity acts as if something else is happening. Nothing else is happening. What you're doing in an almost Proustian way is getting deeper and deeper saturated into the thought.'[11] Feldman clearly relates this to Beckett's answer to the composer's questions concerning his working methods: 'He would write something in English, translate it into French, then translate the thought back into the English that conveys that thought. And I know he keeps on doing it' (Feldman, 'Darmstadt-Lecture', 185). It seems, then, that Feldman's perception of the text is of the repetition in terms varying in small incremental differences of a single idea that is itself without substance or definition, but which is purely, abstractly evocative. In this sense, the words are mere traces of an inexpressible thought, and Feldman's music, therefore, attempts to recreate parallel traces in musical notes. For the composer, the text is a multi-dimensional object, exposing different facets of the same 'non-idea'[12] while giving the impression of change.

The validity of such an interpretation must, however, be questioned. Despite the ineffable character of the libretto and the apparently goalless, pendular movement depicted by its greater part, some kind of closure *is* finally achieved. The status of this repose is certainly dubious, even ghostly, in its emplacement beyond the regions of self or other; the implications of this final stasis are deathly, and the unsayable nature of the resting place suggests its impossibility in terms accessible to our

[11] Morton Feldman, 'Darmstadt-Lecture', in Walter Zimmerman (ed.), *Morton Feldman Essays* (Kerpen: Beginner Press, 1985), 181–213 (p. 185).

[12] Feldman describes the subject of the Beckett opera—life as framed in a shadow into which we cannot see—as a 'good non-idea'. Morton Feldman, 'XXX Anecdotes and Drawings', in Zimmerman, *Morton Feldman Essays*, 144–80 (p. 163).

limited knowledge or understanding. Nevertheless, the possibility of immobility has undeniably been suggested, however negatively: the concept of some kind of end to the continual wandering has been posited, but Feldman does not seem to want to allow for this. The non-specific self-enclosure of the text means that it is dangerously reductive to draw any positive hermeneutical conclusions. Antoni Libera, for example, attempts to interpret the intra-textual relations by their alignments within the oppositional categories of mental ('inner shadow') and sensual ('outer shadow') images, of cognition and existence.[13] It is equally deceptive, however, to ignore the general direction in which the end of the libretto moves, as Feldman's setting does. There is perhaps an acknowledgement of this alteration and its effect in Feldman's comment that: 'I noticed that, as the work went on, it became much more tragic. It became unbearable, while here [in the opera] it's bearable' (Skempton, 'Beckett as Librettist', 6); the composer, it seems, is more interested in the evocation of the endless, shady coming and going than in the implications of a change in this state.

The basis of Feldman's approach to the text, then, was to attempt to render in musical terms the pendular motion of a single insubstantial idea, viewed in varying contexts. The question of the opera's suitability for analysis is, as one would expect, a difficult one. The piece comes late in Feldman's output, well after his experiments with free duration and graph notation, and after his gradual detachment from Cage's aleatoric experimentation through the feeling that 'Cage's idea [that] "Everything is music" had led him more and more toward a social point of view, less and less toward an artistic one.'[14] Feldman reached a point where he felt that a minimal degree of control was necessary for the exploration of the experience of sound and, similarly, his pieces increased their degree of musical incident: as he explained in an interview with Bernas and Jack: 'You can't write *growing* sound with free notation.'[15] Nevertheless, the notion of unfixing sound from its referential associations and from its falsification within teleological narratives remained central to the composer's aesthetic, and the music therefore attempts a certain ' "inbetween-ness": creating a confusion of material and construction'.[16] Certain characteristics are therefore common to both the earlier and later works and, clearly, the libretto of *Neither* had little effect on Feldman's compositional approach: it is easy to make specific compari-

---

[13] Antoni Libera, 'Some Remarks About *neither*', *Journal of Beckett Studies*, 3/2 (Spring 1994), 85–91.

[14] Morton Feldman, 'Give my Regards to Eighth Street', in Zimmerman, *Morton Feldman Essays*, 71–8 (p. 76).

[15] Richard Bernas and Adrian Jack, 'The Brink of Silence', *Music and Musicians*, 20/10 (June 1972), 7–8 (p. 8).

[16] Morton Feldman, 'Crippled Symmetry', in Zimmerman, *Morton Feldman Essays*, 124–37 (p. 136).

sons with the deployment of pitch material and its orchestration in other works (most particularly in the other Beckett-related works, *Words and Music* and *For Samuel Beckett*).

As in most of Feldman's output, lyricism without melody, the unmediated contemplation of sound, and the avoidance of dramaticism through the use of understated dynamics are all evident in *Neither*. Similarly typical is the approach to form as a length of time with minimal divisions, such that the piece is kept going without the demands of causality, thereby exposing the fallacy that artworks should grow organically. Like various minimal artists, Feldman rejects the tendency to see the parts as more important than the whole, agreeing with sculptor Donald Judd that 'The thing is to be able to work and do different things and yet not break up the wholeness that a piece has.'[17] Instead, Feldman's prefers the determination that form is inseparable from direct experience of the material: as David Lee writes with reference to minimal art, 'The *idea* of a piece no longer exists. [. . .] The *idea* is dissolved in the complexity of experience.'[18] Thus any attempt to find micro/macro-structure correspondences, or even to divide the work into sections for examination according to the allocation of material, is nonsensical. Odd moments may suggest growth as if towards a climax, but this is never pursued over any length of time or to any kind of resolution.[19]

Similarly, the deployment of material has, as usual, an arbitrary quality, suggesting the pre-eminence of intuition in the choice and placing of chords. Despite this, however, an examination of the pitch content of the textures reveals the adherence to surprisingly specific parameters for the choice of notes; this combination leaves us faced with 'the feeling one has in Feldman's music of an exact and maddening superimposition of logic and enigma',[20] and, in this sense, analysis of the forces guiding some of the compositional choices and their relevance to Beckett's libretto can, to an extent, proceed usefully.

On the simplest level, the visual division of the text on the page is translated into a kind of formal grid which juxtaposes blocks of non-developmental material. This is described in an interview with the composer as 'a regular arrangement of bars within the system, each system containing half a line of text' (Skempton, 'Beckett as Librettist',

[17] Donald Judd cited in Bruce Glaser, 'Questions to Stella and Judd', in Gregory Battcock (ed.), *Minimal Art: A Critical Anthology* (New York: E. P. Dutton, 1968), 148–64 (p. 155).

[18] David Lee, 'A Systematic Revery from Abstraction to Now', ibid. 195–9 (p. 198).

[19] The most definite impression of growth towards a climax occurs in the gradual thickening of the texture towards and beyond figure 110. Even this, however, disappears suddenly, without any conclusion having been reached.

[20] Brian O'Doherty cited in Peter Gena, 'Freedom in Experimental Music: The New York Revolution', *Tri-Quarterly*, 52 (Fall 1981), 223–43 (p. 230).

6), but this is only the case for some of the work, the entirety not being as simply constructed as this quotation might suggest. The grid starts from the basis of subdivisions lasting for twelve bars, and each of these covers the breadth of one page of score. These segmentations are maintained through into the wordless section that follows the setting of the line 'intent on the one gleam or the other'.

However, the division of the text into half a line per twelve bars is not always strictly adhered to—the longer third sentence is spread over four segments, while the fourth ('beckoned back and forth and turned away') covers only one twelve-bar length. Similarly, the sentence partitions do not always follow the syntactic logic of the text, as in the setting of the fifth sentence ('heedless of the way, intent on the one gleam or the other'), which is split after 'on' rather than after the comma. The inclusion of sections from which the soprano is absent, and the incorporation of the word 'whose' (from the third sentence) into the end of a section in which the soprano is otherwise resting both have the effect of disrupting the system slightly.

From figure 69, part way into the soprano's wordless section, the lengths of the divisions change. The visual representation of each page of score constituting one section remains, but the number of bars included begins to vary to fifteen, eighteen, twenty, etc., and this inconsistency continues to the end of the work. Despite his deliberate indifference to the assumed need of the audience to make out the words, Feldman occasionally chooses to repeat certain words or phrases, as if to mark them off from the rest of the text: the line 'unheard footfalls only sound' is sung twice, and the final word is repeatedly echoed in the plural over the following twelve bars. Similarly, the words 'neither' and 'unspeakable home' are sung nine times and eight times respectively.

Given the constantly changing bar lengths, the varying pulses used within and against the metres, and the apparently arbitrary allocation of words or syllables within the sections, it has to be admitted that the regularity of many areas of the grid is not aurally perceptible. Instead, its use would seem to derive more importance from its value to the composer as a sequence of frames within which to arrange his material (unsurprising, considering Feldman's early experiments with graphic notation and his links with various minimal artists). Nevertheless, as will become clear, the formal layout finds a more audible counterpart in the actual treatment of blocks of material (even if the correspondence to the divisions of the grid is not always absolutely precise).

The time signatures themselves contribute to the unsteady sense of motion to and fro. The opening is quite unstable, but nevertheless hovers around a mean bar length of 2/4, which alternates with the slightly shorter or longer lengths of 3/8 and 5/8 in no regular pattern.

Once the second page of the score is reached, however, the metre is settled into the steady alternation of 2/4 with 3/8, and this remains constant for roughly the first third of the work. From this point on, the time signature patterns become less fixed, changing either from one twelve-bar section to the next, or at least between small groups of the divisions. However, the metres are almost always organized in pairs wherein one of the signatures has both an odd number of beats and a beat length half or a quarter that of the other, thereby combining repetition with unevenness. Occasionally, but far less persistently, the bar lengths are arranged in repeated groups of three or four changing metres (3/4–3/8–2/2–3/8 in the section from the fourth bar of figure 49, for example); any of these patterns create comparable effects of movement in and out across a central position. Ironically though, because of the varying lengths of the pedal notes or of the ostinati that are written across these metres, their effect is all but destroyed: the mean time signature which would seem to provide a central focal point is both present and absent. Again, as with the grid structure, the score reveals an interesting aspect of textual representation which, in itself, remains unheard, but a comparable aural effect is found in the rhythmic organization of the actual pitch material.

Speaking of his interpretation of the text in terms of the impossibility of fathoming either self or unself, Feldman commented: 'I certainly know more than anyone else in my generation what the "self" is in terms of personal music. I had to invent the "unself". I saw the "unself" as a very detached, impersonal, perfect type of machinery. What I did was to superimpose this perfect machinery in a polyrhythmic situation' (Skempton, 'Beckett as Librettist', 6). In this way, many of the sections of *Neither* are composed of layers of differing pulses (even or uneven), or of pedal notes which either begin or end at different times or else incorporate dynamic swells (again either even or, more often, slightly uneven), so as to give the effect of periodicity. The most regular pulses, ironically, would appear to be those created by dynamic variation within sustained notes, and yet this is undermined by the slight variations in the peaks of the crescendos that are bound to occur through the in-built imprecision of 'hairpin' notation. The total aural effect is of confusing layers of pulse; the impression is both that of music in search of a regular metre, and of the implication that there must be some underlying common denominator within the various layers, some mean pulse to which the instruments are working but that cannot be located.

Throughout the majority of the work, similar effects are created by the movement of different instruments in and out of the texture with their own pulsations. The textures as a whole do not always change from one twelve-bar section to another, but the entries and exits of instruments usually coincide with these points. For certain sections, most of the instruments (usually including the faster pulse material) will suddenly drop out of the texture, and an entirely different effect will be created through the use of static chords.

Even here, however, it cannot be said that the effect of pulse—or the exposition of an attempt to find a pulse—has been entirely abandoned. All that has changed is the time-scale; either one instrument (or, often, the soprano) will persist in the reiteration of a single note, even if at a slow and perhaps uneven pace, or else the pitch material of the long, sustained chords will gradually alter, but their incidence will be regular (as in the solo cello and divisi viola section that begins just after figure 30, for example). Only one type of material is ever played in unison, entering accompanied by nothing but intermittent double bass harmonics (see Figure 4.1). Even here, though, within a single line of pitch material, a kind of virtual polyrhythm is created through the repetition of a nine-note melodic figure; each statement of the figure covers two

Fig. 4.1 *Reproduced by kind permission of Universal Edition (London) Ltd.*

bars (3/4 followed by 2/2) by playing four crotchets in the time of the 3/4 bar and five in the time of 2/2, thereby alternating slightly uneven note lengths against the metre. On top of this, each instrument divides the figure into different phrase lengths (varying from three notes to seven), such that both the stress of the beginning of each phrase and of the alignments with bar openings all work against each other.

Taken cumulatively, the effect of the block juxtaposition of rhythmic material is of the not-quite-presence and the not-quite-absence of regularity. If straight rhythmic repetition is allowed to occur, then it can only do so within the constantly changing contexts of orchestration and/or pitch. Otherwise, it will be undermined by the superimposition of other (often irregular) pulses. In an interview regarding *Neither*, Feldman said: 'What I'm trying to do is hold the moment' (Skempton, 'Beckett as Librettist', 6), and he perhaps achieves this as closely as is possible. While we might expect unchanging, static chordal material to be the most appropriate musical expression of a held moment, Feldman realizes the falsity of such a representation in its inability to continue indefinitely: either the staticity inevitably implies expectations of change, or, at the very least, the piece has eventually to end. Feldman's undertaking is more complex, revealing the very attempt to grasp the ungraspable and thus disclosing the 'almost-ness' of the situation.

Writing about Cézanne, Feldman once said that his contribution to art 'was not how to make an object, not how this object exists by way of Time, *in* Time or about Time, but how this object exists *as* Time. [. . .] Time as an Image. [. . .] This is the area which music, deluded that it was counting out the seconds, has neglected.'[21] Feldman's problem is thus to deal with the fact that while music must be played through actual time, he requires it to reveal the experiential nature of time. All music creates a kind of virtual experience of time, but Feldman sees this as mere falsification: the focus should instead be upon the very point of intersection or collision of the two temporal experiences. The concern is with keeping the piece going; his interest—both in this piece, and in his work as a whole—lies with the process of duration extended by means of change and reiteration,[22] with the '*rightness* of the moment, even though it might not make sense in terms of its cause and effect' (Gagne and Caras, *Soundpieces*, 172).

Thus, the various polyrhythmic disruptions of pulse act as a close musical equivalent to the 'something that just hovered' that Feldman had required of Beckett. The impression is both of an elusive and

---

[21] Morton Feldman, 'Between Categories', *Contemporary Music Review*, 2 (1988), 1–5 (p. 3).
[22] 'I'm working with two aspects which I feel are characteristic of the 20th century. One is change, variation. I prefer the word change. The other is reiteration, repetition. I prefer the word reiteration', Morton Feldman, 'Darmstadt-Lecture', 212.

perhaps even non-existent central point of focus and, simultaneously, of the direct experience of the very search for this position of stability.

At rare points in the score, the uneven metrical effects are temporarily abandoned; twice—first in the eighteen-bar section from one bar before figure 72, and then in the thirty-one-bar subdivision at figure 104—a single time signature is suddenly maintained throughout: 3/8 in the first instance, and 2/4 in the second. In both cases, the material is also such that the periodicity is allowed to be perceived through the placing of material exactly on the beat.

At one point, a similarly regular effect is achieved by alternative means: in the fifteen-bar segment from the fourth bar of figure 77, the time signatures gradually lengthen by one semiquaver per bar, starting from the metre of 5/16. Since all the instruments (with the exception of the sustained string notes) play on the last crotchet of each bar, whatever its duration, the evenness of the process is clearly audible. In each of these three isolated cases, then, regularity seems, momentarily, to have been achieved. Yet no sooner has this been recognized than it is retracted, either (as in the single time signature sections) through the return to, or else by the addition of, the old, rhythmically disruptive material. The effect is of a tantalizing revelation of that which has thus far been withheld beneath the surface: the brevity of the experience, however, is such that its substantiality remains questionable. In this way, correspondences begin to emerge not simply between the opera and Beckett's text, but also between the role of the audience's perception of both. Just as the reader of Beckett's text mirrors the text's 'subject', scanning back and forth across the text, attempting to grasp the meaning and understand the strange effectiveness of the work, Feldman creates a parallel effect: the music seems to search for its own centre, while the listener both follows this process and tries to find his or her own focal points in the rhythmic wanderings.

Writing of Feldman's organization of time, Peter Gena cites Brian O'Doherty's comment: 'Time is used to destroy time. The resulting stasis is what opens the way to the spatial idea. And in turn the spatial idea more or less suggests simultaneity, the possibility of seeing all the piece at once' (O'Doherty cited in Gena, 'Freedom in Experimental Music', 230). In this way, it is not simply the formal division of the piece into juxtaposed blocks of non-developmental material which generates the impression of a single multi-faceted object being viewed from different perspectives; the smaller-scale movement from one moment to the next effects the sense of an extended present tense: Feldman attempts to evoke the inescapable directness of the not-quite-apprehendable 'now', and this, in turn, suggests the possibility of the contemplation of the object as if suspended in space.

At the same time, however, the object is always slightly beyond reach, such that its full assimilation remains unattainable: beneath the 'hover-ing' of Feldman's music, time ticks on, passing into the memory. As with many of Feldman's techniques, the influence of minimal art is here apparent in the formal obfuscation of any definition between the lines of internal division and the edges of the work. More specifically, a com-parison can be made with Rothko's blurring of the boundaries between areas of colour: as Wilson Baldridge writes, 'Musical events Feldman moves away from, drawn to what Rothko said about image-disclosure: darker tones work to "slow down" formation of objects, withhold their approach.'[23] Feldman creates a musical equivalent to this complex at-tempt to capture the dynamic moment of experience, the endless deferral of absolute presence, and, interestingly, in the Rome Opera staging, Feldman himself invoked the comparison with Rothko, expressing his concern that the effect of his music and the libretto should not be translated simplistically into the use of a light-source focusing from shadow into light: he wanted the designer to 'make it like a Rothko painting, the gradation of shadows rather than just a kind of easy symbolic visual aspect of shadows' (Feldman, 'XXX Anecdotes and Drawings', 163).

Beckett has on several occasions spoken of the 'consternation' that lies behind the formal composition of his work.[24] He once told Lawrence Shainberg that: 'Being is constantly putting form into danger', and that: 'If anything new and exciting is going on today, it is the attempt to let Being into art.'[25] For Beckett, then, the attempt to express is the (impos-sible) attempt to render both ontological experience and our impotence and ignorance in the face of existence. Like Feldman, Beckett often preferred to express this need for a radical revision of subject-object relations with reference to his favoured modern artists. Writing of Bram van Velde, for example, Beckett describes the success of the paintings in terms of their ability to capture the unattainable object in simultaneity with the need for the act of representation: 'It is the thing on its own, isolated by the need to see it, by the need to see. A motionless thing in the void; here at last is the visible thing, the pure object.'[26]

Thus, Beckett's disintegration of subject, object, and their narrative

[23] Wilson Baldridge, 'Morton Feldman: One Whose Reality is Acoustic', *Perspectives of New Music*, 21/1–2 (Fall/Winter 1982; Spring/Summer 1983), 112–13 (p. 112).

[24] Beckett once said: 'In my work, there is consternation behind the form.' See Israel Shenker's interview with Beckett (1956), in Graver and Federman, *Samuel Beckett: The Critical Heritage*, 148.

[25] Lawrence Shainberg, 'Exorcising Beckett', *Paris Review*, 29/104 (Fall 1987), 100–36 (p. 105).

[26] Translated from Samuel Beckett, 'La Peinture des van Velde', Cahiers d'Art (1945–6), to accompany the 1993 Tate Gallery exhibition, 'Paris Post War: Art and Existentialism 1945–55'.

exposition is the result of this enterprise; it is the necessary effect of the falsity of the neatness and clarity commonly imposed upon artistic content. Hence his comment to Lawrence Shainberg that: 'I know of no form [. . .] that does not violate the nature of Being in the most unbearable manner' (Shainberg, 'Exorcising Beckett', 106). The transience of time and the distortions of memory are constant preoccupations of Beckett's work; these are major sources of the failure to achieve full presence or meaning, and Beckett cannot simply ignore the impotence of the individual caught within the resultant confusion: as he wrote in a review of poetry by Denis Devlin: 'The time is perhaps not altogether too green for the vile suggestion that art has nothing to do with clarity, does not dabble in the clear and does not make clear.'[27] Thus, Feldman's lamenting of the neglect of the true nature of time in music equates with (and *is a part of*) Beckett's determination to break open artistic form and thereby allow access to Being.

For both artists the challenge is formidable, for what is attempted must endeavour to express its own inability to be grasped. The medium of music is simultaneously perfect and inappropriate for presenting the experience of time in such terms; while the lack of any concrete subject-matter allows a more concentrated focus upon the organization of sound within time, the very expectation of a different temporal experience makes it harder for a composer to direct the attention towards this aspect. Similarly, while Beckett's work moves towards a state of music through the disintegration of both the false restrictions of grammatical and narrative coherence and of referentially grounded meaning, thereby giving access to the attempt to grasp the direct momentary experience, this experience is nevertheless constituted by language itself: the subject and its expression have no existence beyond their expression in linguistic terms, and since this, in turn, is part of Beckett's subject-matter, he—unlike Feldman—can never completely abandon the use of language.

Returning, in the light of this, to Feldman's indifference to the audible coherence of the libretto, it could be suggested that the composer effectively overcomes the problem of the different temporalities of music and language through his awareness that the issues evoked by the text are better examined by the very deployment of material than by any attempt to use the music to 'comment' on the text. The simultaneous transience and ever-presence of the experience of Being in time, and the continual effacement of actual presence, are both articulated through the rhythmic functions and their formal juxtapositions, and, moving into the area of

---

[27] Samuel Beckett, 'Intercessions by Denis Devlin', in *Disjecta*, ed. Ruby Cohn (London: John Calder, 1983), 91–4 (p. 94).

pitch, it is found that the deployment of material can be described in similar terms.

Throughout the opera, the non-developmental nature of the grid divisions is compounded by the correspondence between certain types of pitch material and individual instruments. Thus a particular instrument or class of instruments becomes associated with specific notes or chords, and interest is maintained by the reiteration of the various material-types in different combinations or orchestrations. This is very obviously the case with the different kinds of pulsation (in the opening, for example): whenever an instrument re-enters the texture with pulse material (almost always at the beginning of a grid division), it will be with the same pitch or combination of pitches. Certain instruments therefore become very strongly identified with one element, rarely playing anything else. For example, the timpani are very much associated with the tremolo chord of G♭, C♯, and G♮, which is only occasionally varied by the slight augmentation up to A♭ or A, or by the diminution of the lower interval by the use of C♮. Alternatively, material may be passed back and forth between instruments, as is frequently the case with the strings' widely spaced three-note chords—these are often swung between upper strings and woodwind (around figure 9, for example), emphasizing the block orchestration. The pulse material tends to consist of a single note or semitonal pair of notes all very close in pitch class, such that their gradual superimposition fills out a certain block of the chromatic scale, often in several registers simultaneously.

The chordal material is, in contrast, generally built from three-note chromatic clusters. These can either remain in semitonal intervals, or, just as often, can be transposed into widely spaced chords consisting of minor ninths and/or major sevenths. Thus, while the pitch classes remain constant, the effect is of the alternate expansion to intervallic extremes and contraction to their minimization in clusters: movement in and out. Within an instrumental section (in this case, either strings or woodwind), each group will take a different three-note cluster. Frequently, these are then combined in groups of three, such that nine consecutive pitches of the available twelve are covered, and their superimposition fills out patches of sound in the same manner as the accrual of the various pulse materials. An independent pulse will then be formed by the occurrence of each chord at a different point in the bar, or, if the chords are sustained simultaneously, by the various peaks of the crescendos and diminuendos of each instrument. Effectively, this generates several modes of motion to and fro; in addition to the rhythmic oscillations, we are presented with the linear movement of one instrument between the different pitch clusters, the swinging of intervallically related material between different instruments within the same instrumental group, and the passing back and forth of exactly the same material (in pitch and interval) between instruments of contrasting types (as in Figure 4.2).

Each musical parameter is, in this way, isolated, established within a limited range of articulations, and then treated as a variable for organization into different permutations. Importantly, and perhaps not surprisingly, considering Feldman's early interest in graph notation, these processes are clearly delineated by the appearance of the score; both the alternation between contracted and expanded three-note chords and their oscillation between pairs of instruments effect a striking visual image, such that the musical concerns are apparent in various modes of representation. All possible similarities and differences are highlighted, and thus the contexts in which material is heard are varied on all levels: the same pitch in different instrumental colours, differing pitches but in the same intervallic relationships and in varying orchestrations, and, on the larger scale, these whole blocks of material in different superimpositions with one another.

Through the use of such techniques, Feldman avoids the sense of development or eventfulness that would normally result from the introduction of new material; the possibilities are endless and the order in which they will be explored can therefore remain arbitrary. As was found with the examination of rhythm and metre, even when a complete change of character takes place (as in the abandonment of faster pulses in favour of static chords and sparse textures), a certain aspect of the music is made reassuringly recognizable through the recurrence of past chordal structures, or of an underlying pedal note that has been heard earlier in the same instrumentation. Even in the reflective passage for solo cello and divisi violas, where the chordal progression is clearly intuitive and its duration arbitrarily determined,[28] we recognize the transference of the soprano line into that of the cello, and are even reassured both by the semitonal pairs of notes that constitute parts of the chords and by the close semitonal movement that marks the progression between one chord and the next within much of each viola line (see Figure 4.3). Change and reiteration are therefore both present, but only to the minimal degree necessary for the continuation of the piece.

Throughout the work, Feldman seems to play with the notions of presence and absence through the deployment of pitch material. The superimposition of three-note chords wherein each pitch class is

[28] Within the above-cited interview with Howard Skempton, Feldman said: 'What made me determine the length of the instrumental interlude? I can't answer. It's almost as if I'm reflecting. I didn't want a cause-and-effect continuity, a kind of glue that would take me from one thought to another.' Skempton,'Beckett as Librettist', 6.

Catherine Laws

Fig. 4.2 Reproduced by kind permission of Universal Edition (London)
Ltd.

Fig. 4.3 Reproduced by kind permission of Universal Edition (London) Ltd.

different could so easily allow the presentation of the full chromatic gamut. Most of the time, however, Feldman restricts the number of these chords to three, often combining this with a pair of semitones held in another instrument so as to increase the number of pitches present to eleven.[29] Thus, the frustrated attempt to fill the chromatic spectrum seems to correspond to the rhythmic effect of the attempt to find a central, original pulse, and both of these reveal Feldman translating into musical terms the libretto's condition of ceaseless pendular movement. Naturally, the exclusion of a single pitch class is not likely to be aurally detectable, especially within the often wide range of the composer's note distribution, and yet Feldman does use devices that suggest a desire to make his organizational priorities clear. At times, we *are* presented with all twelve pitch classes at once. When this happens, however, it is not normally by the inclusion of the twelfth pitch within the chordal material but, rather, by its separate presentation

---

[29] See, for example, the few bars opening the section from the fourth bar of figure 25, where F♯ is excluded in this manner (apart from its occasional sounding in the soprano part).

within a different kind of material, and often in an unusual range and/or orchestration.[30]

In this way, the listener receives a clear sense not only of the coming and going of material, but, more precisely, of the interdependence of the presence and absence of particular notes; the missing note is made obviously present, and yet will usually remain excluded from the main textural type. It is noticeable how often the isolated pitch is of the same class; while it is not always the same note which is absent, a focus upon two specific pitch areas from which the missing note will be picked is gradually established.

The most commonly used of these two areas is that around F, F♯, and G: a large proportion of the segmentations which omit a single note choose one or more of these and sometimes for more than one consecutive division.[31] In contrast, the other area from which the missing note is commonly chosen is that around C, C♯, and D.[32] The demar-

---

[30] The first appearance of the chromatic gamut, for example, is in the section that begins one bar after figure 6, where the flutes, oboes, and clarinets each have a three-note chord of sevenths and ninths. To this the double basses add a semitonal pair of harmonics, such that the sustained chordal material includes every pitch except F. Continued from the previous sections, however, is the unsteady harp pulse simultaneously sounding E♯ and F, very low in register and emphasized by the instrument's ability to pluck the notes doubly by means of enharmonic tuning: this arrangement of material recurs on several occasions. (See Figure 4.4). Similarly, and even more pointedly, the missing note may enter suddenly, again in a noticeable instrumentation and often part-way through a section, as is the case in the subdivision beginning five bars before figure 27. For the previous two grid divisions, F (again) has been the only note omitted from the pitch clusters, but here, half-way through the section, it enters alone, independent of any other entries and played by the tuba. This pattern of events recurs on occasion later in the work, as at figure 112 where, having been absent for five segments, the F enters at the opening of the subdivision in the bassoons, momentarily at the base of the sustained chordal material.

[31] This is the case in the sections around figures 20 and 21, which omit F♯ and F, F♯ and G (at least until the soprano entry in the final bar) respectively, and in the sections from three bars before 56 and one bar before 57, which leave out all three notes.

[32] For example, C and C♯ are the only pitches excluded from the section around figure 15, and C and D are similarly omitted from that after figure 17. In the reflective chordal section for solo cello and divisi violas, the cello takes over from the soprano, alternating strictly between the notes F and G♭. The viola chords which lie beneath the cello are obviously determined fairly arbitrarily; while the linear motion is often either semitonal or tonal, the adherence to this is variable, as is the direction of the movement. Nevertheless, one particular factor does seem to have been taken into account, and this, again, concerns the pinpointing of these two pitch areas, this time focusing on the notes D and G. For example, while the chords in the grid division from the fourth bar of figure 31 exclude the note G, the two subsequent sections, taken cumulatively, include every pitch class excepting D. Following this, as the cello continues its solo but the accompanying orchestration changes, the division from one bar before figure 35 alternates the presence and absence of the D (emphasizing its omission by the inclusion of the surrounding notes C♯ and E♭ in the same register), while the next section excludes D but focuses upon G and the neighbouring pitches. The chords of the next two subdivisions suddenly exclude both notes before, in the section around figure 38, we hear both simultaneously, emphasized by their orchestration (the D is placed at the base of the chord, in the tuba, while the G is at the top of the clarinet chord). Despite the fact that these presences and absences are clearly indeterminately ordered, and that the excluded note is not necessarily the sole omission, no other notes are treated in this fashion, and the movement continues back and forth between the permutations of their inclusion and exclusion.

Fig. 4.4 *Reproduced by kind permission of Universal Edition (London) Ltd.*

cation of these two areas effectively bisects the octave, giving the effect of passing between two opposing poles of pitch. This is established almost immediately: C is the only note missing from the second section, while F♯ is absent from the next section from which such an omission is made (that starting one bar before figure 5). Nevertheless, the positions of these points are themselves unstable, and they tend to give the effect of marking out general pitch areas rather than specific points.

This rough bisection of the octave is used not only in the isolation of two pitch areas, but also for the opposition of chromatic blocks of material. In many places where the material does not cover all or virtually all of the twelve pitches, the examination of included notes reveals that they fill out all of one patch of pitch classes, the outer-reaches delimited by either C/C#/D or F/F#/G. For example, while the section around figure 16 includes all of the pitches from C# through to G excepting D, that around figure 22 comprises those from G to D♭. Thus the dual presence of the note G (separately allocated to the so-prano) acts as a kind of axis for the pitch territory either side, while the complete absence of the note D pinpoints the other pole. The instability of the territories is again occasionally emphasized by the expansion of the pitch-block boundaries, as in the sections around figures 10 and 11, where the pitches cover C–G, thereby including the areas around both pitch poles and the intervening notes on one side. Thus, the block material can expand outwards to encompass each focal point, or con-tract inwards to pinpoint the exclusion of one or both.

On other occasions, while all or nearly all the pitch classes may be included, the delineation of the two opposing areas is achieved by means of orchestration. In the subdivision beginning one bar after figure 76, the soprano line encompasses the pitches from F to B, while the string chords consist of those from B to E (and also of F# and G, as usual emphasizing the presence of these notes above the others); in this in-stance, the contrast is not simply between two pitch areas, but also between the soprano's linear and the strings' chordal exposition of the territories. The sense of movement between regions is thereby combined with the linear spatial exploration of one area. Again, while the precise pitch correspondences may not be aurally perceptible, the effect is clear: the rhythmic, dynamic, and textural flux back and forth is matched by the linear and chordal expansion and contraction of pitch areas around points which are themselves unable to be fixed. Thus, even the audibility of the compositional procedures and the interdependencies of the ma-terial are subjected to the process of 'coming and going'—the alternate setting up and effacing of various elements is enacted both within the material, and on the external level of audition. This combines with the painterly attention to the score's appearance to explain Feldman's asser-tion of the importance of notation in determining the music itself, rather than as a mere template for realization.[33]

---

[33] 'The degree to which a music's notation is responsible for much of the composition itself, is one of history's best kept secrets', Morton Feldman, 'Crippled Symmetry', in Zimmerman, *Morton Feldman Essays*, 132.

Examining the part of the singer, it becomes clear that it is the soprano line that is responsible for the pitch divisions; for roughly the first two-thirds of the opera, the soprano is restricted to the pitches of F♯–G–A♭ in the upper register, only extending this slightly (upwards, to a top B) in the wordless section. Thus, the choice of one or more of these notes as significantly absent from the orchestral textures is contrasted with their presentation in the brief soprano entries, and this is occasionally emphasized by the unaccompanied sounding of only these notes in the soprano and one or two other instruments. When the singer suddenly re-enters after the tacet following the wordless section (at 'unheard footfalls only sound', one bar before figure 91), the pitch has been unexpectedly shifted down to the note D, which is then intoned throughout the line and for the duration of its repetition. From this point on, the soprano continues to delineate these two pitch areas, moving around either one. This changes only once, for a brief moment, in the last pages of score, when the intervening pitches are, for the first time, covered; the effect is of the temporary breaching of boundaries that, ironically, reveals both their self-imposed nature and—through the inevitable return to the restricted higher region for the repetition of the final words—the inescapability of their definitive power.

The soprano and orchestra, therefore, exist in mutually supportive roles in more than just the traditional sense. With regard to the pitch material, each seems to fix its own presence in relation to the position of the other, and yet neither is at all stable. Both are endlessly shifting in time and in the spatial deployment of their pitches; each attempts to define its aural presence in terms of a lack or an absence in the other, and yet the instability of these elements renders this impossible—the contexts are constantly changing. Despite the eschewal of micro/macro-structure correspondences, the reiteration and variation of limited material enhances the self-referentiality of the work. The close relationships between musical materials serve not as a means of achieving a coherent organic unity, but, in opposition to this, as a means by which the absence of a central point of focus is suggested. Eventfulness is minimized, ironically, through the very realization of the proliferation of possibilities; the internal reflection of material through contextual variation and juxtaposition gives the effect of everything being the shadow of everything else: the original image, if it ever existed, is beyond reach.

In a general statement about his work, Feldman once wrote: 'Essentially I am working with three notes and of course we have to use the other notes. But the other notes are like shadows of the basic notes. [. . .] When after a few years I added another one, I added four notes, because the four notes would give me the relationship of either two minor seconds or two major seconds' (Feldman, 'XXX Anecdotes and Drawings', 169). This seems peculiarly apposite in the current context, relevant to not only the hazy evocative effect, but, more specifically, to both the precise terms of Beckett's libretto, and the incorporation of three-note chords. Thus, the most minimal addition to the material generates a whole field of possibilities, and the correspondence between this method of working and Feldman's description of Beckett's technique of continual translation becomes clear: the increment of differences through repeated translation back and forth between two languages finds a parallel in the accumulation of intervallically related chromatic clusters allocated variously in terms of both register and instrumentation.[34]

The result of both is the infinite shifting of contexts by minute degrees, and the impression of forward momentum is given without the occurrence of any real change. In each case, the skill is such that the technique is fundamental to the evocative power of the content—the two are interdependent, and the use of regular, block material (temporally, instrumentally, and in terms of pitch) combined with arbitrary choices as to the deployment of material-types within these divisions creates the simultaneous effect of rigorous searching and unfocused wandering.

Beckett's use of translation as a compositional method, therefore, corresponds to the constant recontextualization of sound in Feldman's work. Feldman has often spoken of the vital importance of instrumentation—'For me, composition is orchestration'[35]—and of his sense that 'instruments get in the way of sounds, robbing them of their immediacy'.[36] This attitude is, perhaps, the musical equivalent of Beckett's preoccupation with the intermediary distortion of words—'more and more my own language appears to me like a veil that must be torn apart in order to get at the things (or the Nothingness) behind it'[37]—and yet, if anything, Feldman sees his medium as more restrictive than Beckett's:

Beckett's voice is also so prevalent on his stage that it's difficult to distinguish *what* is said from *who* is saying it. As in Guston's painting, we seem to be hearing two voices simultaneously.

---

[34] Feldman himself seems to make this connection, albeit with respect to his general technique: 'What I do then is, I translate, say something, into a pitchy situation. And then I do it where it's more intervallic, and I take the suggestions of that back into another kind of pitchyness—not the original pitchyness, and so forth, and so on. Always retranslating and then saying, now let's do it with another kind of focus', 'Darmstadt-Lecture', 186.

[35] Paul Griffiths, 'Morton Feldman', *Musical Times*, 113/1556 (Aug. 1972), 758–9 (p. 758).

[36] Peter Dickinson, 'Feldman Explains Himself', *Music and Musicians*, 14/11 (July 1966), 22–3 (p. 22).

[37] Samuel Beckett (trans. Martin Esslin), 'German Letter of 1937', in *Disjecta*, 170–3 (p. 171).

For a composer this is a crucial problem: that the means or the instrument you use are only to articulate musical thought and not to interpret it.[38]

The pre-existent nature of musical notes differentiates them from the materiality of words or paint, and this purity, in a sense, excludes the direct 'touch' of the composer: 'The tragedy of music is that it begins with perfection. You can see all the time, while you are looking at a terrific picture, where the artist has changed their mind. I love those Mondrians where you can see it's erased. [. . .] There's nothing like that in music.'[39] Thus, in Cézanne's painting, his 'intelligence and touch have become a physical thing, a thing that can be seen. In the modulations of Beethoven we do not have his touch, only his logic. It is not enough for us that he *wrote* the music. We need him to sit down at the piano and play it for us' (Feldman, 'Between Categories', 4).

Feldman's concern, then, is to create a music with 'surface' definition—'time canvasses' which attempt to capture the direct experience of temporal existence—and hence to give up the control of his material as far as possible while still being able to call the piece his own. The composer, according to Feldman, cannot simply and tyrannically manipulate his material, but must pay real attention to it: 'The composer may have plans [. . .] but the music others' (Dickinson, 'Feldman Explains Himself', 22). The relationship to Beckett's statement that 'the kind of work I do is one in which I'm not master of my material' (Graver and Federman, *The Critical Heritage,* 148) is clear, and such an attitude is vital to the attempt to express the experience of the ungraspable nature of Being. Feldman once wrote: 'What concerns me is that condition in music where the aural dimension is obliterated', moving on to explain that he means this not in the sense of inaudibility: 'I think of Schubert, *Fantasie* in F-Minor. The weight of the melody here is such that you can't place where it is, or what it is or what it's coming from.'[40] The ideal of a sourceless music of surface in relation to which the listener does not know how to fix his or her self is thereby evoked. The endlessly self-reflective, shadowy character of the material and organization of *Neither* can be seen in this light—the treatment of pitch, rhythm, and form, the minimization of eventfulness, and the promotion of orchestration to pre-eminence with regard to the varying presentation of all of these, contribute to the effect of movement around a central absence.

Again, this relates to Feldman's attitude towards the libretto and clarifies this sense of its implications being somehow pre-existent and

[38] Morton Feldman, 'Essay', in Zimmerman, 115–19 (p. 116).

[39] Fred Orton and Gavin Bryars, 'Morton Feldman Interviewed by Fred Orton and Gavin Bryars', *Studio International*, 192 (Nov–Dec. 1976), 244–8 (p. 246).

[40] Morton Feldman, 'The Anxiety of Art', in Zimmerman, *Morton Feldman Essays*, 85–96 (p. 89).

already known; the musical processes attempt to render the impression of the piece having begun before the opening and of it continuing before the end. Thus, while the expected authoritative essence is absent, the terms within which it has been sought revolve endlessly. In this sense, the lack of concern for the intelligibility of the soprano's words can be seen as a fundamental and necessary part of the process of setting this particular libretto.

Beyond the specific correspondences between Feldman's generation of a music that revolves around an unlocatable focus and the subject and articulation of Beckett's text, it is possible to trace analogies with Beckett's general status as a bilingual author. In his book *Beckett and Babel*, Brian Fitch draws attention to the uniqueness of Beckett's position as a writer and self-translator producing each text in both French and English. As Fitch points out, in translating a text, Beckett often made alterations, frequently of single words or phrases, but sometimes of whole passages, such that the two versions of each work are in some senses significantly different. This calls into question the status of the 'work', for neither can be seen as the 'correct' or authoritative version, and yet the two are not the same. Each is dependent upon the other since, while the second text cannot exist without the former, the changes made and its temporal succession suggest its priority.

In terms of the Derridean concept of the supplement, it is this very addition—that which seems to guarantee the presence of an original—which reveals the lack in each, opens up an absence. Thus there is no original, and the status of the work is thrown into crisis through its unstable location in the very movement between languages. The contradictions between the two versions deny the text any existence as a 'whole' other than in some purely hypothetical space within which the differences could coexist. As Fitch concludes: 'Beckett's persistence in producing a second-language version of each and every one of his works is intimately bound up with his conception of his fundamental enterprise as a writer';[41] beyond the content of the works, textual authority is effaced within the actual process of creation (just as Feldman attempts an 'inaudible' music), a fact which serves as the ultimate denial of the viability of effective literary expression.

In the light of this, Feldman's fascination with Beckett's method of repeated translation becomes particularly relevant, especially considering his own view of the importance of orchestration as a kind of musical equivalent to translation. The analogy, however, opens up a problematic area in which certain attitudinal differences begin to emerge. While

---

[41] Brian T. Fitch, *Beckett and Babel: An Investigation into the Status of the Bilingual Work* (Toronto: University of Toronto Press, 1988), 229.

Feldman laments the perfection of music and attempts to create a musical surface by emphasizing the materiality of sound, Beckett seems to move in the opposite direction: the structures of language are broken down, dissolving into something more pure and direct and, ironically—through both the increasing self-referentiality and the deployment of words for their sensual qualities—something more musical.

This situation is, however, more complex than such a simple opposition might suggest, for, despite the apparent divergence, both see the problem in similar terms. While Feldman appreciates the materiality of words and paint in contrast to the purity of music, this is not from any wish to deny music its abstraction, but rather from his concern to make the process of composition its own subject-matter. This approach developed through an appreciation of Abstract Expressionist painting: he gives the example of the way the paint falls onto a Jackson Pollock canvas being clearly formative of the work's subject since 'there are no other allusions to get in the way of the action of what has happened' (Orton and Bryars, 'Morton Feldman Interviewed', 245), and this corresponds to Beckett's attempt to use language in such a way that 'the thing I am trying in vain to say may be tried in vain to be said' (*Three Dialogues*, 144).

In interviews and essays, Feldman often returned to the idea of a music without instruments, a music which would bypass the problem that performers are 'not interpreting the music; they're interpreting the *instrument*, and then the music' (Gagne and Caras, *Soundpieces*, 166). Thus Feldman's attempt to give his music a certain plasticity and Beckett's dissolution of linguistic structures are both results of the need to bypass restrictive intermediary factors, factors which unavoidably falsify the directness of expression by dissociating what is to be said from how it is said: it is Beckett's very negation of referential content which, ironically, focuses attention upon the signifier and emphasizes the very materiality of his medium. While Feldman may believe that the 'impurity' of words restricts their distortion by the performer or the reader and allows the dual articulation of what is to be said and who is saying it—Feldman's 'two voices'—Beckett would seem to disagree, as is shown in the assiduity of his direction of his plays.[42]

Effectively, both Beckett and Feldman use the meeting point of their media—the pure play of their signifiers—to emphasize the self-referentiality of the works. The result, as Bersani and Dutoit have written with reference to Rothko, is that each leads us 'to re-enact what might be called our *extensive identity* in the world, an identity forgotten

[42] Consider, for example, Billie Whitelaw's descriptions of working on a Beckett text by listening to him read it and then following his intonation and timing. See Jonathan Kalb, *Beckett in Performance* (Cambridge: Cambridge University Press, 1989), 234.

or repressed by the authoritative self intent on reinforcing its boundaries in order to know better what is beyond them'.[43]

From this point of view, both attempt the impossible in seeking to render both existential experience and its very ungraspableness. Feldman's assertions that 'For art to succeed, its creator must fail' ('The Anxiety of Art', 91), and that while 'craft is something you do in the light, skill is something you do in the dark' ('XXX Anecdotes and Drawings', 173), seem to align him with Beckett's comments on the impossibility of expression, yet a vital difference remains. Feldman once stated that: 'Where in life we do everything we can to avoid anxiety, in art we must pursue it' ('The Anxiety of Art', 96), but his music in general, and *Neither* in particular, simply does not suggest the level of consternation of Beckett's work. Beckett's later works, including the *Neither* libretto, may have moved beyond the desperation reached in *The Unnamable*, leaving the reader with a shadow of the first person narrator, but the anxiety of the impossible attempt to find a position from which self and other can be melded into the unity of full presence remains. Even this knowledge of the process of refinement in Beckett's output enhances this impression, the works themselves, like their 'subjects', appearing as referentially diminishing shadows of former texts.

In Feldman's case, however, the sense is always of the wealth of possibilities inherent within reduced circumstances:[44] even the above quotation regarding the necessary failure of the artist includes the *success* of the artwork itself, a possibility which Beckett would not admit. In *Silence*, John Cage tells of a car journey on which Feldman fell asleep: 'Out of a sound sleep, he awoke to say, "Now that things are so simple, there's so much to do." And then he went back to sleep' (*Silence*, 72); while the incident may be from early in Feldman's career, the positing of endless creative possibility is equally relevant to later works, including the self-generative properties of *Neither*. Feldman's association with Cage provides an interesting counterpart to his relationship to Beckett and helps the assessment of aesthetic differences; while Cage's assertion that Feldman 'is not troubled about continuity for he knows that any sound can follow any other'[45] may overstate the case in its denial of an element of concern with 'keeping the party going' (Bernas and Jack, 'The Brink of Silence', 8), it serves as a reminder of Feldman's roots in the freedom of the experimental music of the 1950s and 1960s.

[43] Leo Bersani and Ulysse Dutoit, *Arts of Impoverishment: Beckett, Rothko, Resnais* (Cambridge, Mass.: Harvard University Press, 1993), 207.

[44] In an interview, Feldman said: 'Whether it's on the keys of the piano or on the canvas, there are thousands of other possible notes or marks to choose from.' Orton and Bryars, 'Morton Feldman Interviewed', 246.

[45] John Cage, *A Year from Monday* (London: Marion Boyars, 1968), 98.

Feldman's *Neither* may articulate precisely the ceaseless motion back and forth and the instability of the attempt to locate an original subjective point of focus—the contradictions of not-quite-full presence and not-quite-complete self-effacement may be simultaneously delineated without any attempt at assimilation into a unity—but the final state is of the acceptance of the plurality, rather than Beckett's problematization of it. In the dialogues with Georges Duthuit, having spoken of Bram van Velde as the first artist to 'admit that to be an artist is to fail as no other dare fail', Beckett moves on to describe his own inability to make of 'this admission, this fidelity to failure, a new occasion, a new term of relation' (Beckett, *Three Dialogues*, 145) such that the failure could be reassimilated into the terms of an expressive act.

While our reaction to this may be complicated by the appreciation of the expressive power of Beckett's work in the face of its complicity with such negative terms, the quotation nevertheless serves to articulate the difference between Beckett's and Feldman's attitudes towards the problematics of *Neither*: while Feldman can accept contradiction into the equation, Beckett's work achieves both formidable linguistic expressivity *and* the problematization of the creative act.

In various interviews with Feldman, it is easy to identify the coincidence of apparently contradictory attitudes, at once asserting the need for anxiety while emphasizing that: 'Art is distraction' (Bernas and Jack, 'The Brink of Silence', 7) and that: 'Sounds were treated as self-contained counters, and fitting them together was a bit like making moves in a game of chess.'[46] While the permutational form of much of Beckett's later work may suggest the 'art as distraction' approach (and even the reference to chess is appropriate in the light of works such as *Murphy* and *Endgame*), such absolute detachment can never quite be achieved; even in *Quad*, for example, where the four figures work through all their possible combinations in moving around the sides and diagonals of the square, a sense of unease is generated by the direction that they must avoid the centre.

Ultimately, the very concurrence of contradiction within Feldman's attitude indicates the prevalence of a positive approach within which no dialectical justification is necessary, an approach which Nicholas Zurbrugg sees as typical of the all-encompassing, affirmative nature of American postmodernism (strongly influenced by Cage), as opposed to the more commonly recognized European conception of postmodern art as delineating a crisis-ridden culture of exhaustion.[47]

[46] Christian Wolff, 'Taking Chances', *Music and Musicians*, 17/9 (May 1969), 38–45 (p. 39).
[47] Nicholas Zurbrugg, *The Parameters of Postmodernism* (London: Routledge, 1993), 55–6.

Feldman's assertion that he never has to worry about having ideas because they suggest themselves through the process of sitting down to work (Orton and Bryars, 'The Brink of Silence', 247) even denies the artist his or her traditional distress on being faced with a blank piece of paper or canvas. While Beckett's (supposed) inability to master his material forms part of the consternation of his subject, from Feldman's point of view this is not a problem, for to minimize artistic control is seen as a positive action, a step in the direction of true expression.

Feldman thus lies somewhere between Cage and Beckett, adapting the terms of each and presenting them simultaneously in full recognition and acceptance of their inherent contradictions. Feldman, like Cage, 'rejects the limitations of the past rather than worrying about the limitations of the present and the future' (Zurbrugg, *Parameters of Postmodernism*, 12); for Beckett, in contrast, the weight of both his own literary past and that of literary history as a whole hover over his work as a reminder of other heroic failures in the search for expression—he is all too conscious that the very constitution of his words and their meanings is inescapably bound up with that history. Beckett's work is innovative, but through an angst-ridden process of refinement of both his own work and its relationship to literary tradition. Feldman's relationship to the history of Western music is more complex than he would have admitted: despite the early unfixing of sound from the musical canon and its academic study (since 'sound does not know its own history' ('The Anxiety of Art', 86)), later writings seem to make increasing references to past composers.[48] Yet the anxiety within this is purely personal, and, despite changes in compositional style that occurred through the later reconciliation with the guiding force of the composer, it in no way finds its expression in the music.

Clearly, then, the aesthetic correspondences between the work of each artist are many. Both Beckett and Feldman institute a radical revision of traditional subject-object relations, abandoning the falsities of cause and effect dialectics and instating non-teleological structure. Each locates the reader/listener within the instability of the experience itself, rather than allowing the safety of objective contemplation from without. Thus the work comes to exist dynamically within the space of its reception—as Feldman wrote with reference to the painting of Philip Guston, the work is 'not confined to a painting space but rather [exists] somewhere in the space *between the canvas and ourselves*'.[49]

---

[48] In an interview, Feldman described his retreat from Cage's absolute abandonment of artistic control: 'I once told Cage: "John, the difference between the both of us is that you opened up the door and got pneumonia and I just opened up a window and got a cold".' Orton and Bryars, 'Morton Feldman Interviewed', 246.

[49] Feldman, 'After Modernism', Zimmerman, *Morton Feldman Essays*, 97–112 (p. 106).

However, while Beckett retains the sense of a struggle with the semantics and the history of his medium through a process of refinement rather than rejection, Feldman frees sound from the old structures of goal-oriented tension and resolution but, having done so, does not look elsewhere for a means of recasting the anxiety of expression. In this case, the very clarity of Feldman's approach—his appreciation of the 'deity of sound' (Ashley, 'Morton Feldman: An Interview', 364)—precludes any real pursual of anxiety: perhaps (particularly non-tonal) music's unproblematic existence precisely *as* the pure play of deferred presence itself excludes the consternation.

Hence Beckett's paradoxical striving towards such a state in the face of the inability to abandon words. This is again reminiscent of Feldman's acknowledgement that the opera is less tragic than the original text, and it becomes clear that the statement is relevant to the whole opera, rather than merely the rejection of the change in character of the last part of the libretto.

Despite the work's success, therefore, it could be suggested that Feldman's insistence upon a new text was unnecessary; the opera effectively renders the subject and general effect of Beckett's output (most especially the later works) successfully in musical terms, and yet it is clear that this is mainly due to the close affinity between the aesthetic attitudes of the two.

5

Beckett and Holliger

PHILIPPE ALBÈRA
Translated from the French by Mary Bryden

When Heinz Holliger chose to write musical settings for Beckett's *Come and Go* and *What Where*, he was choosing two plays which undoubtedly lend themselves to music: not only does their structure combine the principle of variation with the rondo form, but also the language relinquishes much of its denotative function by concealing from us the very subject of the discourse: it remains secret, or unnamable. *Come and Go* and *What Where* can thus be affiliated with musical scores, in which everything is noted with the greatest of precision (especially at the level of playing directions), but which at the same time require a performance and an interpretation. It is in effect the reader—or the spectator—who is called upon to define the context in which archetypical situations and essentially banal conversation may assume meaning. In shifting Beckett texts into a musical space, Holliger thereby suggests his own interpretation.

COME AND GO

Within the basic structure of *Come and Go*, Holliger applies a process of amplification which, paradoxically, foregrounds something resembling a ritual of extinction. Not only are the three women represented by three instruments of identical register, but they are also multiplied by three (as is the case with the instruments).[1] Thus, the music projects the text onto three simultaneous 'stages', each one defined by a specific register and language (the French, English, and German versions being used concurrently). In strictly logical fashion, the piece is played in its entirety three times. The music therefore implements a transposition in time and space. The 'image' of this can be found in the score: the melismas are not usually synchronized, either within each group or between groups. The musical voices are sometimes staggered, sometimes

---

[1] The work can be played with the whole ensemble, or with a reduced one: for example, the instruments alone, or three flutes alone (or three clarinets, or three violas), etc.

in an echo, a dialogue, or in complementarity. They spread out in an almost organic movement of expansion and consolidation, revealing nodes, convergences, simultaneities. The writing is essentially poly-phonic—a polyphony which is both free, and very controlled. Holliger exploits one of the potentialities of Beckett's text: the play of permuta-tions, exhausting the combinatory possibilities of the three women, reaches to infinity, evoking children's round-songs. But it is undermined by the secret which the women, two by two, whisper to each other concerning the absent one, and by the passage of time, which the circular structure does not manage to hold within its magic circle.

Holliger has made of these absent figures—what is not said or seen—the basis of the musical form. Each repetition of the piece operates a reduction in the aural and verbal resources, together with a weakening of the tone qualities and intensities. Thus, in the second part, the singers only pronounce the consonants of the text, and the perceived sounds (harmonic or multiphonic sounds, noises of keys or breath, various modes of playing, etc.) invade the instrumental space. The second clari-net is exchanged for the bass clarinet, the second flute for the alto flute, and the second viola lowers its last string by one tone. In the last part, the phenomenon is further developed: the voices mime the text, only releasing a few key words ('Oh!', 'Weiss sie es nicht?', 'À Dieu ne plaise', 'alten', 'after', etc.). The sounds rarify, and the intensities diminish until they can scarcely be heard. Then come the contrabass clarinet and the bass flute, which take the place of the third clarinet and third flute, whilst the third viola lowers its last string by two tones. The end is physically perceived as an exhaustion of the possibility of any speech (the piece forms an immense decrescendo, from the initial *fff* to the final *pppp*). Beckett signalled this erosion of time by the nostalgic evocation of a past epoch, of which memories become more and more remote ('Just sit together as we used to, in the playground at Miss Wade's'; 'Holding hands . . . that way'; 'Dreaming of . . . love'), and by the enig-matic last words: 'I can feel the rings'. (In his stage directions, Beckett writes 'No rings apparent'.) It is the image or symbol of maturity as a child's dream, and it takes place in a circular space shot through with the arrow of time.

WHAT WHERE

In *What Where*, Holliger extends the structure of the Beckettian text in a different direction. The voice of Bam (an interior voice, distorted by a megaphone) drags constantly behind it the shadow of the characters whom Bam has had suppressed: Bam, Bom, Bim, and Bem form a chorus of ghosts to which are added the four trombones, within a texture where there is often no difference between voices and instruments. The percussionists crudely evoke the scenes of torture which, in the play, are suggested but never described or demonstrated. All the music exacerbates the mixture of violence and scorn which is characteristic of Bam. If the exchanges, in *Come and Go*, are characterized by tones of confidence, conspiracy, and nostalgia, they function in *What Where* within a mode of interrogation, authority, and resentment. The violence visited upon others results from a wish to know, which remains unsatisfied, and which is turned back upon the one who has begun the procedure. The four characters methodically eliminate one another. Holliger has portrayed the extreme tension of the dialogues between Bam and the others by turbulent, angry music and by changes of tempo, with the accelerandos and ritardandos creating constant instability. The passage of time, symbolized in the piece by the evocation of the cycle of seasons, from spring to winter, also finds its corresponding music: at the end, the sound peters out and freezes.

However, what does appear to be a clear trajectory, up to the reference to Schubert's *Winterreise*—which Holliger does not neglect to cite in the music, even if he does so by means of a negated quotation—is much more ambiguous. Here we find the relationship between circularity and linearity, between infinite repetition and the process of annihilation already present in *Come and Go*, but reversed. The systematic elimination of Bom, Bim, and Bem is integrated into the cycle of seasons, which is forever renewing itself, and into the gesture of Bam, who keeps on switching the light on and off. This gesture allows reassessments of that absurd and terrible scene which is going on inside Bam's own head ('Make sense who may', says Bam at the end). Beckett spoke of the search for an exit: 'C'est une vieille histoire que je ne comprends pas. Je me suis demandé ce que signifie *où*. Peut-être: où est l'issue? La vieille histoire de l'issue . . .'[2] [It's an old story which I don't understand. I wondered what *where* meant. Perhaps: where is the exit? The old story of the exit . . .]. It is also the metaphor of a theatrical moment, of a stage which acts like a tribunal, of the destiny of the Enlightenment, where interrogatory Reason provokes the violence it claims to have overcome. (From that moment we could be said to be approaching the end of a journey which had reached its peak with the song of the prisoners in *Fidelio*, celebrating the return of light, or with the triumphant chord on the word 'Licht' in Haydn's *Creation*. These are two moments of collective celebration which, in Schubert's *Winterreise*, are irrevocably reversed).

[2] André Bernold, *L'Amitié de Beckett, 1979–1989* (Paris: Hermann, 1992), 35.

READING THE MUSIC OF HOLLIGER

In Beckett, time is essentially an interior time, close to dream (or night-mare) time. It is fundamentally non-narratorial, and is presented in an extremely condensed form. However, by the play of repetition, it offers layers of stories and meanings which seem to refer to a subtext—a text which is more explicit, but is inexpressible; the dramatic structure is like the sum total of a deep-rooted reality which is out of direct reach. Holliger has emphasized and developed in his music this latent poly-phony which blurs the edges of an apparently simple shape. Thus, in *Come and Go*, the exclamation which follows the exchange of the secret becomes a motif which is varied each time it occurs. Similarly, when the three women are all together, and silent, Holliger has composed instrumental interludes which, through the interplay of tones, form a sort of musical round, based upon a series of twelve sounds (this 'round' symbolizing the intertwining of the three women's hands). This series nevertheless loses a few notes each time it is repeated. The possibilities diminish, the memories fade. In *What Where*, Beckett has treated the monologues (Voice of Bam) like refrains, of which one or several elements are modified with each repetition, apart from the sentence which marks the passage of time: 'Time passes'. The variations create ambiguities—for example, between 'We are the last five' and 'I am alone', linked to the appearance/reappearance of the characters ('In the end Bom appears. Reappears')—and oppositions: for example, between 'First without words' and 'Now with words', or between 'Good' and 'Not good. I start again', which extends into the movement of switching the light on and off. Holliger has played upon such repetitions/transformations. At the beginning, the phrase 'We are the last five', followed by the evocation of spring, is expressed musically by a great melodic sweep; 'Time passes' engenders a canon for five voices; the last group 'First without words', followed by 'Not good' and 'I switch off', requires a speaking voice (without precise pitches but with directions for movement). After the passage where the whole of the piece is mimed, executed musically by percussion alone, the evocation of spring is absorbed into the canon structure in association with the sentence 'Time passes'. But, further on, when summer is mentioned, this last sentence gives rise to a huge swell of voices, and, at the end, nothing remains of the canon except its skeleton: the voice is solo. Put another way, Holliger has developed the play by means of variations proper to Beckett's text, but in accordance with a purely musical logic. The quality of the textures also brings us back to the dramatic structure of the play, as we can discern in the contrasting writing styles of the timed and non-timed passages of *Come and Go*, in the monologues and dialogues of

What Where, or in the functions of the introduction, transition, and coda in the two works.

By choosing these short Beckett plays, Holliger has voluntarily set himself apart from the conventions of opera. His reference point, as he has pointed out himself, must be sought in the Noh theatre rather than in traditional opera, or even contemporary opera. The instrumentalists, as in Noh theatre, participate in the 'action'—they are not hidden in the pit—and the voices use a very particular register which veers between speaking and singing, and passes through all the intermediate stages. As with Noh theatre, each detail is significant; the tiniest directions, the subtlest modifications, are crucial. Holliger has fused with Beckett in this quest for precision, combined with a maximum degree of expressive intensity. There is no diluting of impact: even the most unusual sounds are integrated into the musical phrase. All Holliger's music *speaks* and *breathes*, in accordance with a tradition which his teacher Sándor Veress passed on to him. Thus it is that the Beckettian text (including the stage directions) has been transposed in concrete terms into a musical language which has its own significance, for Holliger has in a sense composed that part of the text which is unnamable. He has not only exposed the subtexts, but has also brought out the full weight and resonance of each word. The music makes tangible the erosion of time, through the play of repetitions and variations which lie at the heart of the musical discourse, and which give Beckett's language and drama a quality which is wholly musical.

HEINZ HOLLIGER IN CONVERSATION WITH PHILLPPE ALBÈRA

Translated by Mary Bryden

PA. Did you always feel a vocation to be a musician?

HH. Yes, always. At least, from the age of 10, it was absolutely clear.

PA. What about your choice of the oboe?

HH. I heard the oboe on the radio and at the Langenthal Theatre. The sonorousness of the instrument fascinated me, even if what I heard was not very high level.

PA. Your musical training took place in the context of the 1950s. As a composer, how did you situate yourself in relation to the generation which was dominating the world of contemporary music at that time?

HH. I started to write music before I'd even heard of Boulez or Stockhausen. . . . My first contact with Boulez's music, for example, was in 1956. I'd seen a performance in Paris of the *Oresteia*, in Claudel's translation, directed by Jean-Louis Barrault, and with music by Boulez. I remember I couldn't stand the music: there was a lot of vibraphone, which I didn't think sounded suitable for Greek tragedy. Then, in 1957, I heard a concert with the two *Improvisations sur Mallarmé* and the *Marteau sans maître*. This time, I was really struck—especially by the first *Improvisation* (but not at all by the *Marteau*). At that time, I greatly admired the poetry of René Char. . . .

PA. You wrote poetry when you were young, and you still feel very drawn to poetry: was there a time when, like Schumann, you hesitated between poetic writing and musical writing?

HH. No, my poetic activity was juvenile. It was based upon a very strong attachment to Trakl. It was a very direct means of expressing myself, and I think that my later work in music represents something I explored first within poetry. I wrote a lot of poetry while I was at secondary school, and I also translated a lot, particularly Rimbaud. I translated the 'Bateau ivre' with great difficulty, but I didn't get anywhere near Celan's version of it. My poetic activity was really all part of my music.

PA. In your earliest works, there's both great lyricism and great rigour; then you evolved towards using sounds which go beyond the normal range of instruments, and towards a much more provocative kind of music, where the traditional parameters, even the formal parameters, were in some sense destroyed. How did this change occur?

HH. I don't really see all that much difference between the two periods. . . . It's always been the physical side of a sound shift which has interested me most. If I transform a sound, it's not the result which interests me so much as the demonstration of the force behind it. For example, if I use a flattened sound, I want people to be aware of that distortion of a clear sound quality. So in listening to a distorted mode of play, it's always necessary to hear its origin, its full sonorousness. That's why I can say that I'm certainly not seeking sonorousness in my work. It's more, if you like, a form of expressionism.

PA. In the choral pieces which have some religious connotation, like your *Dona nobis pacem* or *Psalm*, you're not so much working on texts, as carrying out a kind of deconstruction of the text, in a way which seems to me parallel to your work on purely instrumental sonority. . . .

HH. I must say in the first place that they're not really religious pieces. *Psalm* is the negative of religious music. Obviously, you could say that atheism is also religious, since one can't deny what doesn't exist. In *Dona nobis pacem*, I only work on the level of syllables; I took a text at random, like Kagel in *Anagramme*. And so I used the six syllables of the title to build synthetic languages, like made-up Claudel, meaningless things, concrete poetry, false Church Latin, and so on. All these texts result from it. . . . I did think of composing a third part, with real extracts from newspapers and radio, using only chaotic sounds and cries. But I never carried that out. Maybe it was in any case too political. I'd thought of including extracts from newspaper articles on Vietnam, especially on the tortures of Mi-Lai, with ironic allusions to the words written by the American astronauts on the moon in 1969: 'We came in peace for all mankind.'

PA. Would you say that your pieces are more linked to drama than to sound architecture?

HH. In *Cardiophonie*, I felt the need to go to the very limit of what was possible, to exhaust the musical resources, and to push expression towards its own annihilation. In my string quartet, there's a kind of inverse movement. The work begins with an extraordinary high-pitched frenzy, and then develops over thirty minutes into a huge ralentando, a descent below the normal ranges and sounds of the strings. The relationships between the tension of the bow, the tension of the strings, and the tempo, form a kind of closed circuit system. The energy decreases to the point where the sound must die away, as if in a kind of death-agony. In the end, you can no longer distinguish between the sound of the bows and the breathing of the players; the movement of the bow then resembles breathing, in and out. It reflects the physical dimension of the sound.

PA. Is there a link between this tendency always to go to the limits, even beyond possible limits, and your fascination for poets who are extending the limits of poetic language, even of rationality?

HH. It's all connected. I didn't 'choose' the poets I've incorporated into my music; it's a question of affinity. They imposed themselves on me. They 'fell into my lap', if I can put it that way, and I 'fell' into their poems. I think there's an eloquence in what we call 'madness' (even if none of the poets within my music was mad), and an openness which has got something prophetic about it. Words and music find a lot of common ground there, much more easily than in a more 'rational' kind of literature, which I associate with an almost empty acoustic chamber. Each word, in effect, radiates out and projects in all directions, and that's where music comes in.

PA. Is it also this prophetic dimension (which brings us back in a sense to the religious question we were discussing earlier) which led you to Beckett's texts? Indeed, in a more general sense, what is your relationship with the theatre?

HH. In spite of my interest in Pinter and in American theatre, I haven't had much contact with modern drama. It's true that I wrote a lot of theatre music between 1957 and 1959, but I never felt a part of the so-called 'normal', institutionalized musical theatre scene. It's definitely

Beckett's drama which fascinates me most. Naturally, I didn't choose the texts which were most striking from the scenic point of view, but ones which were in a sense neglected, not very popular, and not particularly successful. What interested me was the extreme economy of gesture and movement. Each movement has countless meanings; everything is ambiguous. As a musician, I'm also attracted by the musicality of Beckett's texts, even if this musicality seems to exclude any added music. Sometimes, it all seems to take place in an empty room, from the acoustic point of view. No sound can penetrate it; it's a completely closed universe, where you can't hear any echo, not even your own voice. It would be completely idiotic to set such texts to music in the traditional sense, and that's obviously not what I set out to do. In fact, the only theatre which really attracts me is Noh theatre. I always go to it when I'm in Japan. What fascinates me, as in Beckett, is its extreme economy of gesture, and its ambiguity, both of which slice through our own traditional and lucid styles of theatre and cinema. In Noh theatre, the ambiguity is based upon a formal system of traditional gestures, where each movement, each blink of the eye, has a semantic value. I too have to set up for each piece a repertoire of symbols: they're not ready-made for me. The handling of time—the ability to stretch time to the limits of immobility—is also an element which interests me very much in Noh theatre.

With *Come and Go*, I wanted at first just to write an instrumental trio. Then I started to multiply and extend the outline of the piece, which is extremely simple, into space. A projection like that exists in *Not I* as well, but from the basis of a human being who can no longer manage to be an individual: that led me to write a polyphony for as many as sixteen voices. *What Where* is quite different. I respect Beckett's structural idea—a sort of diminishing musical rondo which runs on to exhaustion. *Come and Go* also uses this idea of a rondo, but in a more overt way: it never comes to an end. And, what's more, we don't know the age of the characters. In *What Where*, on the other hand, we know that they are older people, but in an atemporal universe. I wanted to show, rather as in *Not I*, that these four characters, as well as the one overlaid with the recorded voice, form one unity: four grave voices having the same tessitura, the same expression. Sometimes they sing with their mouths closed, or are placed behind the scenes—you never know *who* is singing. It's like the Chorus in Greek tragedy, who makes a commentary and reacts emotionally. This quartet of voices is mirrored by the four trombones, which also form a unity—a kind of *consort*. There's a real blending of voices and trombones, so that you can never really know where the sounds are coming from (and the trombonists sing into the instrument).

PA. The percussion part contains many realistic noises or sounds, played on quite an array of instruments: what's the function of that?

HH. The two percussionists are like clerks: they give the orders for the torture. They're a bit removed. All the sounds they make are highly realistic: the sounds of torture, chains, broken glass, squeaking fingernails on metal, noises of brushes on rusty metal, instruments drowning in water. It's like an undercurrent, a 'trompe-l'oreille' or auditory illusion. Clearly, they're formal symbols, signs which help to define the form: you often find the same gestures being used for identical situations. I also used a somewhat primitive dramatic device: the inter-rogations are always within a rising movement, and the responses within a descending one. But, apart from that, there's no psychological drama in it. Of course, you could say that the voice of Bam is that of God; and, at the end of the performance, he puts out the light. But it's not for me to suggest such an interpretation.

The music for *What Where* is very direct in comparison with *Come and Go*. There's no temporal multiplicity; it's like one solo body. Bam is alone, and everything takes place in his head, as in *Endgame*, where the room *is* the head. That also provides a framework for the three Beckett plays with the lone voice in the middle. *What Where* seems to me to be like a ritual of annihilation—almost a religious piece. You find the cycle of seasons in it as well—from spring to winter—with an allusion to Schubert's *Winterreise*, which is also found in Beckett. The cycle stops because it can't go any further—'without journey'—and, at that time, Beckett kept listening to the *Winterreise*, which I too allude to through the opening melody, 'Gute Nacht'. But it's almost nothing, just three notes. . . . We mustn't forget, either, one important dimension of Beckett's texts: their clownish character, which is constantly present.

PA. At the beginning, did you think of the three works on Beckett texts as being a whole?

HH. No, but I wrote the three works in relation to one another. Nevertheless, they sound very different from one another.

PA. How does the drama of the music express itself in relation to the drama of Beckett's texts?

HH. Music recreates the drama, but using Beckett's directions, which are very precise and which form a kind of choreography. They're always present, whether they're made obvious or hidden by the music.

PA. Did you establish a relationship with Beckett himself, either before, during, or after writing your works?

HH. I think he didn't really like the idea of adding music to his plays. He'd no doubt have hated *Come and Go*, because I used his text as a pretext, and ended up by completely destroying it. With *What Where*, my adaptation was stricter, but I would never have chosen that text if I

hadn't seen the fantastic production of it in New York, directed by Alan
Schneider: those voices went straight into my ear. A production like
that, carrying out to the ultimate degree what Beckett wants, would be
the ideal production for my music. . . .

PA. How did you manage to compose the different layers of *Come
and Go* so that they would be playable in versions that were both
independent and variable?

HH. I worked out something like a triple counterpoint which was
reversible in every direction. Each group represents one voice. First of
all, I wrote the first act for flutes alone, and then I composed variations.
Each group has its harmonic fields, its gestural and temporal characters.
At one and the same time, it must both form a unity, and be heard
independently. There's no hierarchy between the groups: voices and
instruments form one entity.

PA. Your writing contains a lot of melismas which interweave; you
seem to avoid constraining rhythmical structures, based upon pulsations. . . .

HH. I used to have an extreme allergy to pulsed music: maybe because of Boulez. I'm more of a Schumannian—he's the greatest rubato
composer, in my view. But in *What Where*, the music is rhythmically
very strict; sometimes the beat even emerges from the steps. I love the
combination of mobile and immobile time. I write complicated, differentiated, calculated rhythms, but I can't stand chronological time.

PA. Why are you so distrustful of philosophy?

HH. Perhaps because I don't want to know too much. I depend very
much on the unconscious. Composing is a process which is so delicate,
so fragile, that, as soon as you start analysing yourself, or controlling
yourself, you get blockages. I'm interested in philosophy, but I stay at a
distance, perhaps also because I haven't entered deeply enough into
philosophy to be able to link it with my creative work. But I'm not
convinced of the link between music and philosophy: they're two different modes of thinking. I have the impression that philosophy has grafted
itself onto music, as a secondary activity. . . . I used to read a lot of
philosophy at one time, especially Hegel, Kierkegaard, Pascal: now, I'd
rather try to get to grips with an author like Kant. I read a lot, but very
little philosophy. . . .

In fact, I don't think that philosophy, today, is capable of solving our
problems. We must try to progress, but not with the crutches of theory.
Philosophical constructs belong to a logic different from that of music:
transposing it doesn't work. A musical thought is never comparable to
a philosophical thought.

PA. How can it be defined?

HH. It's extremely difficult to transpose a musical thought into words. You can use formulas, to try to get round it, but it's not a good transposition. I think that music speaks in an untranslatable way; it's a meta-language. You can try to describe why such or such a piece is convincing; you can try to find equivalents, accommodations. It's like Klee in his Bauhaus classes: he gives equivalents for a sound, an image, an idea. In the case of music, you use colours, and ideas of light and darkness.

PA. You loathe making commentaries on your own works: how do you picture the 'ideal' listener to your music?

HH. I cling on to what might be an illusion: that someone listening to my music needs to be completely open, without bias, and capable of listening very intently. He or she must be able to listen to what's offered without letting too many preconceived criteria get in the way. I wouldn't like to put barriers between myself and the listener, especially by means of explanations. That's why I don't like writing about my work; this is my way of lying low. I also think that music comes in through your skin; you've got to have a more or less unconscious relationship with it before you bring the intellectual apparatus into play. Think about composers like Haydn or Schubert, who left behind practically nothing on the subject of their works. That doesn't stop me liking composer-writers, like Schumann, or Debussy. . . .

PA. Do you feel rather isolated in the present musical climate, or do you have the feeling of belonging to some kind of 'movement', to a spiritual family?

HH. I've always stayed away from groups and tendencies; I must admit that there aren't many composers who really fascinate me today. For example, a few days ago I heard a recent work by Lachenmann— *Allegro sostenuto*. Well, that'll do me for a year! There was such a creative force there that I felt overwhelmed. But that's no doubt unfair. Perhaps I've simply arrived at a point where I'm feeling the need to concentrate on what, for me, is really essential. . . .

6

End Games

PETER SZENDY
Translated from the French by Veronica Heath

Among the texts Heinz Holliger chose to stage were two 'dramaticules' by Samuel Beckett—*Come and Go* and *What Where*—which, by means of radical reduction, mould the dialogue within a strict combinatory pattern. Hence, the very mechanics of the dialogue are called into question: how can it achieve resolution, how can the end game be reached?

In fact, mathematical and logical games, sometimes associated with chess and its interminable end games, figure prominently in Beckett's dramatic and poetic universe. There is no doubt that, in his novels *Watt* and *Murphy*, Beckett makes use of the most complex and far-reaching combinatory mechanisms. There, these games explicitly go hand in hand with a retreat from reality and a sundering of the links between words and things: 'Watt now found himself in the midst of things which, if they consented to be named, did so as it were with reluctance.'[1] And this rupture abandons language to its own devices, to its infinite play of combinations—one which is explicitly associated with music in *Watt* and *Murphy*.

The allusions to musical incidents which punctuate the narratives of the two novels in effect assume an emblematic function. These incidents form a series of noteworthy events relating to music, and this serialization takes two contrasting forms. A crescendo runs through *Murphy*, reaching its culminating point when the initials of the 'Magdalen Mental Mercyseat', where Murphy works, 'stood suddenly for music, MUSIC, MUSIC'.[2] By contrast, in *Watt*, as Heath Lees[3] has demonstrated, music is subject to a progressive extenuation in accordance with a *diminuendo al niente* pattern.

These two contrasting musical figures both seem to represent processes tending inexorably towards alienation. The crescendo in *Murphy* accompanies an escape from the body—out of reality, out of its spatial

---

[1] Samuel Beckett, *Watt* (London: John Calder, 1963), 78.
[2] Id., *Murphy* (London: Picador, 1973), 132.
[3] Heath Lees, '*Watt*: Music, Tuning, and Tonality', *Journal of Beckett Studies*, 9 (1984), 5–24.

and causal categories—towards the expanses of the mind. In *Watt*, on
the other hand, this escape has already taken place. The inexhaustible
calculations and the interminable lists represent a series of attempts to
reconstitute lost causalities. So Watt is unable to receive any pure,
gratuitous impression—that distinctive impression which was for
Schopenhauer quintessentially musical. His perceptions fade progressively in the face of the endless series of ratiocinations: the *diminuendo
al niente* reflects that fade-out of immediate reality, that failure to be *in
tune* with the present reality.

THE PROBLEM OF REFERENCE

In the dramaticules chosen for staging, it is this same figure of discord-
ance which is represented on a thematic level by the failure to find
ground for agreement within the play of dialogue. What we could call,
to borrow Francis Jacques's[4] term, the 'referential' moment in the dialogue is in fact rendered problematic: it is impossible to establish 'what
the matter is'. And if the 'coreference' poses a problem in this way, it is
due to the inextricable entangling of what logical analysts have labelled
epistemic modalities (those relating to knowledge) and ethical
modalities (those relating to duty and constraint). For what is at stake in
the play in each case is the distribution of knowledge—or of its watered-
down form: belief—as well as its connection with constraint.

COME AND GO — THE INFINITE GAME

Heinz Holliger's *Come and Go* was written between 1976 and 1977.
Beckett's play, originally written in English, was translated into French
by the author himself, and into German by Elmar Tophoven. Holliger's
'mini-opera' makes simultaneous use of these three texts, without modifying them in any way.

Beckett's three female characters have monosyllabic names: Flo,
Vi, and Ru in French and in English; Lo, Mei, and Su in German.
The sequences of dialogue which bring into play all three protagonists
punctuate, like a refrain, the confidences exchanged first by Flo and
Ru, then by Ru and Vi, then by Vi and Flo. Each one of these confiden-
tial exchanges concerns the absent third party, who has left the stage
meanwhile. The pair who are confiding in each other believe that the

---

[4] Francis Jacques, *Dialogiques* (Paris: Presses Universitaires de France, 1979), 153.

latter is unaware of an important event, which will, however, never be mentioned.

The three-handed sequences echo back to an unreal, fantasy past—'dreaming of . . . love'—whose present reality is explicitly denied. Flo's exclamation 'I can feel the rings' is tersely contradicted by Beckett's stage directions: 'no rings apparent'. Thus, the three successive sets of confidences do not lead to any genuine community of knowledge. The epistemic worlds of the three characters remain separate and hermetically closed.

THREE TIMES THREE TIMES THREE

Come and Go is structured around the number 3, which pervades Beckett's play in a wide variety of ways. And it is with the guidance of this 'masterfigure' (*Leitzahl*) that the composer breaks down the dramatic structure. The score is written for nine—three times three—sopranos, three flutes, three clarinets, and three violas. Each character is divided up into three, then linked to three different instruments; the three versions—English, French, and German—are superimposed in a triple counterpoint and separated onto three stages, occupying three different points in space. *Come and Go* is simultaneously performed in three languages, each language corresponding to a homogeneous instrumental trio. Moreover, Beckett's play is tripled in length: the opera consists of three acts, each one equivalent to the entirety of the dramaticule. Thus the multiplication affects both dimensions, of time and of space (Figure 6.1).

As in certain polytextual fourteenth-century motets, the musical texture here takes account of the simultaneous presence of three texts. Nonetheless, no text is confined to any given spatial position, since there is no privileged link between a given language and a given line in the polyphony; the triple counterpoint, within which each trio represents one voice, is completely interchangeable: each of the three languages figures successively on each of the three stages.

In the 'interludes' (*Zwischenspiele*), and the postlude, the composer presents three dodecaphonic series, which, far from having any relationship with, or underpinning in any way the music played in the three acts themselves, creates a distancing effect. It is a true serial citation, conceived as follows: series 2 is the inversion of series 1, played a half-tone higher, while series 3 is a 'filtering' of series 1 in a variation which retains only one note in two (Figure 6.2).

During the two interludes and the postlude (pp. 35–41, pp. 70–5, and

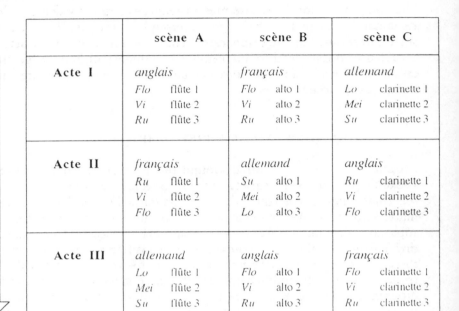

	scène A	scène B	scène C
Acte I	*anglais* *Flo* flûte 1 *Vi* flûte 2 *Ru* flûte 3	*français* *Flo* alto 1 *Vi* alto 2 *Ru* alto 3	*allemand* *Lo* clarinette 1 *Mei* clarinette 2 *Su* clarinette 3
Acte II	*français* *Ru* flûte 1 *Vi* flûte 2 *Flo* flûte 3	*allemand* *Su* alto 1 *Mei* alto 2 *Lo* alto 3	*anglais* *Ru* clarinette 1 *Vi* clarinette 2 *Flo* clarinette 3
Acte III	*allemand* *Lo* flûte 1 *Mei* flûte 2 *Su* flûte 3	*anglais* *Flo* alto 1 *Vi* alto 2 *Ru* alto 3	*français* *Flo* clarinette 1 *Vi* clarinette 2 *Ru* clarinette 3

Fig. 6.1

Fig. 6.2

flûte 1

flûte 2   [. . .]

flûte 3

(a)

	Interlude I	Interlude I	Postlude
Groupe A (*flûtes*)	*Série 1*	*Série 2*	*Série 3*
Groupe B (*altos*)	*Série 2*	*Série 3*	*Série 1*
Groupe C (*clarinettes*)	*Série 3*	*Série 1*	*Série 2*

(b)

Fig. 6.3 (a,b)

pp. 98–101 of the score), each group and each stratum of the polyphony forms a three-voice serial canon (Figure 6.3*a*; p. 35, beginning of the group A canon). Between one interlude and the next, the groups exchange series, in accordance with a permutation which corresponds to that governing the three languages (Figure 6.3*b*).

At the end of each act, just before the interlude, another interpretation of the series is played, in conformity with the following pattern: this time each one is divided up into three groups of four notes, and each of these three groups is interpreted in succession by the three instruments in each

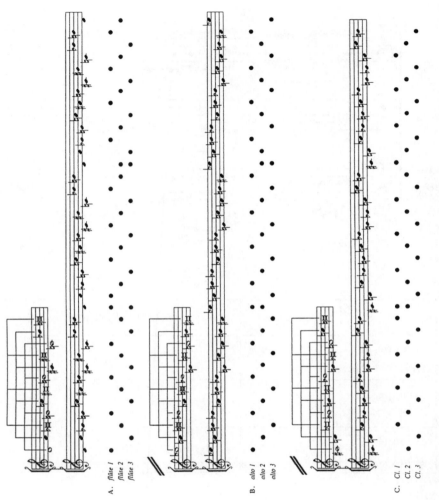

(a)

A. flûte 1
flûte 2
flûte 3

B. alto 1
alto 2
alto 3

C. Cl. 1
Cl. 2
Cl. 3

(b)

Fig. 6.4 (a,b)

trio (Figure 6.4*a*: Act I, pp. 33–5). It is a musical representation of the way in which Flo, Vi, and Ru join hands 'in the old way' (Figure 6.4*b*).

WORDS AND MUSIC

While throughout the play the sung or spoken word is associated with specific pitches, a character's silences are accompanied by indistinct sounds. These two types of writing affecting the instruments related to each singer are represented in the musical score by two graphic notations implying different interpretations and realizations of sounds. When the instrument plays in synchrony with a syllable, word, or phrase sung or spoken by the soprano, when it becomes an 'instrument parlant' [speaking instrument] (p. 75 of the score) its *melos* is represented by thick notes signifying a full, 'expressive' sonority, which surely must be seen as the musical equivalent of the banality of the speeches. When, in contrast, the character is silent, listening, or retreats into the background, the melodic line of the corresponding instrument is transformed into a neutral background of sound, inclining towards imperceptibility. As the composer specifies in the foreword to the score: 'Les petites notes doivent rester indistinctes, à la limite du seuil d'audibilité' [The small noteheads should remain indistinct, at the limit of the threshold of audibility]. And it is this music of silence and dispersal which is the real vehicle of the meaning 'entre les mots' [between the lines].[5]

Sounds are most often scored with non-barred rhythms. The direction and the contours given to the instrumental parts thus become particularly significant. The entrance of a character is marked by gestures which are the reverse of those marking her exit: mirror-image glissandos whose initial and concluding sections are switched round (Figure 6.5), or constant variations of tone along an 'échelle de bruit' [noise scale],[6] traversed in the opposite direction (Figure 6.6). Both dramatic and instrumental movements are performed simultaneously, since 'tous les déplacements scéniques se modèlent sur la durée du processus musical correspondant' [all the stage shifts are modelled on the playing time of the corresponding musical process] (p. 5 of the score). Or, to put it another way (as Holliger explained in the interview cited above), the instrument itself becomes a stage, across which the player moves.

[5] Heinz Holliger kindly agreed to an interview in London on 17 Sept. 1992. Some quotations used here are taken from this (unpublished) interview.

[6] Heinz Holliger, *Entretiens avec Elliott Carter*, trans. from the German by Daniel Haefliger (Geneva: Éditions Contrechamps, 1992), 107

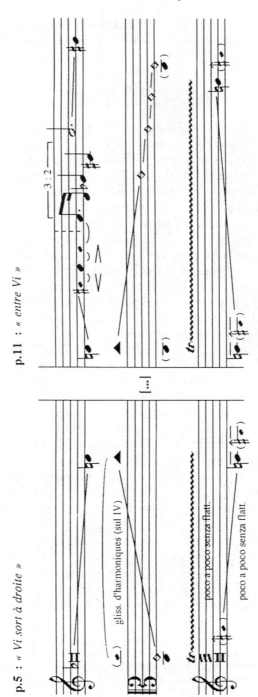

Fig. 6.5

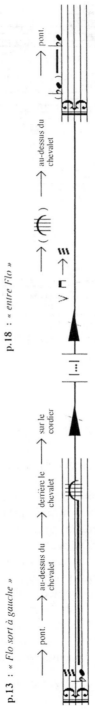

Fig. 6.6

Fig. 6.7

Fig. 6.8

DIMINUENDO AL NIENTE

Once the process is set in motion, the multiplication of the dramatic structure of the Beckettian text is infinite in theory—'cela ne finit jamais' [it is never-ending].[7] However, in practice, it is not immune to an increasing entropy, which disrupts every dimension of the flow of sound.

The text itself undergoes a process of filtration; certain syllables, marked between brackets, are not pronounced aloud—the singer merely mimes the appropriate mouth movements. Between Act II and Act III, all of the words are thus emptied of their vocal or consonant content. Holliger had already devised this method of representing aphasia in 1975, in the first song of Spring—*der Sommer 1*—in the *Scardanelli* cycle. But this negation of the text, engraved and hollowed out as it were

---

[7] Philippe Albèra, 'Entretien avec Heinz Holliger', in programme for the *Festival d'Automne à Paris*, 1991, p. 94.

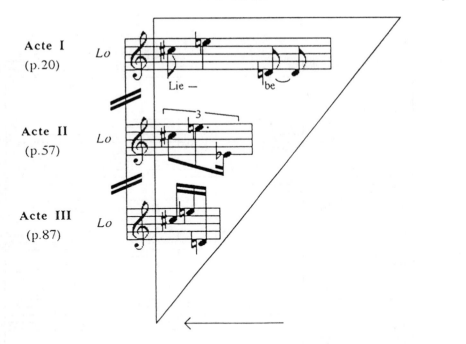

Fig. 6.9

Fig. 6.10

within the polyphony, also echoes back to the paradigm of these 'ghost-structures' which pervade the texture of many of the composer's pieces with their presence/absence. Thus the first song of Winter—*der Winter I*—in the *Scardanelli* cycle constitutes, to use Holliger's own words, a

Fig. 6.11

veritable sound-negative of J. S. Bach's chorale BWV 56, the notes of which become the silences in this piece.

Such a loss of the intelligibility of speech entails concomitantly a variety of losses within the musical message which accompanies it. The melodic structures undergo particularly drastic 'levelling of peaks' and *apocopes* which are clearly evident if we compare the vocal exercises on the words 'love' and 'amour' between the first and last acts (Figures 6.7 and 6.8). The rhythmic figures are subject to irregular but increasing diminutions, like those which affect the melismas on 'Liebe' (Figure 6.9). Finally, it is as if the melodic line is contracted so that the singer and her 'speaking instrument' perform a crasis, so to speak, of the original motif associated with the exclamation 'Oh!' (Figure 6.10).

This entropy also brings about a progressive collapse of the sound pillars which uphold the three-act structure of the opera. The beginning of each act is marked by the formation of a cluster of nine notes, bringing together the three groups of three instruments. In Acts I and II, this cluster remains the same, although it undergoes internal alterations—but in Act III, the entire structure moves a half-tone lower (Figure 6.11). In addition, if the cluster of flutes remains in position close together, the cluster of violas and clarinets also sinks an octave lower.

And this downward slope which condemns the opera to an inexorable *diminuendo al niento* is even perceptible in the tone spaces (cf. Figure 6.11): in Act II, the second flute and the second clarinet take the part of the alto flute and the bass clarinet respectively, while the second viola takes its fourth string down to B♭: in Act III, the third flute and the third clarinet take the bass flute and the counterbass clarinet respectively, while the third viola goes out of tune into A♭.

Finally, in the postlude, the dying away of the serial canons takes on a very specific form. The three instruments at each level go through the series assigned to them (cf. Figure 6.3*b*) at the end of the process of permutation which has extended over the last two interludes, but at each repetition of this series two notes are eliminated, with the result that, prior to the seventh repetition, all the notes in the series have disappeared, leaving silence (Figure 6.12, pp. 98–101, canon of three flutes). And these eliminations are made in accordance with three different patterns (a, b, and c on the figure), these patterns themselves being permutated between the three instrumental trios (Figure 6.13). Thus the three quintessentially Beckettian motifs of reduction, extenuation, and failure to attune are central to the way in which the musical material is worked: *Come and Go* is, as Holliger told me, like 'un rituel de vieillissement de la musique elle-même' [an ageing ritual for music itself]. And the composer echoes V's nostalgic questions with one or two

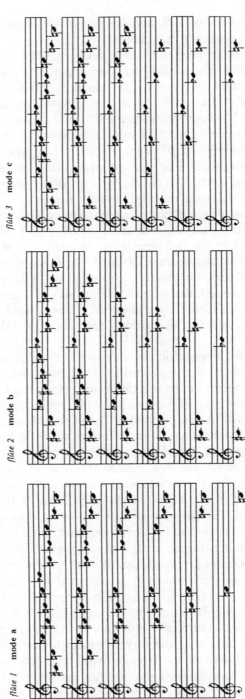

Fig. 6.12

flûte 1	**mode a**	*alto 1*	**mode c**	*clarinette 1*	**mode b**
flûte 2	**mode b**	*alto 2*	**mode a**	*clarinette 2*	**mode c**
flûte 3	**mode c**	*alto 3*	**mode b**	*clarinette 3*	**mode a**

Fig. 6.13

Fig. 6.14 (a,b)

short stylistic exercises: thus, in the German stage version, in the first act, when Vi talks about 'the old days', the three clarinet parts contain a fleeting allusion to Wagnerian chromatism (Figure 6.14*a*, p. 29);—in the next bar, when Vi mentions 'what came after', the instrumental score echoes Webern's stylistic traits (Figure 6.14*b*, p. 30).

THE COMPARTMENTALIZATION OF KNOWLEDGE

In *Come and Go*, the translation into formal terms of traditional situations relating to the fragmentation of knowledge results in a terrible inability to conclude: the dramatic mechanism of numerous classic plays and operas is taken over by a formal system whose logic leaves no room for any resolution of any kind: the dialogue goes round in circles, in the literal and spatial sense of the term.

And if the dramaticule seems incapable of finding a way out of this absurd rotation, the opera makes this impossibility explicit and accentuates it still further: the proliferation and division revolving around the number 3 prohibit any kind of clarification. The composer underlines the loss of wholeness of the personality by means of a triple division into three: linguistic, spatial, and temporal. It is a schizoid situation which could be seen as an exacerbation of Beckett's own problematic bilingualism. Holliger has likened the techniques of composition employed in *Come and Go* to those of Elliott Carter: each group within the triple counterpoint possesses its own unique harmonic fields and gestural characteristics. These are techniques which, for Carter, are related to the operatic universe: 'écrire par couches superposées' [writing in superimposed layers] also means retaining 'des caractères séparés, tout en les faisant coexister dans un ensemble' [distinct, separate characteristics, while simultaneously having them coexist within an ensemble] (Holliger, 102). The organization of *Come and Go* into three differently characterized strata therefore appears as a reflection of the separation of the epistemic worlds of the characters into a polyphonic field of sound.

It is a separation which can never be bridged by repetition. In fact, if *Come and Go* is an *infinite* game, it is because the end has already occurred before the beginning of the action. In Beckett's play, it is not contained within the bounds of the work itself, but in a dreamlike past. In Holliger's opera, it occurs in the prelude, which the composer compares to Munch's expressionist painting, *The Scream*: a long-drawn-out cry—the only triple forte in the entire work—which slowly dies away, giving way to the beginning proper, which is almost soundless (*fast tonlos*). Thus, for Holliger, no inceptive form can come into being until after musical energy has been exhausted, only to diminish further for all that. Because, to use the terminological distinction suggested by Gilles Deleuze,[8] the musical entropy which pervades the play comes from exhaustion rather than from fatigue: if 'on est épuisé avant de naître' [one is exhausted before coming into being], before beginning, then the exhausted being has already exhausted every possibility before realizing any; then there is nothing left for him but to 'end again',[9] *ad infinitum*.

WHAT WHERE: THE FINITE GAME

Heinz Holliger's *What Where* was composed in 1988. Beckett's play itself dates back to 1983. Holliger's 'chamber opera' follows the original English text without modifying it in any way. The opera is dedicated 'to Elliott Carter on his eightieth birthday'. The score is written for four singers—a baritone (Bam) and three bass-baritones (Bem, Bim, Bom)— a tape-recorded voice (V), four trombones, and two percussionists, equipped with a particularly varied range of instruments.

The play's four characters are differentiated from each other by a vowel sound only—Bam, Bem, Bim, Bom. V—Bam's voice—initiates and arranges a succession of cross-examinations within a framework which becomes increasingly complex each time, the outside frame of reference being absent. For either the object of the questioning merely refers back to the preceding bout of questioning, e.g.:

BIM. What must he confess?
BAM. That he said it to him,

or else is itself devoid of a defined referent, e.g.:

BEM. What must I confess?
BAM. That he said where to him.

Thus the play rests on a twofold branching structure, of prescriptivity and knowledge. The reduction in the number of characters is therefore accompanied by the increasing complexity of the system of knowledge.

Beckett himself has suggested that *What Where* could be interpreted as an allusion to torture[10]—an interpretation which is reflected in the way in which the percussion parts are conceived: their realistic quality is nonetheless 'un peu à l'écart' [slightly removed] (Albèra, 'Entretien avec Holliger', 94). For, even more than in *Come and Go*, sounds have a specific function; by linking the musical action to the play's dramatic

[8] Gilles Deleuze, *L'Épuisé*, in Samuel Beckett, *Quad et autres pièces pour la télévision* (Paris: Éditions de Minuit, 1992), 58.
[9] See Samuel Beckett, *For to End Yet Again, and other Fizzles* (London: John Calder, 1976).
[10] See Walter Asmus, 'Réduire . . . Les deux mises en scène de Godot', *Revue d'esthétique* (special number on Beckett, 1986), 349–57 (p. 352).

Peter Szendy

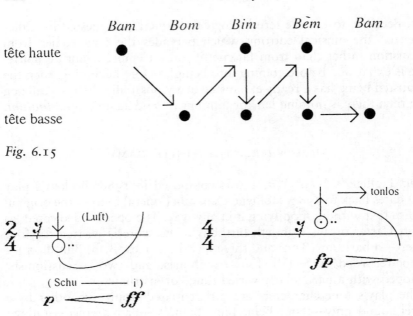

Fig. 6.15

Fig. 6.16

development, they perform as it were the function of 'shifters', as defined by Jakobsonian linguistics: they engage the evolution of the music within the reality of the evolution of the drama. And as the disfunctioning of the referential mechanisms spreads to the play's dialogic structures in their entirety, this hyper-realism—one is tempted to say 'hyper-reference'—seems to work against the grain. Holliger himself compares it to a 'trompe l'oreille' [auditory delusion] (ibid. 94). Sounds, by shifting the musical discourse onto the situation on stage, perform the function of *signals*. For this reason they are actors in a kind of musical mime, towards which Beckett's theatre has an occasional tendency to move.

'FIRST WITHOUT WORDS'

What Where opens with just such an 'act without words'.[11] V calls for a synopsis in the form of a mime: 'First without words'. Using only the entrances and exits of the characters, and with one distinguishing feature, the head position, expressing the characters' attitudes, Beckett

[11] Cf. Beckett's *Act without Words I and II* (in *Collected Shorter Plays* (London: Faber, 1984)).

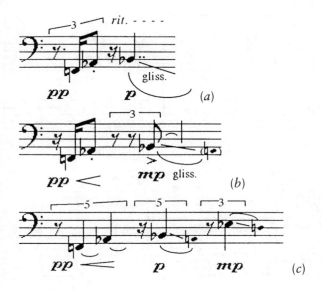

Fig. 6.17 *(a,b,c)*

provides a kind of summary of the play—a spatial reflection of its constituent branching structure. A head held high denotes the dominance of the person who is asking the questions, while a bowed head denotes the submission of the person being questioned (Figure 6.15).

And, as in *Come and Go*, the characters' entrances and exits are linked with ascending and descending musical gestures respectively. So, when 'Bim enters at E, halts at 2 head haught', the third trombone blows into the instrument and creates the impression of a change of pitch by moving from a bass to a treble vowel (Figure 6.16, bar 44). Then, two bars later, when 'Bim exits at E followed by Bom', it is the turn of the fourth trombone to 'breathe in while vibrating the lips' (*mit Lippenvibration einsaugen*), to produce a glissando, on a descending scale this time (Figure 6.16, bar 46).

The figure played by the kettledrum to accompany the first entrance (Figure 6.17*a*, bar 42)—'Bom enters at N, halts at 1 with head bowed'—is undoubtedly one of those formal symbols which underscores the repetition of identical stage actions. In fact, when Bom comes in again (Figure 6.17*b*, bar 82), it is played again with scarcely any variation. And similarly for the entrance of Bim (Figure 6.17*c*, bar 144). Thus the music registers modifications in the pattern of scenes and the linking elements in the play's structure. To quote the composer's own words, the two percussionists are 'comme des greffiers' [like clerks of the court] (Albèra, 'Entretien avec Holliger', 94).

Fig. 6.18 *(a,b,c)*

But the way in which the instrumental or vocal movements provide directions acquires meaning in the context of the dramatic system: 'Les interrogations sont toujours réalisées par un mouvement ascendant, les réponses par un mouvement descendant' [Questions are always represented using an upward movement, replies using a downward movement] (ibid.). The contrary movements alternate according to a sometimes very rapid rhythm of gestures, as in each of the three instances (Figure 6.18*a*, bb. 91–4; Figure 6.18*b*, bb. 103–5; Figure 6.18*c*, bb. 160–5) of the following fragment of the question sequence:

He wept?
Yes.
Screamed?

Yes.
Begged for mercy?
Yes.

The mimed exposition of the form of the play, a schematic and succinct one, is therefore based on the same musical resources of gestural characterization as the alternating patterns which go to make up the question sequences. It is a *responsorial* structure which is, as will be seen, central to the play's semantics.

TIME PASSES

Beckett has set his play within the cycle of the seasons. For, while the branchings-out multiply, 'time passes'; 'it is spring'; 'it is autumn'; and finally 'it is winter'.

The cycle of the seasons already constituted a musical figure for Beckett: the allusion to Schubert becomes evident at the moment when the play ends with V left alone:

> I am alone
> In the present as were I still.
> It is winter.
> Without journey.
> Time passes.
> That is all.
> Make sense who may.
> I switch off.

The Winter Journey ends here, since, 'chez Beckett l'hiver est sans voyage: plus rien ne bouge' [for Beckett there is no travelling in winter: nothing stirs] (Asmus, 'Reduire', 352). Here we see another example of the evocative *diminuendo al niente* present in *Come and Go*. And in the

Without journey

*) 1/2 ton chanté

Fig. 6.19

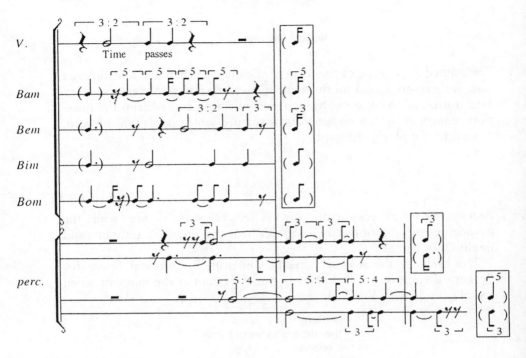

Fig. 6.20

closing bars of *What Where*, when the music has died away, leaving only
a few sounds and V's 'speech song' (*Sprechgesang*), the three sung notes
echo back to the melodic unit which is so characteristic of the incipit of
Schubert's piece, with its pointed rhythm and its half-tone embellishments (Figure 6.19). (This metonymic association between winter, frost,
and paralysis was already present in Holliger's *Scardanelli* cycle, composed between 1975 and 1985.)

In *What Where*, the handling of rhythm is explicitly linked to the
inexorable course of time. Each time V's phrase 'time passes' comes up,
a kind of rhythmic canon of diminishing values is produced by the
instrumental and vocal sections of the opera.

The first time this canon occurs (Figure 6.20) can be considered as a
false start, as V declares a few lines further on:

> Not good
> I switch off
> [...]
> I start again.

The rhythmic values, assigned to different units according to the parts,
correspond in this instance to the following sequence, which is wholly

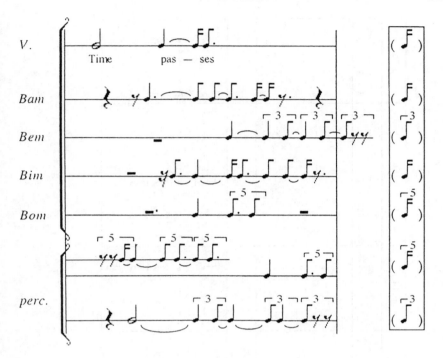

Fig. 6.21

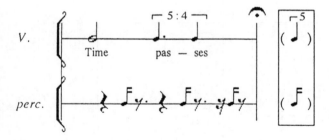

Fig. 6.22

atypical: [8-4-4]. For all the other occasions when this canon occurs, the values are in fact distributed according to the proportions set down by the first terms of a Fibonacci suite: [1-2-3-5-8].

The composer starts off the fragments of this sequence in such a way as to create asynchronic entries, as if the words pronounced by V (Figure 6.21) were followed by a series of echoes, thrown back four times, first by Bam and Bim, with the same values and the same rhythmic units

	p.14	p.20	p.21	p.44	p.66	p.76
V	5 – 3 .	2 – 3 – 5	5 – 3 – 2		8 – 5 – 3	5 – 3 – 2
Ban		8 – 5 – 3				
Bem		8 – 5 – 3				
Bim		2 – 3 – 5				
Bom		3 – 2 – 1				
Trombones		3 – 5 – 8	2 – 3 – 5.			
		1 – 2 – 3 – 5 – 3 – 2 – 1	5 – 3 – 2	5 – 1 – 2		
percussions	8 – 5 – 3	8 – 5 – 3	5 – 3 – 2	5 – 1 – 2	5 – 3 – 2	5 – 3 – 2
	5 – 3 – 2	3 – 5 – 8	2 – 3 – 5.	5 – 1 – 2	5 – 3 – 2	5 – 3 – 2
	5 – 3 – 2	5 – 8 – 3		5 – 1 – 2	5 – 3 – 2	5 – 3 – 2
				5 – 1 – 2	5 – 3 – 2	
					8 – 5 – 3	

Fig. 6.23

(though slightly deferred), and then by Bom and Bem, with the lower values of the sequel and different units.

The last time the phrase occurs, it elicits an echo in B (H, the composer's initials, in the German notation system) from the kettledrums, the lengths of which seem as if they are truncated, intercut with silence (Figure 6.22, bar 252), which is rather reminiscent of the similar emptying which takes place in *Come and Go*. (Figure 6.23 sums up the other repetitions of the phrase: V always traverses the scale of values in a downward direction, except on p. 20; on the other hand, the instrumental parts, and particularly the percussion section, can disrupt the order of these values, so creating permutations within the sequence). By reiterating this rhythmic reduction on each occasion, these rhythmic canons inscribe the formal idea of the play: 'une sorte de rondo musical en diminution qui va jusqu'à l'épuisement' [a sort of diminishing musical rondo—shrinking to the point of extinction] (Albèra, 'Entretien avec Holliger', 94) at the very heart of the musical durations.

LIKE ONE BODY

Likewise, the way that the manipulation of pitch is handled is a reflection of the ramifications which shape the play's dramaturgy. For, as Holliger emphasizes, in *What Where* 'il n'y a pas de multiplicité temporelle, c'est comme un seul corps. Bam est seul, et tout cela passe

Fig. 6.24

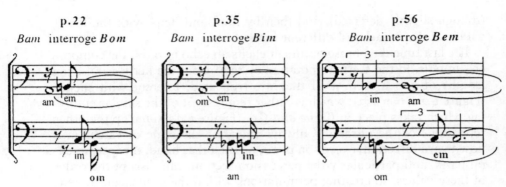

Fig. 6.25

dans sa tête' [there is no multiplication in time; there is, as it were, one body. Bam is alone, and everything happens in his head] (Albèra, 'Entretien avec Holliger', 94). In fact, the orchestration of the play stresses the confusion of tones. 'J'ai voulu montrer [. . .] que ces quatre personnages, y compris celui dont la voix est dédoublée, forment une unité: quatre voix graves ayant une même tessiture, une même expression. Ils chantent parfois bouche fermée, ou sont placés derrière la scène—on ne sait jamais qui chante' [I wanted to demonstrate [. . .] that these four characters, including the one whose voice is duplicated, form one entity: four bass voices which have the same range, the same expression. They sometimes sing with their mouths closed, or are positioned off-stage—it is impossible to tell who is singing] (ibid. 94).

Bam alone, or rather V, his voice, is situated at the top of the tree. And the opera opens with a unison on D which incorporates the four distinguishing vowels of the four imaginary protagonists within a unified figure (Figure 6.24). This D then gives rise to a cluster within the ambit of a minor third—D to F—like a beam connecting the four characters as closely as possible. And the same cluster reforms, transposed by a fourth, at the beginning of each question sequence, the four notes following a different order each time, with the last note bearing the vocal signature of the character being questioned (Figure 6.25).

This cluster can also assume melodic forms. At bar 69, the four characters bring out a corresponding number of virtual possibilities contained within V's motif (Figure 6.26a). Bam enunciates the recurrence of this motif, Bem transposes it down a fourth, while Bim and Bom produce two different permutations on it (Figure 6.26b). And the four trombones undertake an exchange of voices within a verticalization of this same fragment (Figure 6.26c).

At the end of the play, when Bam is once again alone on stage

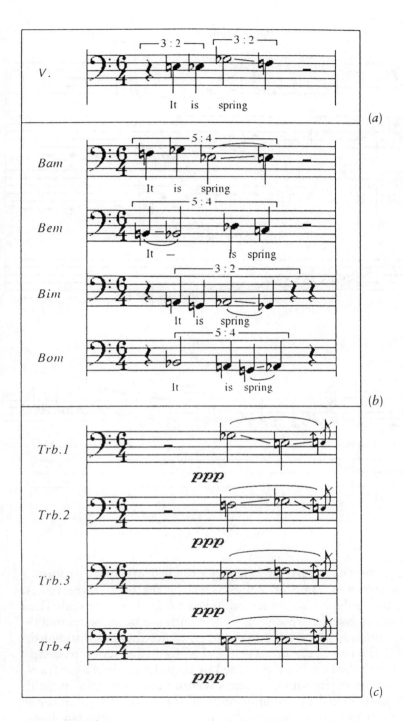

Fig. 6.26 (a,b,c)

Fig. 6.27

Fig. 6.28

(pp. 74 ff.), the vocal parts are arranged in such a way as to form a dodecaphonic series, sung on Bam's vowel by the other three voices, according to a polyphonic framework (Figure 6.27, bars 235–42). Then the three voices give an exposition of the recurrence of the series in a re-established unison, which once again incorporates the four distinguishing vowels (Figure 6.28, b. 245). In this way, the series is clearly associated with the constraint exercised by Bam. Its original form transforms the fusion of the four characters within the unison into an artificial polyphony, belied by the uniformity of the vowel. Its palindromic form describes a strictly symmetrical course: it closes the open fan shape, as brackets are closed.

QUESTIONS AND ANSWERS

The serial structures employed by the composer thus appear to represent an explicit exposition of the modality of constraint which is implicit in the logic of questioning.

As Jaakko Hintikka has demonstrated,[12] any question addressed to anyone can in fact be analysed as consisting of an imperative operator of the 'See to it that [. . .]' type, and a *desideratum* concerning a certain state of knowledge, represented by a subordinate clause to be inserted into the brackets after the imperative operator: 'See to it that I know that P'. And this is most particularly the case with the 'Wh-questions'[13] around which Beckettian dialogue revolves: *What* and *Where*. Each of these questions also implies what Hintikka calls a presupposition. So, the presupposition preceding the key question in the play: 'What did he say to him?'—takes the form '($'x$) [i.e. x exists] he told him x'. And the reply to such a question, in order to be conclusive, must at least satisfy its presupposition.

Now—and here we come to the crux of the mechanism operating in Beckett's dialogue—it is impossible in *What Where* to attest the existence of an x, since all information concerning this unknown quantity is deliberately kept hidden. From this stems a powerlessness to bring the dialogue to a close, so long as there are people, however doubtful their existence, to question. But in that case, how can we explain the assertion that *What Where* is nonetheless essentially a finite game?

The answer lies in the fact that the play's basic figure of temporality is that of wearing-out: in *What Where*, the *diminuendo al niente* which had run through *Come and Go* punctuates each appearance of the emblematic phrase 'Time passes'. Time passes, possibilities are narrowed down, the characters who are subjects for the questioning process disappear. And this dwindling of the modalities of power is thematically represented by the '*respir*':[14] at bar 255, when the cluster uniting the four protagonists occurs for the last time, the trombones hold the note 'as long as breath lasts' (*bis Atemende*).

In *What Where*, the end takes place within the scope of the play, and not in an in(de)finite past or future. And this sense of the imminence— even, one might say, of the immanence—of the end was already present in the first 'successful' playing of V's first insistent phrase: at bar 31, the second percussionist punctuates the ritual of the rhythmic canon of bell plates by scattering sand 'le plus régulièrement possible' [as steadily as

---

[12] Jaakko Hintikka, *The Intentions of Intentionality* (Dordrecht: D. Reidel, 1975), 137.

[13] 'who-, what-, which-, when-, and where-questions are wh-questions' (ibid. 137).

[14] Jean-Louis Tristani defines the *respir* as 'la composante libidinale respiratoire' [the libidinal component of breath], in *Le Stade du respir* (Paris: Éditions de Minuit, 1978), 54

possible]. The hour-glass: is not that the most explicit symbol possible that our days are *numbered*?

OH TO END IT ALL[15]

What Where and *Come and Go* embody two contrary figures within the interplay of dialogue. In *What Where*, the dialogue is framed within a monologue—that of V—and set within the cycle of the seasons: the universe of knowledge, even if it develops in a tree-like configuration, remains essentially one finite entity, diminished by time. In *Come and Go*, on the other hand, the dialogue is fragmented into separate confidences which never succeed in coming together; and the course of time remains suspended, as the same dreamlike past is endlessly recreated.

These two dramatic configurations are inductive of, just as much as they clarify, the organization and the musical content of the two operas to which they have given rise. They are inductive of them, in so far as each opera is a response to a specific dramatic system, adopted as a logical *model*. They clarify them, inasmuch as they constitute verbal *metaphors* for the musical structures already present as features of the composer's works.[16]

The *diminuendo al niente*, the to-and-fro movement between the unison and the cluster, the *scordatura*, the way that the breathing is scored, the presence of negative, void elements, inscribed in the 'hollows' of the texture: these are all features typical of Holliger's style which in the two operas come to be intermeshed with the semantic networks of the Beckett dramaticules. It is this displacement, this transfer of meaning from one plane to another, from musical to textual, which can be truly described as *metaphoric*: it stems from a poetic, even rhetorical, conjunction.

But Holliger also takes the dramaticules as *models*, in the strongest sense of the word. The original play, *Come and Go*, could be considered as a telescoped figuration of the opera—a figuration which is actualized in three different ways in the three separate acts of the opera. And these three actualizations, which exhaust every possible permutation, relate to the original dramaticule in the same way as enumerations relate to a model.[17]

It is particularly striking that we find Beckett himself raising this

---

[15] Cf. the last words of Beckett's *Soubresauts* (Paris: Éditions de Minuit, 1989), 28: 'Oh tout finir'.

[16] Cf. André Riotte, 'Modèles et métaphores: les formalismes de la musique', in S. McAdams and I. Deliège, *La Musique et les sciences cognitives* (Brussels: Mardaga, 1989), 523–33.

[17] Cf. 'Pour qu'il y ait modèle, il faut que [. . .] la représentation soit plus économique qu'une simple énumération d'événements' [In order for there to be a model, the representation must have more economy of form than a mere enumeration of events] (ibid. 526).

question of enumeration and the capacity to be exhaustive, and specifically in relation to opera: 'By definition, opera is a hideous corruption of this most immaterial of all the arts: the words of a libretto are to the musical phrase that they particularise what the Vendôme column, for example, is to the ideal perpendicular. From this point of view opera is less complete than vaudeville, which at least inaugurates the comedy of an exhaustive enumeration.'[18]

The question of closure—or of 'anti-clotûre' [anti-closure],[19] which comes to the same thing—is of course not specific to the musical work. Nonetheless, *a posteriori*, the principles peculiar to serial writing seem closely related to the problematics of open-ended works of art: historically, at least, they have led in that direction.[20] Nonetheless, if the open-ended work of art has seemed to offer a means of actualizing, or not actualizing, the whole spectrum of virtualities in a series, it has never before taken as its theme the advent of the end, the process of ending: the open-ended work is represented as a perpetual process of genesis, eternally inceptive.

Heinz Holliger was able to see more than a facile parallel of serial conventions of spontaneous generation in Beckett's works: *Come and Go* and *What Where* are truly rituals of reduction. By turning upon itself, and bringing to light the mechanisms embedded within the dialogue, Beckett's plot, or the vestiges of it, gives us the spectacle of the end of fiction and the fiction of the end. It is a chiasmus which is reflected in Holliger's music by a treatment of the negative quality which could be compared to that of Lachenmann.

Certainly, some aspects of *Come and Go* do derive from the aesthetic of the open-ended work; but while the opera explores the proliferation of possibilities, and while the text is infinite in theory, in practice it undergoes a wearing-down process: numbering becomes listing. *What Where*, on the other hand, explicitly takes time as its theme. And it is impossible not to see the musical treatment of V's insistent catchphrase, 'time passes', as a reply to Stockhausen's famous article '. . . wie die Zeit vergeht . . . ' [how time passes].[21] For in *What Where*, when time passes, possibilities are exhausted: exhaustivity becomes exhaustion.

---

[18] Samuel Beckett, *Proust, and Three Dialogues with Georges Duthuit* (London: John Calder, 1987), 92.

[19] See Paul Ricœur, *Temps et récit*, ii: *La Configuration dans le récit de fiction* (Paris: Éditions du Seuil, 1984), 38.

[20] Cf. Célestin Deliège: 'C'est en toute logique que l'œuvre ouverte devait résulter d'une telle expérience; c'est en cela qu'elle nous paraît dérivée des conséquences du système sériel' [It is completely logical that the open-ended work should result from such an experiment: and it is in this way that we see it as derived from the consequences of the serial system], *Invention musicale et idéologies* (Paris: Christian Bourgois, 1986), 320.

[21] See *Die Reihe*, 3 (1959), 10–41.

7

Marcel Mihalovici and Samuel Beckett: Musicians of Return[1]

Edith Fournier
Translated from the French by Mary Bryden

'The artist who stakes his being is from nowhere, has no kith.'[2] What Samuel Beckett was saying here, in 1954, of the artist Jack B. Yeats, can be said of only a handful of artists, whether they be painters or poets, writers or composers: those who, without any pretence, 'stake' their entire being in each of their works. Such totally committed artists have no homeland other than their own creative impulse: a spiral ascending from the depths to rise towards the height of beauty. Being the only offspring of his own art, each of these exceptional creative spirits has, in his domain, no 'kith': he is incomparable.

If creative spirits such as these have no kith, they may nevertheless attain kinship when bridges are thrown between different fields of expression. A link can then form between the writer and the painter, the painter and the poet, the poet and the composer. To modify Baudelaire: 'Mon dissemblable, mon frère'. Whether these bridges span a gulf of centuries, or link contemporaries, scarcely matters: artists are of no time just as they are of nowhere.

While individual identities are, then, retained, an intimate, even if transient, communication is established. For the duration of the work undertaken in common, this intimate communication gives rise to a third vibration: one which is, somehow, foreign to the two artistic domains involved, but which nevertheless unites them in one same inspiration, one same beauty.

Such was the case with the encounter between the composer Marcel Mihalovici and Samuel Beckett. Incomparable, dissimilar creative artists, they were yet 'brothers' through the many parallel aspects of their individual endeavours, and 'brothers' too through three works which brought them together, gangways thrown between music on the one side

---

[1] This is a translated and modified version of Edith Fournier's article, 'Marcel Mihalovici et Samuel Beckett, musiciens du retour', which appeared in *Revue d'esthétique* (special number on Beckett, 1986), 243–9.

[2] Samuel Beckett, 'Homage to Jack B. Yeats', in *Disjecta*, ed. Ruby Cohn (London: John Calder, 1983), 149.

and words on the other; 'brothers', then, to the extent of no longer being sure who is the poet and who the musician. It is true that, whether together or individually, Marcel Mihalovici and Samuel Beckett are both poets, both musicians. Both, too, are choristers of silence and return.

Marcel Mihalovici, a Frenchman of Romanian origin, who was born in Bucharest in 1898, but settled in Paris from 1919 onwards, is a composer of whom it has been said that he is 'outside time and fashion'. His work, of an exceptional richness and originality, unites the expression of a fiery, passionate, and lyrical temperament with that of an extreme sensitivity in which delicacy and reserve, rigour and modesty blend together. He is the prisoner of no predetermined musical language: diatonic or chromatic, modal or tonal, even serial when he deems it necessary, he makes use of every possible syntax of musical language with the absolute freedom of a painter whose palette excludes no colour, no marriage of their infinite hues. Strength and gentleness, emotion now released now contained, humour and finesse, 'tensions and relaxations': these are some of the characteristics of his powerful work, which is striking in its intensity and intelligence, and inexpressibly touching.

There are innumerable scores for the most diverse instruments, choruses, ballets, sonatas, *Lieder*, operas, symphonies: no musical form is foreign to him. However, we shall mention here only his five operas: *L'Intransigeant Pluton*, *Phèdre*, *Le Retour*, *Krapp*, *Les Jumeaux*; his Symphony No. 5; and the music for *Cascando*, a radio play which Samuel Beckett wrote for Marcel Mihalovici. Amongst these works, we shall consider in detail only the opera *Krapp*, the Symphony No. 5: 'Que ferais-je sans ce monde . . . ' ['What would I do without this world . . . '], and the opera *Le Retour*.

Marcel Mihalovici does not say that he has seen *Waiting for Godot*. He says: 'Having listened to Sam's theatre, I surmised how important the word is for him. The word has a particular meaning because of its musical resonance.' Mihalovici had, then, 'listened to' *Waiting for Godot* at the Théâtre de Babylone, in 1952. For personal reasons, Mihalovici wished at that very time to compose a work in which, more than ever before, he could 'stake his being', pledge his life. Now for him: 'Spoken language is an additional contribution to musical inspiration.' Won over by 'the Beckettian word', he asked Samuel Beckett to write for him a text for an opera. The procedures proper to librettists doubtless seemed impossible to the writer, too much of a musician himself. He therefore suggested three already written texts to Mihalovici. One was unpublished: 'a sort of parable which develops within a landscape destroyed by a catastrophe. Two characters still survive there: a paralytic and a blind man. They squabble instead of joining their forces . . . '.

The second text was *All That Fall,* and the third was *Krapp's Last Tape,* the play which had just been published.

Marcel Mihalovici opted for *Krapp's Last Tape,* which became the opera entitled *Krapp.*[3] We shall come back to the reasons for this choice of text and theme. But first let us examine the circumstances of this composition: 'an exhilarating time', according to Mihalovici.

I began by inviting Sam and Roger Blin to my flat. After lunch, Blin settled into an armchair and, in the presence of Sam, read, reread, and acted out several times *Krapp's Last Tape.* Using a stopwatch, I recorded, listened, recorded every lapse of time. Heard the words, heard the story. What inspired me was to compose an opera based precisely upon the Beckettian word. I recorded everything because I wanted to be as close as possible to this very word. And, in fact, the opera lasts a bare quarter of an hour longer than the spoken text. We know how much music can extend a spoken text.

Marcel Mihalovici began the score of *Krapp* in Switzerland, and then came back to Paris. Samuel Beckett henceforth followed the elaboration of this work, day after day, for months.

Sam used to come round every evening. I would show him my score and play to him on the piano what I had composed. Sometimes, he would set forth a criticism, and suggest precious modifications. Sam is an excellent musician. And the draft sheets I had prepared for the German and English translations of the work include handwritten annotations by Sam.

The composer and the writer met one another then, not only on the basis of that instinctive emotional perception proper to music (a perception whose primacy Beckett stressed), but also on the basis of the lyrical prosody. Time and sounds are the composer's materials. A composer needs to be able to craft duration and acoustic vibration meticulously, and to be a rigorous mathematician, attentive to time-values, rhythms, harmonies; to their periodicity, their conjunctions, and variations. In *Krapp's Last Tape,* as in his later works, whether literary or dramatic, Samuel Beckett bestows a fundamental importance upon sounds, rhythms, cadences. He is rigorously attentive to resonances, echoes, variations, and silences. The musicality of his writing takes on an increasing importance. As the verbal density diminishes, the rhythmic intensity grows. His liking for mathematics merging with his sense of balance and of musical architecture, Samuel Beckett's writings have truly evolved into musical scores.

Marcel Mihalovici says: '*Krapp* contains leading themes: not leading

[3] Marcel Mihalovici, score of the opera *Krapp* (Paris: Heugel, 1961). First broadcast 15 May 1961 (France III). Performed by the Bielefeld opera at the Théâtre des Nations, Paris, 3 July 1961.

themes in the Wagnerian sense! But harmonic compounds, rhythms or even musical sweeps which continually animate the score. The most important theme is that of the woman in the rowing-boat. This scene of ecstasy recurs three times. In the opera *Krapp*, the music is the same, but, each time, another instumental compound accompanies it: wood-wind, strings, or light percussion.'

Krapp posed Mihalovici problems which fascinated him. Two voices were needed: one of the older Krapp, and one, recorded, of young Krapp. They required different qualities in tone, then, and yet they had to be sung by the same performer. This problem, like the others, was solved musically with a subtle perfection.'There was also the difficulty of choosing moments when I could introduce more precise musical forms, such as the *Lied* (*Krapp* contains two *Lieder*), or the sonata (monothematic), and the variation.' At the beginning, the mime allows Marcel Mihalovici to establish in a prelude all the elements and all the incipient themes which will later be taken up and developed.

There was yet another major problem. Music exalts the spoken word. Now the Beckettian word is extremely restrained and sober. It was therefore necessary to bring the lyricism inherent in the music into accordance with this language without betraying that verbal restraint. On the other hand, however sober the Beckettian word may be, his language is nevertheless poetic: this is not a contradiction in terms. But in an opera, says Mihalovici, 'the text runs the risk of duplicating the music, yet it is the music which must create the poetry'. 'However', he adds, 'Sam's poetry does not disturb the poetry of the music: on the contrary, it instigates it.' What, then, is this particular poetic quality of the Beckettian word which allows for it not to 'disturb' the music? In Beckett's work, poetry and music are already present within the word: 'His poetry does not disturb me because Sam is a musician', says Mihalovici.

This problem of the conciliation of lyricism and sobriety, of musical exaltation and verbal restraint, seems also to be solved in a manner which might appear paradoxical: each in his own way, Marcel Mihalovici and Samuel Beckett both have the rare gift of encompassing silence (which is just as much an essential material as sound or word) within their respective art forms, endowing it with emotional hues and expressive possibilities.

'The experience of my reader', Beckett had already written in his *Dream of Fair to Middling Women* (1932), 'shall be between the phrases, in the silence, communicated by the intervals, not the terms, of the statement.'[4]

---

[4] Samuel Beckett, *Dream of Fair to Middling Women* (Dublin: Black Cat Press, 1992), 137.

Besides the numerous pauses which the text of *Krapp's Last Tape*[5] contains, silence is often evoked in it: 'Extraordinary silence this evening, I strain my ears and do not hear a sound' (p. 58). 'Never knew such silence. The earth might be uninhabited' (pp. 61 and 63). And even Krapp asks himself the question: 'Did I ever sing? No' (p. 58). What a challenge for a composer, to have to put these words into music and have them sung! A challenge which Mihalovici meets in full, and triumphs over with a rare felicity, without ever committing the least travesty. In the opera *Krapp*, this leitmotiv of silence gives rise to particularly beautiful passages: an intense throbbing animates them.

Well before the period of his later works, *Quad* for example, where the word has totally disappeared in favour of the play of movement, sound, and light, Beckett was already evoking, in a letter to Axel Kaun (1937), the need to achieve the transposition into the field of literature of what music had already been able to recruit: pauses and silence. And he mentions Beethoven's Seventh Symphony to illustrate his point. Mihalovici, who was not familiar with this letter, expresses himself in identical fashion: 'In *Krapp* I respected these several pauses. All the time I thought of Beethoven, for whom pauses are music.'

After deriding the word by the multiplication of words, the writer espouses silence. Beckett thus achieves this literature of the 'non-word' which allows him to capture, to feel 'a whisper of that final music or that silence that underlies All'.[6] The music of Mihalovici is amongst those which know how to underlie 'All'.

We have mentioned the recurrences which have a fundamental importance in the writing of Samuel Beckett and which contribute to the musical structure of his work. These repetitions are never artificial devices of structure. Structure and meaning blend into one another. These constant echoes take on a variety of aspects. Sometimes it is the endless repetition of the same sentence, an identical chord struck from time to time. For example, 'who(m) else' (in *That Time* and in *Rockaby*), the most searing, simple, and poignant expression of solitude possible. Sometimes, it is the return to the beginning of the work which must be wholly and endlessly repeated: the Dantesque spiral of *Play*. At other times, it is the reiteration of the same sentence, either minutely modified, or augmented by a term which amplifies it:

> another like herself
> another creature like herself.[7]

[5] Id., *Krapp's Last Tape*, in *Collected Shorter Plays of Samuel Beckett* (London: Faber, 1984).

[6] Id., 'Letter to Axel Kaun', trans. Martin Esslin, in *Disjecta*, 172.

[7] Id., *Rockaby*, in *Collected Shorter Plays*, 275.

In this case, which is so frequent in Samuel Beckett's œuvre, the return has the same value as that which is called 'recurrent series' in the field of mathematics: a series in which each term is a dependent variable of the terms immediately preceding. Each new statement both encompasses and exceeds the one before. It embraces all possible adaptations of the first statement.

In this self-obsessed to-and-fro movement, in those themes, variations, or recurrences, in these 'old rounds',[8] it is always a case of the rememberer who mutters or harks back to the past, of being able to say: 'that time when . . . '. It is a return to the past in order to tell it or to invent it, with all its possible variations, 'till just one of those things you kept making up to keep the void out just another of those old tales to keep the void from pouring in on top of you the shroud' (*That Time*, 230). It is a return to the events of the past, in order to prove to oneself ('whom else'!) that one exists. Thus it is with Krapp who, incarcerated in himself, with no elsewhere to go back to, splits himself up indefinitely, from spool to spool as from mirror to mirror, to hear himself as was, perhaps.

In Samuel Beckett's work, nostalgia is predominant: 'Never but the one matter. The dead and gone. The dying and the going.'[9] But the return which nostalgia implies is destructive. The photographs, the images of past days (so present in *Company*), are finally 'torn to shreds and scattered. [. . .] Ripped from the wall and torn to shreds one by one. Over the years. Years of nights' (*A Piece of Monologue*, 266). Then there is nothing left but to remain fixed, face to the bare wall, 'dying on' (ibid. 166), without any possible return.

Unless one hums, timidly, mechanically, Winnie's old-fashioned music-box tune: 'Though I say not | what I may not | let you hear',[10] a return which is the prisoner of an inanimate mechanism.

The theme of return has, in the lyrical work of Marcel Mihalovici, a predominant importance also. It has the force of an impulse from the depths: an impulse which he claims had for a long time remained mysterious and subconscious. Each of his operas adheres to it in a different way. *L'Intransigeant Pluton* is concerned with the myth of Orpheus, and therefore with a descent to hell to obtain the return of Eurydice. In *Phèdre*, the dreaded return of Theseus brings about the fateful ending. *Le Retour* (based upon one of Maupassant's short stories) could be linked to the myth of the return of Ulysses. With *Les Jumeaux* (based upon Plautus's *Menaechmi*), it is the return to oneself, other and yet identical. Obviously, the return of Krapp to his past was

[8] Samuel Beckett, *That Time*, in *Collected Shorter Plays*, 231.

[9] Id., *A Piece of Monologue*, in *Collected Shorter Plays*, 269.

[10] Id., *Happy Days*, ed. James Knowlson (London: Faber, 1978), 82.

the fundamental element which attracted Mihalovici to this text which inspired him so profoundly.

Whatever form it takes—and they are manifold—the return is always illusory or mythical. It is dream, hope, nostalgia.

In Marcel Mihalovici's work, the theme of return is imbued with nostalgia for former places, events lived through elsewhere, at earlier times. Nevertheless, however haunting and poignant the regret may be, this nostalgia never takes on the tone of a languid melancholy. Sombre or luminous, discreet or menacing, his music has too much vigour for that. Completely given over to his dream of return, the composer re-members and hopes, much more than he regrets (in *Le Retour* in particular).

To Nietzsche's question: 'Have you ever wished for the same thing to happen twice?', Mihalovici would no doubt reply: yes. Samuel Beckett makes Krapp reply: 'No, I wouldn't want them [my best years] back' (*Krapp's Last Tape*, 63).

What Samuel Beckett calls 'the need to recognize oneself' (i.e. as having been), comes up against 'the need not to recognize oneself' (i.e. to escape from the consciousness of self). 'Out of this conflict art is born', he says.[11] For Krapp, resurgent memories are clouded over with disillusion, and the return accentuates the separation between the two disjointed elements of one's own being.

What Marcel Mihalovici calls 'the unconscious concept of return' merges with nostalgia. In his work, return reconciles, and his art emerges out of this reconciliation. However, far from making it incompatible, this contrast enriches their encounter. And from this conflict-free contrast emerges the beauty of a shared work: *Krapp*.

In his desire to come 'as close as possible to the Beckettian word', Marcel Mihalovici was equally faithful to the general colouring of the play. In *Eleutheria*, one character says: 'Tout aspire soit au noir, soit au blanc. La couleur, c'est la syncope'; [Everything aspires to be either black or white. Colour is syncopation].[12] *Krapp's Last Tape* is a wholly black and white play, where colour intervenes three times, in three syncopations, with the evocation of lost love. Similarly, in the opera *Krapp*, all the musical thematics rest upon the contrast between a heavy, hollow, profound darkness, and a violent, intense, menacing light. And, three times, after the passages which herald the ecstatic scene, the musical syncopation intervenes, by means of a rupture, to enhance

---

[11] Mme Fournier has explained to me that the phrases within quotation marks within this paragraph emerge from conversations with Samuel Beckett concerning what he described as 'les deux besoins', and are not textual citations [*Ed.*].

[12] Samuel Beckett, *Eleutheria* (Paris: Éditions de Minuit, 1995), 112. The English translation of this quotation, and of the subsequent one, is by Mary Bryden.

and colour the memory of the beloved woman, of love cradled in the rowing-boat.

Does music 'translate' the word? The task of the translator is more humble than that of the composer. The translator does not create. Music transposes the spoken word into another realm which, as we have seen, is both different and yet not unfamiliar. The composer is not content with merely presenting a mirror in which the work of the writer would be reflected. It is more a matter of passing mysteriously through the mirror. Music is that world beyond the looking-glass, where the spoken word finds itself again, different yet neither inverted nor deformed.

The only translation Marcel Mihalovici had to do was to 'translate the music' for the German and English versions of this opera. Meticulously attentive, down to the least detail, to the values of the vowels, open, closed, high or low, as he was with all the phonetics of any given word, Mihalovici had accordingly to modify sometimes the musical prosody which he had composed for the French text.

The case of the Fifth Symphony is quite different. Mihalovici had already composed this symphony, the outcome of a creative impulse of a uniquely musical nature, without the contribution of any verbal inspiration.

Asked one day to suggest a poetic text as a theme for the Prix de Rome competition, Mihalovici chose to put forward to the candidates the poem by Beckett which begins: 'que ferais-je sans ce monde sans visage sans questions'; ['what would I do without this world faceless incurious'].[13] By some mysterious affinity, this poem (so close to *Rockaby*), which sums up in fifteen simple, beautiful lines the whole of Samuel Beckett's work, and which is already music itself, evoked in Mihalovici, like an echo, the memory of his own Fifth Symphony. Perhaps he had the feeling, upon reading this poem, that he had already 'thought it in music', to use his own expression. He therefore took up again the score of this symphony, and modified it entirely. 'I rewrote my symphony so as to be able to integrate this poem into it. I feel that Sam wanted this poem to be murmured, whereas I transposed it into a great lyrical flight.'

After a thematic exposition, a singer (mezzo-soprano), placed at the back of the orchestra, comes forward singing the beginning of the poem. She stops beside the conductor's podium and falls silent. Then rings out a very long and violent scherzo. The third movement follows, which could be seen as an elaborate variation on the first: near the footlights, the mezzo-soprano then sings the entire poem. 'Vocal inflections, introduced by descending fourths, and thematic inflections clearly recall the first movement of this symphony.'

[13] Both the French and the English versions of this poem are in Samuel Beckett, *Collected Poems in English and French* (London: John Calder, 1977), 58 and 59 [*Ed.*].

The first line is thus set forth, proposed. Then the whole symphony follows, without words. The sonorities and the orchestration somehow imagine the words to come. At the end, the singer seems to confirm all that the music alone has already told us. This symphony in which, according to Mihalovici, 'the *cantabile* blossoms' forms a close and perfect union with the poem.

A man of great culture, willingly talkative and capable of holding fascinating conversations on so many diverse topics and areas of knowledge, Marcel Mihalovici, like Samuel Beckett, dislikes commenting upon his own work. It is the characteristic of great creative artists to remain silent about their own creative work. Of course, they are quite right. Their works of art, as such, speak for themselves.

Valéry compared prose to a stroll from one place to another, and poetry to the movements of a choreography.

One can listen to music, play or compose it, not tell of it. One character in *Eleutheria* says: 'Ce n'est pas une chose qu'on peut raconter. C'est un peu comme la musique'; [It's not something you can explain. It's a bit like music] (*Eleutheria*, 126).

To say more about this encounter between the words of Samuel Beckett and the music of Marcel Mihalovici would be to add words to words about a writer who strips himself of them, and to betray the musical emotion of the composer who escapes them.

For those who stake their being, it is clear that art is both 'parfaitement intelligible et parfaitement inexplicable'; [perfectly intelligible and perfectly inexplicable].[14] Their greatness is in simplicity, the rarest and most mysterious thing to be found.

Let us listen, then. Listen, indeed, provided this opera, this symphony, and the others, be played, performed, interpreted, and recorded in France. Here's the rub, an unforgivable omission.

So, listen if you may. And, without striving to explain the inexplicable, 'merely bow in wonder' ('Homage to Jack B. Yeats', 149).

Paris, August 1985.

[14] Samuel Beckett, 'Le Concentrisme', in *Disjecta*, 42.

8

That Time: Samuel Beckett and Wolfgang Fortner

BRIGITTA WEBER
Translated from the German by Julian Garforth

PRELUDE

Wolfgang Fortner ranks amongst the most important German composers of the post-war era. Born in Leipzig in 1907, he grew up with the tradition of church-music associated with the city, the concerts of Hermann Scherchen and the premières of the Leipzig Opera and, by 1931, he was already appointed as teacher of composition at the newly founded Institute for Church Music in Heidelberg. Both here and at his subsequent places of work in Detmold (1954–7) and Freiburg (1957–73), he established his reputation as one of the most sought-after teachers of composition of his era. After the Second World War, along with Wolfgang Steinecke, Fortner founded the Kranichstein Summer Schools for New Music; from 1964 he conducted the Musica-viva-concerts in Munich as successor to Karl Amadeus Hartmann.

In addition to his continuous academic work and his involvement in numerous politico-cultural committees, up to 1950, he composed for almost all genres: church-music works, works for mixed a-cappella choir or for choir and orchestra, chamber music works, solo concertos, and compositions for full orchestra. The only genre for which he had not composed was music theatre.

Even in 1950, Fortner claimed: 'It is still very doubtful whether I shall ever write an opera.'[1] At this juncture, he was already over 40 years old. It seems likely that the actor and director, Karl Heinz Stroux, was the crucial motivating force which led to Fortner composing five major operas in the space of some twenty years. After 1945, Stroux repeatedly asked Fortner for music for his own stage productions, as well as for Federico García Lorca's *Blood Wedding*. The resulting stage music was so important in its own right that Fortner then conceived his first opera from it. It was premièred in June 1957 in Cologne and ranks today as

---

[1] Wolfgang Fortner, 'Zur Situation des musikalischen Theaters', *Die Welt*, 5 Oct. 1950. (This, and other quotations from German within this chapter, are rendered into English by the translator, Julian Garforth.)

one of the most successful operas of the post-1945 music theatre. It has thus far undergone twenty-two new productions in total.

After the one-act *opéra bouffe*, *Corinna*, adapted from Gérard de Nerval (1958), Fortner set another of García Lorca's dramas to music: *The Love of Don Perlimplín and Belisa in the Garden* (1961–3). For the full opera *Elizabeth Tudor* (1968–71), Fortner broke precedent by not referring directly to a work of fiction, but had a libretto written by Mattias Braun. In 1977, Fortner composed his last work for the music theatre up to his death in 1987: *That Time*, based on Samuel Beckett's play. Both Beckett's text and Fortner's composition are to be interpreted autobiographically as late period works.

BECKETT'S *THAT TIME* IN
WOLFGANG FORTNER'S COMPOSITION

Samuel Beckett wrote *That Time* in 1974–5. In Friedrich Hommel's description: 'The sole character of the piece, the "Listener", does not act; he hears. He hears his own voice, which is divided into three strands, by the author [Beckett], designated 'A', 'B', and 'C'.[2]

In April 1976, on the occasion of the author's seventieth birthday, Suhrkamp published a bilingual edition, and the play received its world première at the Royal Court Theatre in London on 20 May of the same year. Later that year, Beckett directed the piece for the Schiller-Theatre in Berlin, where it received its German première on 1 October.

Fortner's composition of *That Time* ends with an indication of the date of completion: 28 December 1976. It was Fortner's speediest literature-based composition.[3]

The motivation for the composition is unusual. Fortner had got to know Beckett at the Academy of Arts in Berlin; in an interview, he recounts:

We got to know each other in Berlin, when we were both living in the Academy of Arts for three weeks or more [. . .]. One day I went down to the breakfast room. He was sitting there totally alone by the window. I went up to him and asked him, 'Are you Beckett?' 'Yes.' Then I said, 'I am so-and-so.' 'Ah! Hm, hm.' I said, 'May I sit with you?' and the result of this meeting was that we breakfasted together every day for two weeks. [. . .] At that time he was directing a play of his for the studio-stage at the Schiller-Theatre. But as he was

---

[2] Friedrich Hommel gave an introduction at the world première of Fortner's *That Time* which appears in the study-score published by Schott Musik International, Mainz, ED 6739, p. 9.
[3] The world première was on 24 Apr. 1977, in Baden-Baden (musical director: Manfred Reichert).

not going to the première [. . .], he gave me his tickets and said, 'Please go for me and tell me afterwards what it was like. We will meet in such-and-such a wine bar.' That is what we did, along with his publisher.[4]

Unfortunately, it is not clear from these comments when this first meeting took place, and which première Fortner attended. An enquiry at the Academy of Arts revealed that there were only two occasions when Beckett and Fortner were there simultaneously: Beckett was a guest at the Academy from 9 August until 22 September 1971, Fortner from 13 to 28 September 1971; Beckett resided at the Academy in 1976 from 29 August until 2 October; Fortner spent only a short time there from 29 August until 3 September 1976. It seems most likely that Fortner attended the German première of *Happy Days* in place of Beckett, which took place on 17 September 1971 in the Schiller-Theatre Werkstatt, but the possibility that Fortner became aware of *That Time* via his contact with Beckett himself cannot be ruled out.[5] [*Ed*: The later date is confirmed in James Knowlson's 1996 authorized biography of Beckett. This refers to Beckett's appointment books for 1976 and 1977, which record meetings with Fortner on 30 August 1976 in Berlin, and on 16 November 1977 in Paris. Knowlson states: 'At the end of August 1976, while directing in Berlin, he met the Heidelberg-based composer, Professor Wolfgang Fortner, who wanted to set *That Time* to music (and saw him again a year later once the problems had been solved and the work finished).'[6]]

A copy of the Suhrkamp edition mentioned above exists in the estate of the composer, which is now housed in the Bavarian State Library in Munich. Along with corrections to printing errors made by an unfamiliar hand[7] are numerous entries made by Fortner, the majority of which relate to the underlining of single words or passages in the English text. In the front dust jacket as well as twice in the course of the text, Fortner noted down a series of sketches for the composition.[8] Motivic material is partly in note form, and with no key indication, rendering the structures unclear, and only partially sketched out in alphabetical order.

Further details have been included in the following analysis. First,

---

[4] Interview with Robert Sanderson, in 'Samuel Becketts Schauspiel *That Time* in der Vertonung von Wolfgang Fortner' (unpublished MA thesis, 1984), 115 ff.

[5] In response to my enquiry at the Academy of Arts, Frau Ingeborg Lübold wrote: 'I know from Wolfgang Fortner that his *That Time* composition can be traced back to his "breakfast conversations" with Samuel Beckett.'

[6] James Knowlson, *Damned to Fame: The Life of Samuel Beckett* (London: Bloomsbury, 1996), 655. (See also n. 83, p. 822.)

[7] The corrections are entered with a very fine black felt-tip pen on pp. 28, 38, 50, and 52.

[8] The outline was apparently not altered further after its original conception. The very clear sketch on the front dust jacket corresponds to the present composition; on p. 26 is a scripted sketch, and on pp. 63 ff. the ending of the last phase is noted down once again.

each part is separated and, in each case, first Beckett's text and then Fortner's composition is examined. At the end of the individual analyses, there is an attempt to define the central concepts of 'time' and 'temporality' in Beckett's writing and to compare them with Fortner's interpretation.[9]

Fortner adopted the text of the piece completely and set it to music in the original language. He also adopts Beckett's dramaturgy in that he only leaves the 'Listener' visible (as a mute actor).[10] All the performers remain invisible to the audience behind screens. Fortner conceives the voices as Baritone (A), Mezzo-soprano (B), and Female speaker (C), and accords each of them an accompanying instrument (respectively, piano, guitar, and harpsichord). In order that the individual parts and instrumental sounds can be unlocalizable, and can mingle with each other as much as possible, Fortner adds live electronics.

There is a deviation from Beckett's version in that Beckett specifies three identical voices; Fortner, in contrast, makes use of different vocal divisions.

A further, decisive alteration of the text is discussed later: when Fortner asked Beckett for his permission to set the piece to music, he had mentioned at the same time his basic compositional idea: 'I had a definition, which is naturally a bit audacious: "Do you know what, I'm going to make a Super-Beckett out of you"' (Sanderson, '*That Time*', 116).

Voice 'A' and Piano

A attempts to explore the terms 'that time' and 'that last time' and imagines himself from the point of view of passers-by: 'the passers pausing to gape at the scandal huddled there in the sun where it had no warrant clutching the nightbag drooling away out loud [. . .] and the old green greatcoat your father left you' (3/A2, A4).[11] The man who 'went back [. . .] to look was the ruin still there where you hid as a child' (1/A1), was—as always—taken over by the ferry, in order to establish that [there was] 'not a tram left in the place only the old rails [. . .] all rust'

---

[9] A further interesting parallel between Beckett and Fortner can be drawn here. Evi Mertens compares Beckett's *That Time* with T. S. Eliot's *Murder in the Cathedral* in her study, 'Identität in der Grenzsituation des Alters: Eine Studie zum Motiv der Lebensretrospektive in ausgewählten Dramen von T. S. Eliot, Peter Ustinov und Samuel Beckett' (dissertation: Aachen, 1983). Both works are said to have as their central theme 'the basic function of a retrospective [. . .], the introduction of a biographical past dimension, without which an understanding of identity cannot develop' (p. 182). What is striking is that Fortner had already composed his *Aria* in 1951, based on precisely this work of Eliot.

[10] Stage directions, pp. 11 ff. (The page references in this analysis refer to the study-score of *That Time*, published by Schott-Musik International, Mainz.)

[11] The figures relate to the relevant phase and paragraph.

(1/A1, A2), 'all closed down and the colonnade crumbling away' (2/A2). And the man 'gave up and sat down on [. . .] someone's doorstep' in 'the pale morning sun' (2/A3). Whilst he waits [for it] 'to be time to get on the night ferry' (2/A3), he remembers his childhood, in which he [used to] 'slip off when no one was looking and hide there' (1/A3), where 'none ever came but the child on the stone among the giant nettles with the light coming in where the wall had crumbled away' (3/A1), 'with your picture-book' (1/A3) 'or talking to yourself [. . .] out loud imaginary conversations [. . .] now one voice now another till you were hoarse and they all sounded the same' (1/A4). So, just as the man stayed in the ruins as a child 'well on into the night some moods the moonlight' (3/A1), whilst 'they [were] all out on the roads looking for you' (1/A4), he asks himself, crouching on the doorstep, 'what for place might have been uninhabited for all you knew like that time on the stone the child on the stone' (2/A4), and he notices that he so sat on 'making it all up on the doorstep as you went along making yourself all up again' (3/A3). 'For the millionth time forgetting it all' (3/A3), another woman enters his memory—'she was with you then' (1/A3)—and his favourite refuge: 'Foley was it Foley's Folly bit of a tower' (1/A3).[12]

In order to reach the night ferry, the old man goes 'neither right nor left not a curse for the old scenes the old names not a thought in your head only get back on board' (3/A4). And he adds: 'and away to hell out of it and never come back' (3/A4). The questions—whether the remembered childhood was unhappy, whether the way back (both then as now) represented flight, and, if so, whether from life or from memory—remain unanswered. The central message is the recognition of a lifelong, solipsistic existence: 'no question of asking not another word to the living as long as you lived' (2/A2).

Just as the past-tense form is puzzling here—surely the visible head on the stage is not that of a dead person?—everything which A describes is relived memory: A begins with 'that time you went back that last time' (1/A1) and ends with the words 'or was that another time all that another time was there ever any other time but that time' (3/A4).

[12] The words 'Foley's Folly' have remained indecipherable in the context of the Beckett text. The German version, 'Tuohys Tuskulum', offers no further assistance with interpretation. An interesting connection appears with a specific film technique—the 'foley technique'. Nothing else could be established concerning this technique other than that it related to particular sound effects, and was named after Ed Foley, who worked in Universal Studios. (See Elisabeth Weis and John Belton, (eds.), *Film Sound, Theory and Practice* (New York: Columbia University Press, 1985), 407). It is widely known that Beckett was interested in the medium of film during these years.

[Eoin O'Brien identifies 'Foley's Folly' as Barrington's Tower, a ruined tower in the foothills of the Dublin mountains, only a mile from Cooldrinagh and a favourite retreat for Beckett when a boy (see Eoin O'Brien, *The Beckett Country* (Dublin: Black Cat Press, 1986), 27–30) Ed.].

Fig. 8.1 © Schott Musik International, Mainz, Germany

The piano part is the instrumental part which is employed thematically in the most stratified way.[13] Fortner introduces certainly the most
important motif at the beginning of the composition: two three-note
clusters which, in the course of the instrumental introduction, are introduced in semitone steps, one after the other, into the three-note harmony
(Figure 8.1).[14]

The second cluster proves to be a retrograde inversion of the first one,
in that the ending and beginning notes of the mirror axis form a tritone
interval.[15] In this respect, Fortner deepens Beckett's division of the
streams of memory into three parts—perhaps corresponding to the
temporal possibilities of awareness of 'yesterday', 'today', and 'tomorrow'—in that he not only adds three stringed instruments, but expounds
a three-note motif as the first motif which, transposed and reflected by
three whole-tones, then demonstrates synchronism in the harmony of
both the three-note clusters. In this and in transposed forms, it is the
central motif of this part: it denotes the change of the remembering
character from his early childhood to the final resignation. The three-
note chord A♭–A–B' represents a spatial variant of the cluster which
unites the time-related concepts 'long ago' (pp. 15 and 20 of score), 'to
look was [the ruin]' (p. 28), 'the end' (p. 50), 'till it was night and time
to go' (p. 83) and '[and never] come back' (p. 90).[16] In addition, Fortner
here uses tone-painting and mood-defining motifs which consolidate the
clustering further (Figure 8.2). Moreover, a septuplet and a related
triplet motif—suggesting animation via the rhythmical precision—con-
nect the memories which are directly linked with childhood.

[13] Fortner apparently paid great attention to this part from the outset. In the Suhrkamp
volume, it is this part which is supplied with most note-sketches. Numerous passages are
marked with thematic notations from a to e, although they rarely correspond to the composition in question. On pp. 36 and 37 of the text, Fortner noted two different twelve-note series,
both beginning with the notes F♯–A–F, which can in this instance be placed under the
instrumental and vocal parts (cf. the harpsichord part in *Adam*). However, it must be stressed
that, overall, more small-scale structures than twelve-note ones define the composition.

[14] Compare the end of the composition (p. 91). The harpsichord part repeats this piano
introduction, in that the harmony remains open.

[15] Fortner had originally noted the cluster in the same way. Presumably for the sake of better
legibility, the standardized spelling is present in the printed text.

[16] This motif concludes A's textual and musical part.

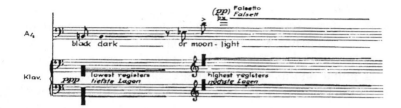

Fig. 8.2 © Schott Musik International, Mainz, Germany

Voice 'B' and Guitar

Shortly before the end of this stream of memory are the words: 'hard to believe you even you made up that bit till the time came in the end' (3/B3), 'that time in the end [. . .] when you tried and tried and couldn't any more' (3/B4). The question as to what he was trying to do so determinedly can be answered by the following explanation: 'no words left to keep it out so gave it up [. . .] and let it in' (3/B4). From these final lines, it becomes clear that the memory, which seems to be a love story, is an illusion, invented at that time: 'you kept making up to keep the void out' (1/B4).

In contrast to A—the old man's memories of his childhood, in which he constantly invented stories and recounted them to himself in allocated roles—here it is the image of a couple, 'on the stone together in the sun [. . .] at the edge of the little wood' (1/B1) or 'together on the towpath' or 'together in the sand' (2/B1), who never turn to each other, but remain in silence next to each other 'in a daze no sound not a word only every now and then to vow you loved each other' (1/B2).

The child who talked to himself has grown into a young man who, from time to time, murmurs a confession of love to an imaginary lover—up until the point when he sees through the self-deception. Here it says, as A too expresses: 'so gave it up gave up' and B remembers: 'and nothing the worse [. . .] and little or nothing the worse little or nothing' (3/B4).

In the instrumental introduction, the guitar[17] plays three different five- to six-part chords. The lowest two and/or three fourth-intervals of each chord (open strings) remain the same; each time, the highest note is symmetrically a minor third higher than the preceding one. If the notes

---

[17] Interestingly, on p. 13 of the Suhrkamp volume, Fortner noted 'harp'. According to this, the original conception pitted the piano and the harpsichord against the harp. In Fortner's other opera compositions, harp and guitar are closely associated with regard to their illuminating capacity of expression. The substitution seems to be dictated by technical considerations in production.

of the three chords are extended to form a scale, a full scale results, which comprises three minor seconds from the additive interval sequence minor-second/major-second (two minor-seconds/two major-seconds). The three chords and the scale contain the complete motivic material of the guitar and its accompanying vocal part.

Above all, chromatic sections from the scale are varied in a rhythmical manner (Figure 8.3). The continuation for hours on end in silence, and the circling of time without end, without result, are evident in the retrograde movement (see score, pp. 86 ff.) (Figure 8.4). 'That time' is

Fig. 8.3 © *Schott Musik International, Mainz, Germany*

Fig. 8.4 © *Schott Musik International, Mainz, Germany*

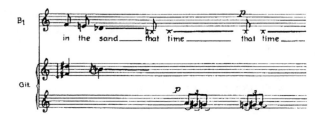

Fig. 8.5 © Schott Musik International, Mainz, Germany

accompanied by a melody which recurs time after time (Figure 8.5).[18]
These notes originate from the scale and represent, like all variants of
chromaticism, a linear treatment of the three-note cluster of the piano
part.

Voice 'C' and Harpsichord

On the basis of Voice C's comments, B's memories and A's questioning
search become clearer. Repetitions (and variants) of the C phrases such
as 'was your mother' (1/C2, cf. 1/A2), 'to hell out of there' (1/C1, 1/C2,
cf. 2/A3, 'to hell out of it' 4/A4), 'the old green greatcoat' (1/C2, 'the old
green holeproof coat' 2/C4, cf. 2/A4, 4/A4), and 'not a sound to be
heard' (1/C2, cf. 'no sound' 1/B1, 1/B2; 'no sound' 2/B4; 'not a sound'
4/B4) show C in a conciliatory function, even when the semantic context
is reversed. A remembers that he used the situation 'when no one was
looking' (1/A3) to escape from parental authority, whilst C entered the
public buildings such as 'the Portrait Gallery' (1/C1), 'the Public Library' and 'the Post Office' (2/C4), 'when no one was looking' (3/C1).
The central experience of B, his inability to go on in this way, deciphers
this distortion 'always having turning-points and never but the one the
first and last that time' (2/C1). C's other comments explain birth as the
single turning point: 'that time curled up worm in slime when they
lugged you out and wiped you off and straightened you up' (2/C1) —
with 'you started not knowing who you were' (2/C2). Life is the state of
being 'sunk in your lifelong mess' (1/C4) and C regards the dust as proof
of the actual passage of time, 'said come and gone [. . .] no one come and
gone in no time' (3/C4).

The murmuring whispering, through which B expresses his love for
his imagined partner and which reminds A of all the conversations with
himself of his childhood, here takes on an additional dimension: 'mut-
tering to yourself who else' (1/C4).

[18] See score, p. 42. The retrograde movement is again typical here. Cf. pp. 75, 82, and 84.

Fig. 8.6 © Schott Musik International, Mainz, Germany

For C, the solipsistic self-experience is linked to permanent suffering, yet represents at the same time the sole possible means of existence.

The harpsichord part which accompanies C[19] is based on a twelve-note series (Figure 8.6). The second half of the series is related to the first as a retrograde inversion; within a six-note sequence, the intervals of minor third-fifths are repeated in a retrograde movement and the boundary intervals of the sixth-seventh notes and the first-twelfth notes also form fifths. This completely symmetrical series structure corresponds to the Beckettian concept of time in the retrograde synchronism.

Fortner develops various motif structures, which exhibit similarities with the other instrumental parts, but which stem from the twelve-note series. The often extensive sequence of different variants is surprising. A larger, related note-example may clarify this (cf. score, p. 16) (Figure 8.7).

The first half of the series is expounded in a retrograde variant; in the numerical sequence, an anticipation of the note after next always appears before the following one. 'Always win[ter]' represents a retrograde flow of the ten-note motif, before a somewhat irregular repetition of the outer-notes accompanies the repetition of the word 'always'. The sustained third interval leads up into the inversion of the motif which begins with a suspended note. The note repetition C♯–C″ already represents, in terms of rhythm and interval, a further variant of the repetition E♭–B″, just as the interval A–E′ to B–D′ does. 'Street out' is set to music in a similar way to 'rain': after the inversion, the numerical sequence is taken up again just as at the beginning. 'Cold' and 'rain' represent a concentration of the previous intervals; here, both the intervals of the adjacent and opposing notes in the motif are integrated—a further inversion variant. Both the five-part chords, which support the words 'seat' and 'slab', are, in terms of intervals, inverted variants of the series interval. 'To hell out'—one of the less frequently recurring passages of

---

[19] Strangely, in the Suhrkamp volume, there are no musical notes relating to Voice C. Presumably, Voice C and the harpsichord were conceived chronologically after the other two parts; the structural rigidity and the numerous compositional connections with the other parts support this. The twelve-note structure in question does not correspond to the two series depicted on pp. 36 and 37 of the Suhrkamp volume.

Fig. 8.7 © *Schott Musik International, Mainz, Germany*

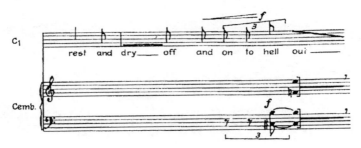

Fig. 8.8 © Schott Musik International, Mainz, Germany

text and music[20]—can be regarded as a circular movement within the notes of the motif (Figure 8.8). The compositional material of the first section of the harpsichord part proves to belong to the motif, without ever previously having been expounded in its original form.

Within the following sections, numerous motivic variants are developed, through which—presumably owing to their close relationship—a coordination can be established which is less linked to words.[21]

The use of motifs constructed in other ways is even more striking. A chromatic melos, for example, always indicates a semantic connection: nearly all the textual passages in which time is mentioned explicitly, or indicated implicitly, are set to music chromatically.[22] This exhibits itself in the first instance as simple descending or ascending lines,[23] melodically based chromatic rhythmical patterns,[24] or (because of the simultaneous retrograde inversion), as the 'clothing' of the chromaticism which is reminiscent of the central motif.[25] To a certain extent, the external manifestations of being bound to a particular moment in time, like the Christmas bustle, the clinking of the pens on their chains during the filling out of forms at the Post Office, are here linked with the feeling described by the speaker (which seems to be equally bound to a particu-

---

[20] See p. 21 '[to] hell out', p. 48 '[till they] put you out in the [rain] at closing-time', p. 69 '[pushed] open the door', p. 73 '[fear] of ejection'. The same motif accompanies the phrase 'to hell out', which appears twice in the piano part; see pp. 57 and 89.

[21] In the same way, for example, 'was your mother' (p. 20), is not emphasized by means of another motif, but is set to music like 'raining' or 'someone famous in his time' (p. 27) is set in parallel fashion to 'always win[ter]'.

[22] 'That time' and '[someone famous in his] time' (see pp. 16, 27, and 83), are linked to the 'Portrait Gallery', and belong thematically to the central motif.

[23] See 'drawing near then dying away' (p. 24), 'bustle Christmas bustle in off the street' (pp. 67 ff.), '[till it] dawned' (p. 77). The most chromatically dense variant—'[with all] the forms and the pens on their chains' (pp. 69 ff.)—also belongs here.

[24] See '[somewhere] when no one would be looking in off [the street]' (pp. 58 ff.), and 'to say nothing of the loathsome appearance' (p. 75).

[25] See 'prince' (p. 28), '[with] age' (p. 29).

Fig. 8.9 © *Schott Musik International, Mainz, Germany*

lar moment in time) of being stared at by others because of his unsightly appearance.

The chromaticism which turns inwards,[26] and the three-note cluster which is familiar from the piano part, which accompany all C's inner experiences of time, also belong here.[27]

A melodic-rhythmical variant of this cluster traces the remembered career of C, which is related to the text (Figure 8.9).[28] C views his standpoint at the end of his life as unchanged from that at the beginning—'curled up worm in slime'. The melody is no longer taken up in the third phase in the same rhythmical way; rather, the static variant of the three-note chord expresses the futility of the lifelong searching.[29]

The chord anticipates the end of the C-phase as a variant of the cluster which, at the same time, marks the end of the composition. 'Gone in no time' corresponds (with the exception of the harmony cluster D–D#–E) to the exposition of the piano part. Fortner links the end of his composition with the beginning, and thus underscores Beckett's attempt to explore time and existence within the passage of time, in that, according to B, the recess of the sound-cluster suggests the absence of a result or a solution.

[26] See 'age and dirt' (p. 27), 'with dirt and antiquity' (p. 47), but also the 'turning' of the pages of old books (p. 90). The composition of *Adam* and 'who it was saying' (pp. 45 ff,) belong equally in this context. In the musical example there is a printing error: instead of E♭, it should read E, as in the parallel passages.

[27] See '[that] time' (p. 40), '[was that the] time [or was that another] time' (p. 41), '[was that the] time or [was that another] time' (p. 46: B instead of A#), '[that was another] another [place]' (p. 63), '[was that the] time' (p. 78), 'another place' (pp. 78 ff.), '[in no] time [gone in] no time' (p. 91). Compare the end of the harpsichord part with the piano introduction from pp. 12 ff: the harmony D–D#–E is left open. Expansions of the cluster up to the ten-note series link the setting to music of 'time' with the representation of 'age', which is marked by a chromatic melody. See '[like] time could [go]' (p. 66), 'another time' (p. 63), '[and] all as you were you were not as they' (p. 77), 'another time' (pp. 78 ff.), '[something to do] with dust something the dust [said]' (p. 85), 'this dust whole [place suddenly full of] dust when you opened your eyes from [floor to ceiling nothing only] dust and not a [sound]' (pp. 90 ff.).

[28] See '[you could never] be the same' (p. 35).

[29] See 'not a sound' (p. 90), and '[not a] sound' (p. 91).

The central significance of the three-note cluster must be emphasized
in this context once again. In the analyses of the individual parts, the
different motivic variants were presented, which here should be viewed
in their entirety: the cluster supporting 'that time', as well as the variants
mentioned, are structurally reflective forms, which represent musically
the 'coincidence of the non-coincidental' in the often only brief moment
of the cluster sound. This only seems possible in the form of human
memory; our imagination, not least formed by the logic of language,
may not be able to manage this easily. Beckett's paraphrasing defini-
tions, such as 'or was that another time all that another time was there
ever any other time but that time' (pp. 89 ff.), or 'year after year as if it
couldn't end the old year never end like time could go no further that
time' (pp. 66 ff.), remain as auxiliary constructions. Fortner can manage
without these auxiliary constructions, since his medium can show that
which is not linguistically tangible. By using motivic associations, he can
create references directly via space and time. Fortner's 'audacious description' of the 'Super-Beckett' should be viewed in the context of this
background, since although the individual phases in Beckett's version
are always heard one after the other, Fortner has placed them over each
other in places (Figure 8.10).

Fortner does basically retain Beckett's sequence of parts. In the first
two phases—which he separates from the last one by an instrumental
entr'acte, after the first run-through of the parts, in each case—two parts
overlap, so that all three parts can be heard together briefly in a concentrated form in the final, fourth section. In this way, Fortner gains two
new dimensions over Beckett's text: the structural inversion of the third
phase—beginning with the concentrated coincidence of the parts, then

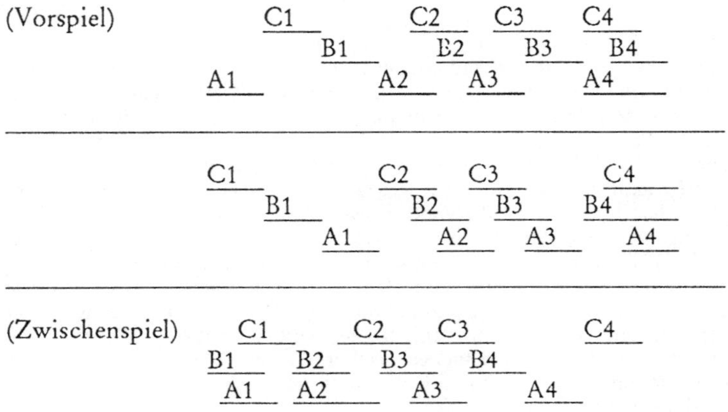

Fig. 8.10 © Schott Musik International, Mainz, Germany

overlapping as two, and finally a successive run-through of the parts—
accentuates yet again what is intended as content, and the overlapping
of the parts in phases, as well as the additional alienation achieved
through the live electronics, shows, more clearly than a mere successive
run-through could, the stratified form and the speed of the human
memory.

POSTLUDE

Ulrich Pothast's study, *Die eigentlich metaphysische Tätigkeit: Über
Schopenhauers Ästhetik und ihre Anwendung durch Samuel Beckett*,[30]
takes as its basis the observation that Beckett 'turned Schopenhauer's
aesthetic into a very personal instrument, which allowed him to interpret Proust's work, as well as to define his notion of his own vocation as
a writer very early on and very decisively' (p. 27).

In the light of the claim of Deirdre Bair, Beckett's first biographer,
concerning 'the strong biographical underpinning of so much of his
writing',[31] *That Time* should be examined as writing in the context of
Pothast's analyses.

According to Pothast, Beckett assumes the forms of cognition of
subjectivity from Schopenhauer, redefined:

Moreover, space, time and causality represent the order of the world of experience [. . .]; but time has gone beyond the priority which Schopenhauer accorded
it, out into this world to become an all-conquering, corrupting structure which
colours everything, in relation to which individuals do not act as unconscious
users, but literally as victims and prisoners. The reality of the temporal is [. . .]
not, as Schopenhauer suggests, confined to the present. Rather, there is a reality
of the future (pale and monochrome) and one of the past (multi-coloured and
exciting), and the latter is even 'stored' for the duration of our life and can be
enhanced. Through this hypothesis, Beckett supplies his aesthetic model with a
reservoir of objects of artistic work, which Schopenhauer, because he only
allows everything which is real to exist in the present, could have seen and
conceived less well. (Pothast, *Die eigentlich metaphysische Tätigkeit*, 183 ff.)

Beckett's 'Listener' in *That Time* can be understood as being like many
heroes in Beckett's drama and novels: with the exception of the resting
head, the 'Listener' remains disembodied; he says nothing himself, but
instead listens to three different voices irresolutely and without control.
In this state of 'unconscious memory', different experiences from various eras of his life appear to him. The mixture of these memories which
well up represents the sole source of information to the audience concerning a person about whom it is said in one of the memories: 'could

[30] Frankfurt am Main: Suhrkamp, 1982.
[31] Deirdre Bair, *Samuel Beckett: A Biography* (London: Vintage, 1990), Introduction, p. x.

you ever say I to yourself in your life' (2/C1). B's memories signify the development up to the renouncement of the 'habit', the experience of which is depicted as 'nothing the worse' (3/B4). The countless, remembered attempts to identify temporality, to make it fixed—'when was that'; 'that time'; 'or was that another time'; 'was there ever any other time'—culminate in the moment of the irresolute (involuntary) listening. Artistically transformed, the past, remembered experiences, which lie beyond time, space, and causality, coincide with the momentary condition of listening. In this sense, in *That Time*, Beckett presents the situation of an 'adequate union'; *That Time* is the artistic expression of Beckett's 'metaphysical activity'.

Numerous comments can be extracted from Deirdre Bair's biography which hint at Beckett's identification with the 'Listener'. A few examples are worth mentioning.

For many years, Beckett wore an 'old battered green raincoat [which] had a pocket permanently distended by the bottle of stout he carried in it' (Bair, *Samuel Beckett*, 132). Beckett also visited museums and libraries with great regularity—particularly when he was not inspired by his own work. Bair writes about his activities at Easter 1933 by way of example: 'Beckett began to use the Trinity library, and soon became a familiar figure as he sat hunched over a book, his shabby raincoat draped on the back of his chair' (ibid. 171). During subsequent visits to Dublin, 'he spent long solitary afternoons in the National Gallery' (ibid. 200) and during his time in London '[owing to financial reasons] he could only go to art galleries and museums on free afternoons or when the rate was reduced' (ibid. 203).

When the phrase 'to hell out of it all and never come back' (3/A4) appears at the end of A's memory, this could represent an analogy of Beckett's final departure from Ireland.

These examples only offer one possible means of interpreting *That Time* in an autobiographical way.

Fortner set both the multi-dimensionality of the streams of memory to music and the biographical dimension as well. The uniqueness of a self-quotation in Fortner's opera work can serve as proof of this (Figure 8.11). Fortner quotes the harpsichord introduction of Belisa's first love canzona[32] from the García Lorca drama *The Love of Don Perlimplín and Belisa in the Garden*. The quotation first appears at the beginning of

[32] See score to *The Love of Don Perlimplín and Belisa in the Garden*, p. 21. The three quotations—pp. 40, 47 ff., and 90—relate exclusively to the first three bars of the harpsichord introduction. The quotation on p. 40 of the score of *That Time* corresponds to the first three bars of the *Perlimplín* score, p. 47 to the inversion of the three bars, plus new variants on p. 48. Page 90 corresponds to the last two bars of the harpsichord introduction. Owing to reasons of space, the significance within Fortner's œuvre of the canzona and of the opera (which was conceived fifteen years previously), cannot be explained adequately here. For Fortner, *Perlimplín* represented the most important figure of identification.

Fig. 8.11 *(a)* *From* In seinem Garten liebt Don Perlimplín Belisa. © *Schott Musik International, Mainz, Germany*

Fig. 8.11 *(b)* *From* That Time. © *Schott Musik International, Mainz, Germany*

the second phase with the word 'you' and thus also draws in the immediately preceding and following context thematically: 'could you ever say I to yourself in your life turning-point that was a great word with you before they dried up altogether always having turning-points and never but the one' (2/C1).

Here, and in both of the other quoted passages, Fortner refers to the possibility of a 'turning-point' which is linked to the opposite of 'you' and also to Perlimplín, who expected to be married to Belisa. The confrontation with the self and the insight into the impossibility of change occurred on the wedding night. Here, in *That Time*, Fortner sees in the confrontation with the depiction a similar kind of potential climax. Shortly before the end, both of Perlimplín and of the 'Listener', is the longing for the impossibility of the individual will.

This self-quotation may be understood subtly and uniquely in its confessional character, but it also represents, beyond this, the demarcation of Fortner's setting to music of Beckett's literary version: indeed, Fortner achieves an increase in the possibility of remembering unconsciously with the musical methods mentioned above. Yet, on the other hand, the semantic unities which emerge most clearly in the canzona quotation hinder the actual approach to 'true reality'. Through the semantic scoring of several passages, which assume disproportionate importance within the whole, Fortner's interpretation represents—in Schopenhauerian terms—consciously directed memory.

9

'Something is Taking its Course':
Dramatic Exactitude and the Paradigm of Serialism in Samuel Beckett

HARRY WHITE

I

There are moments in *Waiting for Godot* that proclaim with painful vividness the infirmity of our moral condition: the incapacity of speech or gesture to countenance the abyss and horror of the times. But again, I wonder whether we are dealing with drama in any genuine sense. Beckett is writing 'antidrama'; he is showing, with a kind of queer Irish logic, that one can bar from the stage all forms of mobility and natural communication between characters and yet produce a play. But the result is, I think, crippled and monotonous. At best, we get a metaphysical *guignol*, a puppet show made momentarily fascinating or monstrous by the fact that the puppets insist on behaving as if they were alive.[1]

A remarkable feature of *Waiting for Godot* is that it constitutes not an end, but a beginning. A body of work, including Beckett's own dramatic writings, is derived from it. Notwithstanding George Steiner's eloquent (if dismissive) characterization of *Godot* as a dessicated epilogue to tragic drama, the modal integrity of Beckett's voice has long been acknowledged as a vital presence in post-war European theatre. His work is at once a persuasion towards the absolute condition of silence and a wager on the intelligibility of dramatic discourse nevertheless. The strategic inventories of that discourse, in which language attains to a fundamental critique of meaning, ironize and undermine the accord between rhetoric and experience which signifies intelligence in the classical drama. Beckett's disengagement from that accord, no more

---

[1] George Steiner, *The Death of Tragedy* (London: Faber, 1974). See also the same author's introduction to *George Steiner: A Reader* (Harmondsworth: Penguin, 1984): 'The undoubted genius of Beckett, the talents of Pinter, still strike me as essentially formal. In their plays, we find an internalized epilogue to an eroded tragic vision. The brilliance and the grief lie in the language' (p. 10). Steiner's identification of an essentially formal and linguistic brilliance modifies his earlier dismissal of Beckett's position.

famously apostrophized than in the satirical indictments of *Endgame* ('I'm warming up for my last soliloquy'[2]) is not an abrupt repudiation. Although the Beckett landscape is perhaps uniquely severe and unremitting, there is a striking contradiction between its condition of nuclear wilderness and the resolute precision by which this is rendered and imagined.

This precision can seem to engender cruelty. Throughout Beckett's work, the assault on human dignity is so vigorous that a perpetual misery settles like fine dust on the human condition. It is misery relieved by humour but rarely by compassion. Beckett's vision transcends pity and terror to such an extent that any form of redemption is removed from the conspectus of emotion and feeling which his characters so variously envisage. Never to have been born is always best: the alternative condition, life itself, is a collage of humiliation, anguish, and wearisome despair. When happiness is glimpsed, it is only as part of a cycle which inexorably turns to further disappointment or stasis. When Nell observes in *Endgame* that 'nothing is funnier than unhappiness' (*Endgame*, 20), she intonates the distortions of Beckett's humour which so relentlessly attenuate the prospect of humane recollection. Nell would prefer to remember happiness as an idyllic afternoon on Lake Como, but Nagg obliterates this decency with a donnish yarn.

The blind and maimed quartet in *Endgame* suffers coherently. It is not the chess paradigm alone which bestows this intelligibility, but the narrative and chronological strategies by which this strange family history is disclosed. The play romances the luxury of the past by comparison with the privations of the present. As with *Godot* before it, *Endgame* concedes the past. This is true not only of its allusions to Shakespeare, and the concept of play which informs the text, but more particularly of that slow disintegration whose final phase is enacted in the present tense. The anterior existence of lives which have come to inhabit the barren terrain of *Endgame* is crucial to Beckett's purpose precisely because the representation of those lives depends on theatrical conventions which secure the plausibility of the action itself.[3]

These conventions are decisively subverted in the plays which follow *Endgame*. Even in *Krapp's Last Tape*, where the past itself determines the obsessive movement towards paralysis, Beckett dispenses with that temporal continuity which underpins his earlier work. Krapp attempts to move on, to make a fresh start with a new tape, but he ends by

[2] Samuel Beckett, *Endgame* (London: Faber, 1964), 49.
[3] Although *Endgame* constantly subverts these conventions—('This is what we call making an exit' (p. 51))—the play notably advances in naturalistic sequences which sustain the illusion of realist drama.

reverting to 'box three, spool five'. The motionless silence which ensues is a final abrogation of narrative design. The prospect of a stable present disappears. A new kind of dramatic discourse takes its place.

Deirdre Bair has observed of *Endgame* that it 'marks the beginning of [Beckett's] preoccupation with dramatic exactitude, his need to specify every nuance and gesture that may take place on his stage'.[4] It is this preoccupation which gives rise to the development of a distinctive theatre in which Beckett's reification of language entails a disengagement from the pre-eminence of verbal discourse. In its stead, a radically hermetic amalgamation of diverse elements—linguistic, gestural, visual, musical—governs the structural integrity of Beckett's controlling presence as a dramatist. It may be valid to judge this presence as 'antidrama' against that tradition which Beckett eclipses: this is Steiner's position, as we have seen, in *The Death of Tragedy*. But there would seem to be grounds for a different reading. Such a reading depends on Beckett's position as a definitive exemplar of modernism.

'Modernism' is worth a moment's scruple. The sheer tenacity of Beckett's influence in the theatre as high priest of the absurd (and of 'alienation' in particular) ironically obscures the systematic scrutiny of that accord between language and experience which distinguishes his dramatic imagination. The heterogeneity of that imagination is taken to represent its essence: 'no symbols where none intended'.[5] Beckett's reinvention of theatrical discourse is so drastic that he appears as the exponent *ex nihilo* of a 'disconsolate art of incompetence'.[6] On one vital level, this is self-evidently the case. It is difficult, if not impossible, to find a directly intelligible precedent for *Godot*, just as (for example) it is impossible to contemplate *The Birthday Party* without the precedent of that play.[7] But in terms of sheer number and imaginative exploration, few of Beckett's plays enjoy this kind of afterlife. The early masterpieces do not negate the fact that Beckett's integrity of voice gains from a wider comparison than that which the theatre affords. Rather, it is music, and specifically the aesthetic and techniques of serialism, which offers a sovereign precedent for the extreme condition of Beckett's dramatic vocabulary.

This reading cannot be advanced in terms of empirical proof. Although references to music are legion in Beckett's writing (dramatic and

---

[4] Deirdre Bair, *Samuel Beckett: A Biography* (London: Vintage, 1990), 491.
[5] The concluding phrase of Beckett's *Watt*.
[6] See Seamus Deane's 'Joyce and Beckett', in his *Celtic Revivals: Essays in Modern Irish Literature 1880–1980* (London: Faber, 1985), 124.
[7] I exclude the precedent of individual writers (such as Kafka) whose influence is variously manifest in Beckett's work. It is the unprecedented nature of *Waiting for Godot* as a play, together with its subsequent impact on the theatre, which is in question here.

otherwise), they are not especially significant for the purposes of evincing his kinship with the strategies of total serialism.[8] Of far greater relevance is the deadpan distribution of sucking-stones in *Molloy*: the comic precisions and anxieties of that famous episode can scarcely be confined to a single interpretation, but its poker-faced parody of serial technique stands out with pedantic gusto from the surrounding text. The painstaking description of different methods by which sixteen stones are or might be sucked in strict succession is so patently suggestive of serial technique that Beckett's unawareness of the latter is hardly tenable. My concern is not to prove such awareness, but rather to establish the compelling affinity between Beckett's comic preoccupation with the integrity of sequential order (he uses the word 'series'), and the same preoccupation in musical serialism. The chess game in *Murphy* may provide a precedent for this episode from within Beckett's own work, but it is not one which enjoys the close parallels of serial organization discussed here.

It is not the *parody* of serialism, however, which confirms the presence of a similar technique in Beckett's post-war drama. No e*xact* parallel can be maintained between the principles of total serialism and similar procedures in the plays which follow *Endgame*. Moreover, I am particularly anxious to disavow the suggestion that Beckett consciously adopts a musical structure (serialism) in the construction of his later plays. It is the affinity, and (to an extent) the influence of such a structure in Beckett's work which bears scrutiny. Nevertheless, the argument to be examined here proposes that serial technique offers an instructive paradigm for those procedures by which Beckett attempts to resolve that crisis of meaning which he discerns in language and which he himself deliberately foments. Celia's musings in the third chapter of *Murphy* address that crisis in notably apposite terms: 'She felt, as she felt so often with Murphy, spattered with words that went dead as soon as they sounded; each word obliterated, before it had time to make sense, by the word that came next; so that in the end she did not know what had been said. It was like difficult music heard for the first time.'[9]

That last sentence is not an unreasonable description of Beckett's art, especially in the plays which follow *Endgame*. But the comparison with music can be taken a good deal further: it obtains with particular force with regard to structural organization, the repudiation of realism, and the elemental condition of language in Beckett, all of which powerfully summon the analogue of serial composition.

[8] See Heath Lees, '*Watt*: Music, Tuning, and Tonality', in S. E. Gontarski (ed.), *The Beckett Studies Reader* (Gainesville, Fla: University Press of Florida, 1993), 167–85, for a discussion of the presence of music in Beckett's writing.

[9] Samuel Beckett, *Murphy* (London: Pan, 1978), 27.

It is clearly not my purpose here to suggest a literal mapping of serial technique in the texts of Beckett's plays, but I do mean to suggest that the origins, development, and application of that technique provide a durable model of (musical) thought by which these plays attain to formal coherence and relativity. An underlying condition of this argument is that fundamental consensus which exists between tonality in music and realism in literature in so far as one is related to the other. This consensus is so well established by literary history as to be almost unremarkable, save for the compelling modernist parallels by which it is reinforced in retrospect. Certain of these parallels are very easy to instance.

The appearance of *Ulysses* in 1922 and of Schoenberg's first serial compositions (including the Piano Pieces, op. 23 and the Piano Suite, op. 25) in the following year, mark crucial developments in modernist fiction and music respectively. Joyce's stream of consciousness and Schoenberg's serialism are not only seminal techniques, they are plainly decisive resolutions of a more general crisis of expression in art. That these techniques profoundly determined the outgrowth of a radical aesthetic in literature and music is of course a commonplace, but the precise contours of this influence are less readily understood. The relationship between Joyce and Beckett, for example, can be glossed in terms of this influence in ways which are notably suggestive of the relationship between Schoenberg and Anton von Webern. The bond of discipleship applies in either case, and more precisely the bond of technique. The more nearly these comparisons are made, the more tenable they become: it is not simply that Joyce inheres in Beckett and that Schoenberg inheres in Webern, but that the degree of dependent difference between them is in either case so unmistakably similar.

It is difficult to characterize that difference here, but to do so is vital to the essential argument of this chapter. Vivid contrast is the easiest means of intelligible access in this case, as in the contrast between Joyce's verbally heroic largesse and Beckett's concentrated parsimony of discourse on one side, and the messianic compulsion of Schoenberg's reanimation of large-scale musical forms (opera, concerto, cantata) by comparison with Webern's scrupulous reductionism on the other. On both sides, reciprocity defines the relationship of master-builder (Joyce, Schoenberg) and the 'master of undermining' (Webern, Beckett).[10] Beckett's temptation to silence is perhaps the most conspicuous signature of his art. His music is so intensely drawn to the template of mathematics that it begets the sterile configurations of total

---

[10] George Steiner uses the latter phrase of Beckett in his preface to the second edition of *Language and Silence* (London: Faber, 1985), 13.

serialism. The *musica arcana* of Boulez, Stockhausen, and Babbit in the
1950s and early 1960s proclaims this 'flight from the neighbourhood of
language'.[11]

Beckett's contribution to this retreat from the word can be construed
on two levels. One of these is well argued and I need not establish it at
length here: the crisis in humane literacy which, more than any other
factor, characterizes modernism finds its most compelling expression in
drama through the agency of Beckett's own writing. The plays mediate
that crisis by degrees: the comparatively stable narratives of *Godot*
(which admit nevertheless a wholly original tonality and structural
design into the theatre), the transitional structures of *Endgame* and
Krapp's Last Tape, in which certain paradigms (chess, recorded
memory) establish and then dismantle the conventions of the present
tense, and the formally controlled experiments of the plays which follow
(beginning with *Act without Words I*), gradually but systematically
disclose its fateful consequences. The unnerving exactitude with which
Beckett inspects the disintegration of meaning is itself a symptom of the
decline which his work unremittingly surveys.

The second level is arguably more difficult to apprehend. George
Steiner provides a vital clue to its perception:

Where poetry seeks to dissociate itself from the exactions of clear meaning and
from the common usages of syntax, it will tend towards an ideal of musical
form. This tendency plays a fascinating role in modern literature. [. . .] More
recently, the submission of literary forms to musical examples and ideals has
been carried even further. In Romain Rolland and Thomas Mann, we find the
belief that the musician is the artist in essence (he is *more* an artist than, say, the
painter or writer). This is because only music can achieve that total fusion of
form and content, of means and meaning, which all art strives for. Two of the
foremost poetic designs of our time, T. S. Eliot's *Four Quartets* and Hermann
Broch's *Death of Virgil*, embody an idea that can be traced back to Mallarmé
and *L'Après-midi d'un faune*: they attempt to suggest in language corresponding organizations of musical form.[12]

These aspirations are also embodied and realized in Beckett. In particular, the 'total fusion of form and content, of means and meaning' is one
which is constantly espoused in the later plays. The immediate consequence of this espousal is that language behaves as something other than
itself. The recomposition of sentence structure by which 'the same old

---

[11] See George Steiner, 'The Retreat from the Word' (1961), reprinted in *Language and
Silence* (London: Faber, 1985), 30–54, esp. pp. 42–3.
[12] See 'The Retreat from the Word' (1961), reprinted in George Steiner, *Language and
Silence* (London: Faber, 1985), 30–54 (pp. 47, 48). It is notable that Beckett is conspicuous by
his absence from Steiner's essay, despite its analysis of linguistic decline and the influence of
mathematical and musical analogues in post-war European literature.

moans and groans from the cradle to the grave'[13] are made not merely bearable but formally tenable is more than a question of radical adjustment. The status of language is downgraded from that of sole intelligencer to compositional technique. Every sentence in the later Beckett is conditional, strategic and contingent, and the principal contingency is form. In play after short play, a constituent series of shards and fragments is scrupulously deployed, scrutinized, varied, and discarded, so that a design briefly comes into being and then disappears. To contemplate these texts as random impulses, or as lyric explorations of voice, is to eclipse that essentially musical conception of meaning which underwrites them. One may as well regard Webern as a tonal composer as ignore the strategic formality of Beckett's demeanour. His later work, in short, invests language with the function of music. But not only language: posture, lighting, appearance, movement, time, space, and sound are so completely structured that music itself unobtrusively consorts with them in the realization of the text. No less than in Eliot or Broch, music in Beckett functions not primarily as a literal presence, but as a structural precedent. The plays themselves show this to be the case.

II

> Serialism: compositional technique in which the twelve notes of the
> chromatic scale are arranged in a fixed order, the 'series', which can
> be used to generate melodies and harmonies, and which normally
> remains binding for a whole work.[14]

By now, I hope that it is clear that my application of a serial paradigm to Beckett's work rests on a version of literary history which situates his technique in the aftermath of a notably heroic modernism. Although George Steiner reads Joyce's fiction as 'an exuberant counterattack [. . .]' against the diminution of language' ('Retreat from the Word', 50), I am more persuaded by that diminution as (in part) an aesthetic reaction *to* Joyce. If Joyce's work 'more than any since Milton, recalls to the English ear the wide magnificence of its legacy' (ibid. 51), Beckett's abstemious precisions appear to countermand that prodigality of linguistic resurgence which suffuses the night-world of *Finnegans Wake* in particular. Beckett's recrudescence of language is chronologically and aesthetically in sequence to Joyce's plurality of discourse. In the same way, the avatars

---

[13] Samuel Beckett, *Rough for Theatre I*, in *Collected Shorter Plays* (London: Faber, 1984), 70.
[14] Paul Griffiths, 'Serialism', in Denis Arnold (ed.), *The New Oxford Companion to Music* (Oxford: Oxford University Press, 1983), ii, 1668.

of total serialism, beginning with Webern, draw sharply back from the passionate espousal of Schoenberg, whose music evinces a fundamental (if superficially paradoxical) continuity with the tonal past. Although Schoenberg began by proclaiming that he had 'broken the bonds of a bygone aesthetic', and although Alban Berg could speak of having 'shattered the holy commandments of tonality', their music eschews the cerebral introspection and severe withdrawal implied and realized by Webern's encounter with serial technique.[15] I see no merit, however, in advancing an *exact* parallel between Webern and Beckett: no reasonable account of cultural history supports it. What I do perceive is an essentially formalist demeanour by which music and language respectively are stringently recomposed. In Webern, this demeanour is self-evidently achieved through the agency of serialism. In Beckett, the paradigm of serialist technique, and principally the disclosure and organization of a strictly limited series of linguistic and non-linguistic elements, offers a formal model by which his later plays may be understood.

The comparative brevity of the plays which follow *Endgame* (notwithstanding the singular exception of *Happy Days*) attests to Beckett's disavowal of conventional structural norms in his later work. Each play examines the possibility of structure afresh, and each declares a formal disposition of materials with increasing rigour. It is this disposition which validates the concept of serial technique as an instructive paradigm.

Act without Words I conveys the serial clarity of this development in Beckett's later work for the stage. Although few of the plays dispense with language completely, this piece countenances a theatre deprived of the sovereignty of language in its very title. To classify it as a mime is beside the point: the sequence of visual, gestural, and musical elements which comprise it constitutes in effect a metalanguage, whose terms are strictly limited: a man is flung upon the stage in dazzling light, and everything that happens, everything that is seen and heard, is derived from this opening move. When the man attempts to quit the stage, to break out, as it were, from the series, he is flung back on. All he can do is to react to each preordained event and reflect accordingly. Deprived of actual language, the text of *Act without Words I* becomes a sequence of events in which form and content are synonymous. The symbolic address of this sequence is distinct from its structure (the intelligibility of objects which appear and disappear is a trope in Beckett's work which is not unique: it is recovered, for example, in Harold Pinter's *The Dumb Waiter*): what I am concerned to identify here is the significance of the

---

[15] For a useful account of Schoenberg, Berg, Webern, and the differences between them (as in their respective applications of serial technique), see Oliver Neighbour, Paul Griffiths, and George Perle, *The New Grove Second Viennese School* (London: Macmillan, 1983).

pattern itself. In *Act without Words I*, this pattern depends on the recurring whistle, the descent of objects (the tree, the scissors, the carafe, the cubes, the rope) and their systematic withdrawal. One speaks guardedly of a sequence and its retrograde, but the lucid progression of Beckett's text encourages such a reading. Without words, the strategic intelligence of this pattern is all the clearer, even if its referential meaning is deferred. Beckett does not introduce elements at random into the series: the withdrawal of objects and the man's failure to respond to the whistle confirm both the rules of play and (retrospectively) the sequence of which it is made.[16]

When actual language is reintroduced into Beckett's drama, the exactitudes of this series are rarely attenuated. *Cascando*, for example, a 'radio piece for music and voice', enlists a similar pattern of serial control, in which the paradigm disclosed in *Act without Words I* obtains, notwithstanding the different elements of the series itself. In *Cascando*, those elements are verbal and musical, and each is of the same gravity as the other.[17] The equivalence which Beckett draws between the musical and verbal utterances in *Cascando* stems from a prevailing concept of absolute control which once again neighbours total serialism. The degree of formal exactitude countenanced by Beckett here strikingly extends to his notion of dramatic personae: 'Opener', 'Voice', and 'Music'. When this kind of abstraction supplants the convention of dramatic character, the distance between Beckett's earlier work and the later plays is all the more apparent. The illusion of individual personality sustained by Vladimir and Estragon, by Hamm and Clov, and even by Krapp himself, disappears. In its place, Beckett deploys those fragmentary cyphers of verbal, musical, and gestural intelligence which regulate the structure of his later plays. Although *Cascando* is not hermetic in the context of Beckett's writing as a whole—(the declarations, 'I'm afraid to open. | But I must open. | So I open'[18] are themselves explicitly paradigmatic of the famous conclusion to *The Unnamable*[19])—its structural manipulation of voice and music affirms a sequential design unique to the requirements of this play. It is not the nature of (Marcel Mihalovici's) music which is pre-eminent in *Cascando*, but its formal designation in the text. Its representation as a series of ellipses confirms this precedence. The reproduction of the notes on the page would distract from the functional and structural condition

---

[16] It is the withdrawal of objects in this play which confirms the limited condition of the series.

[17] This equivalence is also established in *Words and Music*, in which 'Music', 'Words', and 'Croak' function as characters.

[18] See Samuel Beckett, *Cascando*, in *Collected Shorter Plays*, 142.

[19] i.e. 'you must go on, I can't go on, I'll go on' (to say nothing of Clov's similar formula in *Endgame*).

of the music as an element in the threefold series (the Opener's direc-
tives, the verbal and musical equivalences) upon which *Cascando* is
constructed. When the story of Woburn which is filtered through this
series finally lapses into silence, the permutations of the sequence (for
Beckett's purposes, at any rate) are exhausted. Here, too, it is salutary to
distinguish between possible interpretations of *Cascando* and its systematic reliance on sequential order. The play may or may not disclose a
poetic of verbal disintegration—(the incapacity to stabilize the Woburn
narrative suggests that it does)—but its means of articulation are
strongly indentured to a coherent pattern or structure.

  This tensely ironic relationship between exactitude of structure and a
disintegration of verbal meaning is nevertheless one which itself tends to
underwrite the serial paradigm which I have sought to identify in this
chapter. A characteristic feature of (total) serialism is precisely that
discord between the pellucid intelligibility of the tone-row (series) and
the radical break from the musical past (tonality) which its application
engenders. Thus in Webern's String Quartet op. 28, for example,
the permutations of the series are realized by means of contrapuntal
techniques which themselves belong to the tradition of modal and
tonal discourse. The absolute repudiation of tonality which Webern's
serialism envisages is, as a consequence, in deliberate contrast to the
canonic precision of his structural technique. In a similar way, Beckett's
quest for a nearly absolute condition of textual control appears to
contradict the narrative disintegration of meaning which his later plays
espouse. In *Come and Go*, for example, the permutations of a single
exchange between Vi, Ru, and Flo engage a ceremony of posture,
appearance, decorum, and patterned movement, all of which is prescribed with a (by now habitual) level of detail that aspires to the
precision of music. The more exacting this ceremony, the more confined
the temporal duration of play. Here, too, the precedent of Webern is
extremely suggestive.[20] In *Come and Go*, Beckett espouses such a degree
of authorial precision as to nullify the question of interpretation. All
extraneous matter is expelled from the 'ideal space' in which the play is
enacted. The natural intonations and postures of human discourse are
systematically excluded from this arena, and in their place Beckett
unfolds a controlled series of images, sounds, utterances, by which the
paradigm of 'total serialism' achieves its closest impact.

  When a dramatist prescribes '*Voices*: As low as compatible with
audibility. Colourless except for three "ohs" and two lines following',[21]

---

[20] In many of Webern's mature instrumental works, for example, the duration of individual
movements is a matter of seconds rather than minutes. Such radical concentrations of musical
structure prefigure the intensity of Beckett's later plays.

[21] Samuel Beckett, *Come and Go*, in *Collected Shorter Plays*, 197.

the inert landscape of *Breath* is not far away. Although Beckett draws back from the precipice of silence in the plays which follow *Come and Go*, he does not relinquish the aspiration towards absolute control. Nor does the sequential rigour weaken. In *Quad*, on the contrary, 'a piece for four players, light and percussion',[22] the preoccupation with serial structure is so intense that it wholly usurps the possibility of dramatic play. In its stead is the series itself, with all its permutations amounting to some twenty-five minutes of patterned pacing, and the human condition reduced to monk-like configurations upon a square.

Beckett's negotiation between these almost obsessive exactitudes and his interest in the theatre *per se* is perhaps most successfully achieved in *Not I* and its gentle epilogue, *Rockaby*.

In both plays, a woman's voice, and thereby a verbal sequence, is in the ascendant. It is hard not to conceive of one as the obverse of the other, given the strident rhetoric of *Not I* as against the rhythmic caress of *Rockaby*. But in either case the same principles of structural technique remarkably apply. The vehement denial of a first person pronoun in *Not I* apostrophized by the title and underscored by the severe condition of Beckett's tableau (the apparently suspended Mouth, the silent witness of the Auditor), is achieved and sustained by a feverish hysteria which self-evidently threatens intelligibility, and is yet made bearable by virtue of sequence. The motion of this sequence is circular: the maddening logorrhoea which Mouth enacts and endures is critically contained by it. In addition, the fourfold physical movement which Beckett describes as one of 'helpless compassion'[23] confers upon the text those vital *caesurae* through which it attains meaning. When the play turns back upon itself in its pitiful preoccupation with premature birth, a whole life has been surveyed in fitful contemplation of its loveless beginnings. The inevitable disintegration into 'unintelligible' sound at the end of the play is thereby redeemed and dramatically justified. At this pitch of intensity, Beckett's mimetic exactitude requires precisely these interventions of narrative coherence—the sequence itself—by which a crucial distinction between sheer disturbance (the gibberish of the insane) and theatrical representation (the drama as intelligencer of compassion) is precariously maintained at the close of *Not I*.

If *Not I* represents the extreme edge of Beckett's *rapprochement* between structural clarity and the abyss, *Rockaby* notably marks a more relaxed encounter between form and feeling. Here too the terms are disclosed with compelling exactitude: the lighting, the woman (W), her physical description and demeanour, the chair, the movement of the

---

[22] Id., *Quad*, ibid. 291.
[23] Id., *Not I*, ibid. 215.

chair, and the woman's recorded voice (V), establish a sequence which is all the more explicit because of the verbal repetitions which dominate the text. The nocturnal mood which these repetitions generate is mantra-like in effect, but of greater moment, perhaps, is the fourfold division of the piece, a division which closely parallels the fourfold movement in *Not I*. That the beginnings of section one and section three are identical (as in sections two and four) confirms the lucidity of structural sequence in *Rockaby*; that Beckett repeats the pattern 'to herself/whom else' in the first and second sections confirms the relationship with *Not I* in thematic terms.[24]

Because of its explicit serialism, *Rockaby* appears to make a virtue of resignation. The rhythmic structure of the intonations and repetitions (together with the rocking motion) comprise a lullaby to the demise of the spirit. The syntactical transparencies of the text accommodate a simple narrative of the dying woman who contemplates in the fourth section her own mother's decease. The obscene interruption of this sequence ('fuck life'[25]) confirms the sequence's structural importance and easeful tenor of gentle decline. This jarring imperative does not belong to the series: it recalls the man flung back upon the stage in *Act without Words I*. By breaking the series in this way, Beckett signals the lasting silence which constantly threatens to engulf his later plays. 'Fuck life' is a rhetorical energy which breaks the charmed boundary of the sequence itself. Such an abrupt modulation can only lead to the close of play.

The modal precision of Beckett's later work for the theatre (and associated media) does rank as an outstandingly consistent feature of his style. The idea of movement through formal strategy, of dramatic advancement by means of an unfolding structure, would appear to inhere in Beckett's writings almost from the beginning, so that the distillation of this idea in the later plays enjoys a clear precedent not only in *Godot* and *Endgame*, but in early (prose) works such as *Murphy*. The sense that 'something is taking its course' abides in Beckett and underpins the surface collapse of narrative structure. His works confront the void, but they do so with a degree of structural finesse that defies the chaos and diminishment which he envisages as the human condition.

The quest for structural clarity becomes paradigmatic of a quest for meaning against the tide of meaninglessness and defunct tradition. This

---

[24] 'to herself/whom else' is a becalmed version of '. . . what? . . . who? . . . no! . . . she! . . . SHE! . . .' (p. 222), which occurs towards the close of *Not I*. It is as if the woman in *Rockaby* has gained a vital measure of self-acceptance which defiantly escapes the tortured diction of *Not I*.

[25] Samuel Beckett, *Rockaby*, in *Collected Shorter Plays*, 282.

quest is adumbrated in serial composition, which also posits a radical reorientation of (musical) intelligibility. 'Like difficult music heard for the first time', Beckett's later plays may profit from an analytic model which rationalizes their insistent exactitude. 'Nice dimensions, nice proportions', Clov remarks of his kitchen in *Endgame*. But there are also other dimensions and proportions in Beckett, for which serial music provides an instructive precedent and an enlightening analogue.

10

Proust and Schopenhauer: Music and Shadows

JOHN PILLING

Beckett's only extended assessment of what music might mean occurs toward the end of his first commercially published book, the critical essay *Proust* (1931).[1] Like much else in *Proust*, though rarely elsewhere in the essay so explicitly, Beckett's discussion is effectively applied to Schopenhauer, his source the celebrated excursus on music in the fifty-second chapter of volume i of *The World as Will and Representation*, but with account taken also of chapter 39 of volume ii ('On The Metaphysics of Music').[2] Beckett's *Proust* book is throughout predominantly 'metaphysical', irrespective of whether or not music is its focus, as indeed it could hardly help but be with so much of Schopenhauer contributory to its making. Yet there is much in the coda to *Proust* that finds no echo in Schopenhauer, or at best only a muffled one, just as there is much in *Proust* that either blurs or misrepresents what is to be found in Proust himself.[3] Given Beckett's own status as a writer, albeit with a reputation only established long after *Proust* (and with *Proust* but a small, ancillary part of it), this admixture of subjectivity is naturally of more than passing interest, and in any event cannot easily be gainsaid by very virtue of its existence. As Beckett must have realized, however, the context in which it appears is not only dependent upon Schopenhauer for the details of its argument, but is also an exemplification, or illustration, of one of Schopenhauer's most profound convictions: that words can 'speak only of the shadow' and must therefore inevitably misrepresent what they claim to embody. From this point of view, the confident way in which Beckett states that: 'The influence of Schopenhauer on this aspect of the Proustian demonstration ['the significance of music'] is unquestionable' (*PTD*, 91) lends itself to a shadowing which makes the Beckettian 'demonstration' no less demonstrably the product of Schopenhauer's influence.

---

[1] My own quotations are from *Proust, and Three Dialogues with Georges Duthuit* (hereafter *PTD*) (London: John Calder, 1965).

[2] Quotations are from *The World as Will and Representation* (hereafter *WWR*), vols. i and ii, trans. E. J. Payne (New York: Dover Publications, 1966).

[3] See particularly Nicholas Zurbrugg, *Beckett and Proust* (Gerrards Cross: Colin Smythe, 1988), chs. 5, 6, 7, and 8.

The Beckettian 'shadow' is, ironically enough, present in the first significant utterance made subsequent to this: 'Schopenhauer rejects the Leibnitzian view of music as "occult arithmetic"' (*PTD*, 91). What Schopenhauer actually does is much less of a rejection than Beckett says it is: 'We certainly have to look for more than that *exercitum arithmeticae occultum nescientis se numerare animi* ["an unconscious exercise in arithmetic in which the mind does not know it is counting"] which Leibniz took it to be. Yet he was quite right, insofar as he considered only its immediate and outward significance, its exterior' (*WWR*, i. 256).

A similar Beckettian shadowing follows hard upon this: for whilst Schopenhauer certainly 'separates [music] from the other arts', his reason for doing so is not that 'music is the Idea itself', but that 'music is by no means like the other arts, namely a copy of the Ideas, but a *copy of the Will itself*'.[4] Beckett proceeds to separate himself from Schopenhauer still further in his development of this theme:

This essential quality of music is distorted by the listener who, being an impure subject, insists on giving a figure to that which is ideal and invisible, on incarnating the Idea in what he conceives to be an appropriate paradigm. Thus, by definition, opera is a hideous corruption of this most immaterial of all the arts: the words of a libretto are to the musical phrase that they particularize what the Vendôme Column, for example, is to the ideal perpendicular. From this point of view opera is less complete than vaudeville, which at least inaugurates the comedy of an exhaustive enumeration (*PTD*, 92).

The 'listener' who distorts here is actually Beckett himself, since there is no such listener thus characterized in the pages of *The World as Will and Representation*. Schopenhauer, who is much more interested in the composer of music than he is in the person who hears it, never speaks directly of the distortion which the latter experiences, and for good reason. Schopenhauer's world is so very much a matter of separated elements ('in the composer, more than in any other artist, the man is entirely separate and distinct from the artist' (*WWR*, i. 260)) that there is really no need for him to insist upon the disjunctions involved. Beckett, however, straining to complete a task that had by this point (almost at the end of *Proust*) become irksome, is very much the slave of

---

[4] *PTD*, 91–2; *WWR*, i. 257 (Schopenhauer's italics). This is one of the many excellent points made by J. D. O'Hara in an essay tracing Beckett's deviation from Schopenhauer through *Proust* as a whole: 'Beckett's Schopenhauerian Reading of Proust: The Will as Whirled in Representation', in *Schopenhauer: New Essays in Honor of his 200th Birthday*, ed. Eric von der Luft (Lampeter: Edwin Mellen Press, 1988), 273–92. O'Hara, however, assumes (on the authority of Deirdre Bair) that Beckett 'must have had at his disposal [. . .] actual volumes of Schopenhauer' (p. 275) which he had open in front of him. Yet surely the very degree of deviation involved renders this unlikely.

his needs, and in his own words—but from our point of view as listeners reorientating them towards the composer of *Proust*—'insists on giving a figure to [. . .] what he conceives to be an appropriate paradigm' (*PTD*, 92).

In the first of these insistent statements the keyword is 'distorted'. In the second, 'a hideous corruption' is the most eye-catching and expressive phrase. Nowhere in *The World as Will and Representation*, however, is Schopenhauer ever quite so negative in his assessment of opera. In chapter 24 of volume ii, treating opera alongside 'great historical paintings' and 'long epic poems', he observes that, with certain exceptions (*Hamlet, Faust,* and the opera 'Don Juan' (*Don Giovanni*) are mentioned), all such works 'contain an admixture of something insipid and tedious that restricts the enjoyment of them to some extent' (*WWR*, ii. 410). Yet this brief suggestion of a fretted tolerance is almost immediately tempered by Schopenhauer's comment a sentence or so later: 'But that this is the case is a consequence of the limitation of human powers in general' (ibid.). Similarly, in chapter 39 of volume ii of *The World as Will*, in the discussion of opera which forms part of 'On the Metaphysics of Music', Schopenhauer never suggests that the libretto of an opera, inferior though it may (and in some sense must) be to the music of one, is as negligible and damaging as 'a hideous corruption'. If words are to be 'incorporated in the music', Schopenhauer says, 'they must of course occupy only an entirely subordinate position, and adapt themselves completely to it' (ibid. 448). What for Beckett in *Proust* seems, in spite of his anti-moral stance,[5] almost an immoral offence on the part of opera is obviously nothing of the kind for Schopenhauer. The philosopher is concerned only to reaffirm the 'superiority of music' and to pause to reflect for a paragraph or so upon how an opera libretto functions from its inferior position: 'From its own resources, music is certainly able to express every movement of the will, every feeling; but through the addition of the words, we receive also their objects, the motives that give rise to that feeling' (ibid. 449). Far from being 'a hideous corruption', the libretto is, for Schopenhauer, an 'addition'; enabling rather than disabling expressivity, even in a context of 'limitation'.

Volume i of *The World as Will* is even less harsh towards the humble efforts of the librettist, and indeed the relative brevity of Schopenhauer's treatment of the subject is a reflection of how straightforwardly he sees it. Opera and *Lieder*, Schopenhauer tells us, 'should never forsake [the] subordinate position [which they allocate to their verbal elements] in

---

[5] 'Proust is completely detached from all moral considerations' (*PTD*, 66).

order to make them the chief thing, and the music a mere means of expressing the song' (*WWR*, i. 261). For Schopenhauer, the super-ordinate position of music is governed by its status as 'embodied will', which explains music's ability to make 'every picture, indeed every scene from real life and the world, at once appear in enhanced significance' (ibid. 263). Schopenhauer's emphasis is everywhere on such enhance-ments, whereas Beckett's falls, and falls very forcefully, on distortion, impurity, and corruption. Beckett, in the coda to *Proust* (and indeed throughout *Proust*), is writing in a spirit of division and dualism, leaning hard on one note in a given scale the better to call its opposite into question. Schopenhauer is, by contrast, at pains to emphasize that dualist differentials are subsumed in an unchanging singular reality. For Schopenhauer, '[the possibility] of a relation between a composition [music] and a perceptive expression [words] [. . .] is due [. . .] to the fact that the two are simply quite different expressions of the same inner nature of the world' (*WWR*, i. 263). It is precisely in this connection, or rather in preparation for this judgement, that Schopenhauer speaks, for once and once only, of 'vaudeville', a form which is implicitly situated by him at the opposite end of the spectrum to the position occupied by opera. Beckett obviously remembered that Schopenhauer had alluded to vaudeville, but with the sixteen 'abominable' volumes of the NRF edi-tion of Proust to read through in a mere matter of weeks,[6] and presum-ably with no edition of Schopenhauer to hand to refer to,[7] Beckett must have taken the line of least resistance and decided to emphasize the opposition between opera and vaudeville. 'Opera', Beckett insists, 'is less complete than vaudeville, which at least inaugurates the comedy of an exhaustive enumeration' (*PTD*, 92). It is obviously of much less importance to Schopenhauer than Beckett makes it seem. For Schopenhauer, it is a way of reaffirming the superiority of music over words, in that 'the same composition is suitable to many verses' (*WWR*, i. 263).

Beckett muddles the eminently clear Schopenhauerian waters still further by linking his own sense of 'vaudeville' to the structural device of repetition upon which music depends, the 'da capo' which Beckett considers a 'beautiful convention'. Schopenhauer, as elsewhere, is more restrained, though no less approbatory; for him the repetition signs (which would be 'intolerable in the case of works composed in the language of words') are 'very appropriate and beneficial', for—as he

---

[6] *PTD*, 'Foreword'. Beckett told me in August 1969 that he had read *A la recherche du temps perdu* twice in the summer of 1930 before writing *Proust*.

[7] 'Schopenhauer: *Werke*' heads the list of 'Books sent home' (to Ireland from Germany) in the 'Whoroscope' notebook held in Reading University Library's Beckett International Foun-dation (MS 3000). But the only date given in the vicinity is from 1936.

goes on to say—'to comprehend [music] fully, we must hear it twice'.[8] But there is nothing in Schopenhauer which explicitly links 'vaudeville' and the *da capo*, whereas Beckett situates them alongside one another. Both are, for him, 'testimony to the intimate and ineffable nature of an art that is perfectly intelligible and perfectly inexplicable' (*PTD*, 92), itself something of a testimonial to Schopenhauer, albeit one which leaves out what for the philosopher is the *raison d'être* of musical composition. Schopenhauer writes: 'The inexpressible depth of all music, by virtue of which it floats past us a paradise quite familiar and yet eternally remote, and is so easy to understand and yet so inexplicable, is due to the fact that it reproduces all the emotions of our innermost being, but entirely without reality and remote from its pain' (*WWR*, i. 264).

Beckett was either unable or unwilling to attribute to music such a benign and curative role, preferring instead to leave readers of *Proust* to ponder, in perplexity if not pain, the paradox whereby an 'intelligible' art form can nevertheless remain 'inexplicable'. This was a paradox which Beckett was particularly fond of and one he would use again in his spoof lecture 'Le Concentrisme', given to the Modern Languages Society of Trinity College Dublin after he had submitted *Proust* to Chatto and Windus.[9] It must have given Beckett great pleasure that, unbeknownst to his public in 1931, he was not only recommending 'the beautiful convention of the "da capo"', but actually (*sotto voce*, as it were) demonstrating it, having redistributed the elements he had retained from his reading of Schopenhauer.

'Perhaps I overstated Proust's pessimism a little', Beckett once admitted;[10] as Nicholas Zurbrugg has shown conclusively in *Beckett and Proust* 'perhaps' and 'a little' testify to Beckett's mastery of understatement. Yet the remark is of considerable interest notwithstanding, and lends itself to an adaptation in which the name of Schopenhauer, the 'pessimist' *par excellence*, replaces that of Proust. Much of *Proust* borrows from Schopenhauer, whether tacitly or by acknowledgement, and expresses the philosophy of *The World as Will* with little or no distortion. But this is not the case in the coda, and it remains a moot

---

[8] *WWR*, i. 264. This may, at some level of consciousness, have stimulated Beckett to write of Murphy's words (to Celia in ch. 3 of *Murphy*) that they were 'like difficult music heard for the first time' (London: Picador, 1973, p. 27). For Schopenhauer, apparently all music heard for the first time would be more or less difficult.

[9] *Disjecta*, ed. Ruby Cohn (London: John Calder, 1983), 42: 'parfaitement intelligible et parfaitement inexplicable' (said of Mozart). From the correspondence with Thomas MacGreevy held at Trinity College Dublin, it is evident that Beckett must have given his spoof lecture either in late October or early November 1930. *Proust* was sent to Chatto & Windus by mid-October 1930.

[10] In conversation with the present author, Paris, Aug. 1969. See my *Samuel Beckett* (London: Routledge & Kegan Paul, 1976), 16.

point whether Beckett was simply working from a fallible memory, or whether his own developing creative vision—with words so very much a 'shadow' and a limitation—was beginning to generate its own refractory music.[11]

---

[11] See Brigitta Weber's discussion, elsewhere in this volume, of Ulrich Pothast's study, *Die eigentlich metaphysische Tätigkeit: über Schopenhauers Ästhetik und ihre Anwendung durch Samuel Beckett* (Frankfurt am Main: Suhrkamp, 1982) [*Ed.*].

Interlude: Memories

Music in the Works of Samuel Beckett

WALTER BECKETT

When I was a young boy in the early 1920s, I lived with my family in Foxrock, County Dublin. At that time, Foxrock was a fashionable suburb with a sprinkling of houses, surrounded by countryside. I remember my mother being able to walk through fields to visit Sam's mother in their house in Kerrymount Avenue. It was more a friendly relationship rather than a close-knit family one. Later in life, both Sam and I were to attend the same school, Portora Royal School in Enniskillen, and later still the University of Dublin, Trinity College, albeit at different times.

The music in the works of Samuel Beckett may not be apparent to the general reader, but a study of his works yields a surfeit of surprises. The music is largely brought about by his use of language, the paring down of words and the length of time given to pauses or silences, thereby creating a rhythmical whole. Pauses or silences are essential in his writings, particularly in his most famous work, *Waiting for Godot*. Here we have words and pauses in counterbalance. The quick interchange of phrases—'his friends, his agents, his correspondents, his books, his bank account'—and later—'it's the rope, it's the rubbing, it's inevitable, it's the knot, it's the chafing'—are reminiscent of an operatic recitative. Lucky's tirade is an aria carried along by the word-endings, the repetition of words and the use of alliteration. It is a wonderfully complex piece of writing which comes as a complete contrast to the short phrases of Gogo and Didi. Lucky is a magnificent character. The very names of Gogo and Didi are more musical and rhythmical than Estragon and Vladimir, and the use of the repeated consonant in both names is a staccato repeated note.

One of the most musical works is *Krapp's Last Tape*. It is a very short work. From start to finish it is extremely rhythmical. This is achieved by both the flow and the nature of the words. In the passage beginning: 'Past midnight. Never knew such silence. The earth might be uninhabited. (*Pause*.)', I hear at this point a diminished seventh chord F D B A♭, followed by an indescribable chord of F D♭ B G. This type of chordal colour permeates this work. The reiteration of the vowel sounds with the short sentences and the pauses create a flowing melody broken by these chordal colours, giving a complete musical passage. I feel that Sam, with his musical knowledge—he was a competent pianist—conceived and wrote his works in a rhythmical fashion as if they were music. Words to him were notes. They had to be clear to the ear and at the same time create a word picture. The sound was to be carried through from one word to the next in the same way that an accomplished singer carries the sound, on the breath, through from one note to the next.

I, as a musician, was stunned by these colours in his works when they were first performed. They were different from those of other writers. They were new and exciting in their starkness and clarity. One of the first extracts of his works that affected my own composition was the second poem of *Quatre poèmes* (that which begins 'je suis ce cours de sable qui glisse' ['My way is in the sand flowing']). This poem is a two-part piece of music with a thin texture for voice and flute. All life, it seems to me, is summed up in these nine very sparse lines. It is an uplifting work whether read in the original French or in the English translation. The phrases are repeated in the same way that musical phrases are repeated. There is a concentrated interplay of vowels and consonants which adds to the intensity.

The most telling and awe-inspiring of his phrases is the phrase 'Imagination Dead Imagine'. Again the repetition, again the pauses, for the phrase is not meant to run together. One must stop and be enveloped in the music of each sparse word before proceeding to the next. In so doing, what a wealth of thought, inspiration, and musical colour is opened before us.

12

Beckett's Involvement With Music

Miron Grindea

Samuel Beckett's lifelong passion for music remains one of the most fascinating aspects of his creative work. André Gide wrote a long essay on Chopin as well as some lapidary mentions in his *Journal*, but there is an element of histrionics in his remarks which now renders them rather unconvincing, whereas Sam remains as 'secretive' a musician as Julien Green, who, in his ninety-fourth year, still finds solace in his interpretations of Schumann.

Beckett could play for hours on end. His choice of piano works reflected the solidity and happiness of his communion with music from his childhood in Dublin, then later on in Paris, or whenever he could find an instrument in good condition. The composer who spoke most to him was Schubert, whom he considered a friend in suffering. He much preferred Beethoven to Mozart, because he admired his life of struggle and constant searching, in contrast to Mozart's natural facility.

In 1954, he invited me to his apartment in the Rue des Favorites, not far from the Porte de Versailles in Paris. I expected to have a literary discussion, or to talk about the friends we had in common, such as Seumas O'Sullivan and his wife Stella. Instead, for more than an hour, we were chatting about the pianists we both loved—Dinu Lipatti, Clara Haskil, or Monique Haas, the radiant wife of Marcel Mihalovici, and a brilliant interpreter of Bartók's piano music. (He particularly loved her playing of the Third Piano Concerto). Beckett never missed an opportunity to listen to Bartok, whom we considered the greatest inspiration for his late creation. With Marcel Mihalovici he developed a close friendship, and this led to a most important collaboration: Mihalovici wrote the music for *Krapp* and *Cascando* on libretti by Beckett.

I met Beckett again in Paris when he moved to his last residence in the Boulevard Saint Jacques, and then in London, in the foyer of the Riverside Studios. As usual, we found ourselves almost immediately involved in the main topic—music—which was so much part of our lives.

Beckett was very fond of the piano sonatas of Haydn—a composer he mentions in his novel *Murphy*.[1] Beethoven remained a revered composer. Pointing out a passage in the first movement of the Seventh Symphony, in which, after a fortissimo, there follow two bars of silence, Beckett asked: 'What happens during that silence?' On another occasion, Mihalovici recalled Beckett's 'dislike of the inexorable purposefulness of Bach'.

In a letter I have received recently, Edward Beckett, Sam's nephew, a very fine flautist, recalls being introduced by his uncle to Marcel Mihalovici and his wife Monique Haas. He remembers his uncle playing the piano: Haydn, the easier Beethoven sonatas, a little Chopin, and—perhaps his favourite—accompanying himself in Schubert songs. There was, he says, a piano both in the Boulevard Saint Jacques flat and in his house in Ussy. Edward Beckett studied the flute at the Paris Conservatoire, and recalls his uncle coming to hear his annual 'concours', and to some concerts he gave, including one at the Sorbonne in July 1967, playing the Mozart D Major Concerto with the Irish Chamber Orchestra. Beckett also accompanied his young nephew to some concerts: one such concert was Sviatoslav Richter playing Schubert sonatas, at the Salle Pleyel.

Occasionally, an unusual comic element would enhance the atmosphere. John Beckett, a cousin of Sam's, a gifted composer, sat down at the piano after the final performance of *Endgame* at the Royal Court Theatre and improvised some hilarious variations on the *Marseillaise*, to the delight of Beckett, who responded by singing several bawdy Irish songs. . . .

During his short period as a lecturer at Trinity College, Dublin, Beckett found great joy in his music-making, particularly as his elder brother provided him with a piano. Luck was on my side recently when I had the pleasure of talking to one of Beckett's contemporaries at Trinity. Arthur Hillis, a nonagenarian, remembers vividly how they used to listen to gramophone records, mostly Schubert and Debussy.

There is also at Trinity College a vast correspondence in which Beckett describes to his close friend Tom MacGreevy the concerts which he attended. In 1937, when cultural life in Berlin was tarnished by the excesses of the Nazi regime, he rarely missed an opportunity to express his horror at National Socialism, denouncing Furtwängler for his approval of the regime, and criticizing his performances of Wagner. On the other hand, he often expressed his admiration for Victor de Sabata.

---

[1] See early part of ch. 10: 'The decaying Haydn, invited to give his opinion of cohabitation, replied: "Parallel thirds"' (Samuel Beckett, *Murphy* (London: Picador, 1973), 110) [*Ed.*].

Beckett's passion for music offers a vast field of exploration into this aspect of his personality. John Minihan, a great portrait photographer, has taken many photographs of Beckett at the Riverside Studios. One of these shows Beckett listening to popular Irish music. These unique testimonials appear in a new fine art edition, a source of delight to Beckett's followers.[2]

[2] See John Minihan, *Samuel Beckett: Photographs by John Minihan*, with an introduction by Aidan Higgins (London: Secker & Warburg, 1995) [*Ed.*].

Part II

Music

13

Beckett and Music

An Interview with Luciano Berio

MARY BRYDEN. You made the connection between Samuel Beckett and music many years ago, in your *Sinfonia*. Could you say a little about the genesis of that work?

LUCIANO BERIO. I composed the *Sinfonia*, which is for eight voices and orchestra, in 1968. The third, central section of this work develops many different musical layers which are partially generated by the Scherzo of Mahler's Second Symphony. The text, sung and spoken by the eight voices, is taken from Beckett's *The Unnamable*, and it generates other verbal layers. It would be too complicated to describe the musical criteria behind the employment—analogous in some respects— of a musical text by Mahler and a literary text by Beckett. They are immensely distant from each other, but at the same time they share an awareness—different though it is—of time past: Mahler developing it and commenting upon it, Beckett stoically pre-empting it and systematically suspending it.

MB. You have been enormously wide-ranging in your choice of modern literary 'quotations' within your musical compositions: Brecht, Joyce, Eliot, Pound, etc. Do you find anything intrinsically 'musical' in Beckett's writing?

LB. I've always thought, even before working on *Sinfonia*, that Beckett's writing is very musical. But it's very difficult to describe what this 'being musical' means. I suspect that, as with everything else in Beckett, this question also defies analysis, even on a purely metaphorical level. Maybe it's precisely this ability to elude analysis that makes Beckett's writing so musical. It constantly prompts interpretation but, at the same time, it refuses to provide any meaningful or useful instrument. Like music, Beckett's writing seems to say what cannot be spoken.

Beckett's pseudo-narrative situations don't imply future perspectives. There's no future, but only the experience of the present, a moment-by-moment accumulation of facts revolving upon themselves: time is suspended. As with music, there can be an enormous phenomenological distance between the smallest factual detail and the poetic and obscure Beckettian design. But, whereas in music, part of the meaning is based on exploring or inventing paths going from the smallest, practical details to a global design, in Beckett's writing the two dimensions are kept separate from each other: the paths go nowhere and the global events are indifferent to the obsessive description of the details, of those pseudo-paths.

MB. Is there, then, no level on which music can encompass these 'pseudo-paths'?

LB. I think there is. It seems to me that there's a connection between the obsessive, pseudo-realistic descriptions of Beckett and the non-realistic, non-representational experience of music. Meanings, in Beckett, seem to take place and shape somewhere else, behind the shoulders of the speakers, of 'narrators' like Hamm, Estragon, Vladimir, Krapp, and in spite of them. This may also be the case in music, when a meaning seems to appear 'behind' a performance, taking shape in spite of the awkward physicality of an unknown player.

MB. Do you see Beckett as a 'case apart' in this respect?

LB. One could say that Kafka and Joyce are at the roots of this tendency to be at the same time both abstract, and concretely, fastidiously precise. However, there's one thing that is peculiarly and 'Beckettianly' musical: it's the fact that, most of the time, those Beckett pseudo-characters (from *The Unnamable, Endgame, Krapp's Last Tape*, etc.) don't know who they're talking to: to themselves? To us? To another pseudo-character? To an audience? They don't even know what they're really talking about. This is why the laughing and the tears, the comic and the tragic, coexist in Beckett in a profoundly inextricable way: one which has never really been experienced before. That's an issue, and a very musical one, that music theatre should approach again soon, possibly with the blessing of Mozart but, more importantly, under the auspices of Samuel Beckett.

14

Beckett and Music

An Interview with Philip Glass

MARY BRYDEN. When did you first become interested in Samuel Beckett's writing?

PHILIP GLASS. It was in Paris, which of course is a very good place in which to become interested in Beckett! That would have been in 1964 or 1965.

MB. Did you become interested through the experience of seeing his plays, or of reading him?

PG. Almost entirely through the theatre, when I was in Paris. But I had already read the Trilogy, in the early 1960s, before going to Paris. You have to remember that this was over thirty years ago, and at that time Beckett was pretty much an unknown figure. He stayed that way for a long time. I can tell you a funny story about that. In 1955, I happened to be passing through London, on my way to New York, and someone offered me tickets to a play at the Arts Theatre Club. I had never heard of the writer, and turned down the invitation that night. It turned out to be *Waiting for Godot*. The first production. I could have seen it! But I missed it.

MB. One thing you mention in your book[1] is your interest in the music of John Cage and of Morton Feldman, at that time, in the 1960s. Both of them were interested in Beckett's work as well. Was this influential upon you?

PG. No, I came to it independently. What interested me particularly at that time were the parallels I saw between Beckett and four other writers: William Burroughs, Brion Gysin, Allen Ginsberg, and Paul Bowles. I knew all of them, although in the case of Paul Bowles only by means of correspondence. These four writers wanted to create a non-narrative literary form, and it seems to me that their experimentation with 'cut-ups', with non-consecutive narrative, is very close to what Beckett is doing in *Play*,[2] where he takes three monologues and intercuts them to form one story, fracturing the straight narrative form. I remember one particular conversation with Gysin about these connections. He

[1] Philip Glass, *Music by Philip Glass* (ed. with supplementary material by Robert T. Jones) (New York: Dunvagen Music Publishers, 1987).

[2] Philip Glass's music for *Play*, for two soprano saxophones, was written in 1965 [Ed.].

was certainly aware of Beckett's writing, although I can't remember now the details of what he said.

This fracturing of narrative by the use of non-narrative or abstract elements is not unlike what David Hockney was doing with photography some twenty years later. By looking at his polaroid portraits you see the same thing from different angles, and you build up a composite, of which each picture is only a fragment. The composite forms a whole picture, but a somewhat different one from the individual elements. Interestingly, Hockney relates that directly to cubism, and to the multi-perspective painting of Picasso.

So, coming to *Play* as I did, at that time, I saw immediately a historical and cultural association with these other writers and movements.

MB. Was there any special reason for choosing *Play*?

PG. I wasn't the person who chose it. Our small theatre company—JoAnne Akalaitis, Ruth Maleczech, David Warrilow, and myself as composer—decided with the director, Lee Breuer, that *Play* fitted our abilities. We were living in Paris at that time, and we had just done a production of *Mother Courage*. It struck me that there were very interesting parallels, not only between Brecht and Beckett, but also between Genet and Beckett. You have only to think of a play like *Les Paravents*, and how that piece is put together. Bring together in your mind a major play by Beckett, a major play by Brecht, and a major play by Genet, and there you have assembled the most interesting and important playwrights of the twentieth century.

MB. Did you notice anything explicitly 'musical' about Beckett's writing?

PG. Not necessarily. The musical issue was not so much continuity versus discontinuity. It was more a question of tonality than of structure. I experimented by trying to deal with these ideas in a straightforward structural way, but found that it didn't produce what I wanted, so I more or less dropped the idea. Parallel issues may emerge, but parallel solutions are more difficult.

MB. You use the word 'reductive' about your own music at one point in your book, and some of your early work has shared the description of 'minimalist' which is sometimes applied to Beckett's later writing. Do you find these terms useful?

PG. In the case of my own work, the term might have been applicable thirty years ago, but it would not be an informative or helpful description now. Indeed, it would only cause confusion. In the case of Beckett, the dynamic is rather different. By *Oh les beaux jours* you have the quintessential Beckett. After that, his work displays further and further refinement.

MB. Did you ever meet Beckett?

PG. No, I never actually met him, although I lived for a long time in the same city, and was engaged with his writing. Within the group which became the Mabou Mines company, we decided to appoint David Warrilow and Fred Neumann as our contacts with Beckett. Both of them were bilingual. They would just go and see him to discuss things.

MB. Do you know whether Beckett ever heard your music?

PG. I have no idea.

MB. Fred Neumann says in the interview he gave to Jonathan Kalb[3] that he did discuss the question of music with Beckett.

PG. Oh, we always sent him the music. He didn't reply. His initial position was usually that the music was an intrusion. However, with a little conversation, he would in the end allow it to happen. David and Fred provided the necessary contact with Beckett. Generally, as a group, we respected his privacy, to the degree that we didn't want to intrude upon him any further than was necessary.

MB. In your music to Beckett's texts, are you providing an alternative shape to the writing, or does the writing have its own rhythms and shape, which you incorporate into your music?

PG. What you do with pieces like *The Lost Ones*, *Mercier and Camier*, or *Company*,[4] is that, within the context of a theatre modality, you provide another medium. This medium can be supportive of the written text, but it doesn't replace it in any way. It may be an extension of it.

MB. You mentioned David Warrilow just now, and I find it very interesting that Warrilow has spoken of the Beckett actor as being like a musical instrument to be played by Beckett. So too has Billie Whitelaw. How do you feel about this? Is the voice alone enough? Or can music add something else?

PG. I remember talking to Doris Lessing once. I did an opera based on one of her novels.[5] She said to me very early on: 'Why do you want to do this?' I said: 'Well, I can say things in music that can't be said in words'. She clearly accepted that. She said: 'Oh', and we never discussed it again. Music has fluidity. It exists in a world without objects and colloquial complications, and so we have a certain freedom in music which we don't have with words.

MB. So you see your music as something which enhances the words rather than corroborating them.

PG. Of course.

[3] Jonathan Kalb, *Beckett in Performance* (Cambridge: Cambridge University Press, 1989), 206–11.

[4] Philip Glass's scores for these theatrical adaptations, with the Mabou Mines company, date from 1974, 1979, and 1983, respectively [*Ed.*].

[5] Philip Glass, *The Making of a Representative for Planet 8* (1988) [*Ed.*].

MB. In your book, you say interestingly of your setting for *Play* that it is 'a series of five or six short pieces separated by equal lengths of silence' (*Music by Philip Glass*, 35). You also mention being influenced by John Cage's book *Silence* (p. 37). As a musician, do you see silence as an integral part of your work?

PG. Yes, I do. And I did then. I saw the silences as places where the narrative or the words would become unadorned, so to speak. In the silence, they would emerge in a certain way with more clarity. In any case, the difference between narrative and background music, and narrative and non-background music, can be quite enormous. In no case was the music in the foreground.

MB. You also mention in your book the phenomenon of repetition in *Play*. You describe how you became puzzled by the fact that, each time you viewed the play, you 'noticed that the emotional quickening (or epiphany) of the work seemed to occur in a different place' (p. 35), despite all the given elements of performance. Correspondingly, you also describe your own score for the piece as being 'a very static piece that was still full of rhythmic variety'. Was this mirroring dynamic a coincidence?

PG. No, it wasn't just coincidence. I was really trying to learn from Beckett. You have to remember that I was quite a young man at the time: maybe 27 or 28. I was just finding my own voice. Narrative in those days was a big problem for me, as it was for many people. I was using the structures that Beckett provided, and the dispersion of the narrative, as a clue to a new way of working in music. About ten years later, I wrote a piece called *Einstein on the Beach*,[6] which was based upon that new way. The interval between the two pieces consisted of ten eventful years of music, but I would say that *Play* to *Einstein on the Beach* represents a through-line of work. There were other influences, some of which I mentioned earlier, but the fact was that, as soon as I began to write the music for *Play*, I was dealing with Beckett, and so Beckett became the prime influence within the array of solutions to that problem of narrative which so many artists were grappling with at that time. Beckett was the person I was relating to at that moment, and his writing had a real impact on my work.

[6] Philip Glass, *Einstein on the Beach*, opera in four acts (1975–6). For Philip Glass Ensemble, vocal soloists and chorus. Created with Robert Wilson [*Ed.*].

15

The Indifference of the Broiler to the Broiled

ROGER REYNOLDS

PING (1968) BY ROGER REYNOLDS WITH TEXT
BY SAMUEL BECKETT

In 1966, just before leaving for an extended stay in Japan, I saw a production of Samuel Beckett's *Waiting for Godot* in Minneapolis. I can still recall clearly the rush of excitement by which I was consumed during Lucky's virtuoso monologue. What stunned me then was the juxtaposition of excess and control that this work manifested. Although it exceeded (exhilaratingly) the boundaries of what I had thought theatrically viable, it was, at the same time, parsimonious, spare and precise in its detail. The uniqueness of its author's vision was unmistakable.

In Tokyo, my wife and I collaborated with Japanese musicians and artists in producing a series of bi-national concerts and also a festival under the name of *Cross Talk*. This, in turn, brought us into contact with the composer Toru Takemitsu, who was planning a major festival of his own, 'Orchestral Space '68'. I was invited to do a new work for this occasion, and determined that it would be a response to Beckett's writings. As it happened, I came across a copy of the February 1967 issue of the English magazine *Encounter*, in which was printed Beckett's short prose text *Ping*. It seemed as remarkable as *Godot*, but in a different way. Here, an initially limited repertoire of unexceptional words and balanced phrases was relentlessly—though not systematically, I noticed—permuted, adjusted, augmented. Again, as in *Godot*, the fascination was not to be found precisely in what the text said, but rather in *how it said*, and in the implications and emotions that arose as one pressed on through its disconcerting web of slight differentiations and ambiguous associations:

All known all white bare white body fixed one yard legs joined like sewn. Light heat white floor one square yard never seen. White walls one yard by two white ceiling one square yard never seen. Bare white body fixed only the eyes only just. Traces blurs light grey almost white on white.

As I look back on this time now, it is surprising that I did not consider responding to Beckett's challenge—(everything he did seemed to me a challenge, if not willed so then simply as a result of his relentless self-consistency)—by composing with small motivic pitch cells that could be permuted in a fashion that would emulate the author's verbal behaviours. Rather, my reaction was to move towards the perils and excitements of the unruly images and emotions that arose out of the field of his apparently chaste words. Although I had not done anything of the sort before, I decided to write music that rested upon improvisation, positing a rather small number of boundary conditions and hoping to elicit from within them for the ear the sort of emanations that arose in the mind as a result of his way with words.

In my letter to Beckett of 30 June 1967, I wrote that *Ping* had 'provided the sort of provocation I respond to best, the sensing of content, of potential, without immediate comprehension' (surely something of an understatement).

I have in mind lyrical music, though not melodic in any traditional sense—generally slow to change, but sustained and richly textured. *Ping* was printed without structural indications other than the sentence-like units, and I am not clear on what you intend with regard to silences (spacing). It is clear from your other works that spacing is important. I have my own reactions. . . .

. . . I would, of course, welcome suggestions from you, and would hope to consult with you as work progressed, but I am perfectly prepared to undertake this process by myself if you approve.

I included with my letter recordings of compositions that I had done on texts of Wallace Stevens (*The Emperor of Ice Cream*) and Melville (*Blind Men*) which were intended to 'suggest the sort of thing I have in mind for *Ping*'. On 13 July 1967, Beckett responded from Sardinia, thanking me for my letter which he had received the day before, and granting me permission to proceed with the *Ping* project. I set to work immediately.

In the letter to Beckett I had stated that: 'The magnetic tape accompanying the performance would be played stereophonically so as to increase the audience sense of submersion. It would include not only sound materials of a musical nature, but words as well. These I would like spoken by very old and lean voices.'

I wrote to three elderly male friends in the United States, arranging for each of them to be recorded in a reading of the *Ping* text. My intention was to create a montage of these distinct voices, alternating among them word by word or even syllable by syllable. When the tapes arrived, and I began intercutting them, it unexpectedly but quickly became clear that individual readings, however determinedly laconic, carry with them so much contextual information, so much that is of an interpretative nature, that they cannot productively coexist. Such a montage would have

Fig. 15.1 A projection instance from the visual presentation of the text for Ping

been inappropriately comical. It would have encumbered with irrelevancies the distilled essence of Beckett's prose in an inappropriate and destructive fashion. A tape component remained in the picture, however, because of a chance circumstance.

We were living in an older wood-frame house in Tokyo, and winters were an ordeal. The intermittent ignition of the water heater was unpredictably accompanied by a piercing shriek of inhuman and corrosive vigour. Strangely, we both came to look forward to its incursions with an attitude not entirely unlike that which I described above in relation to the performance of *Waiting for Godot*. This 'cry' became for me an unbidden vocalization from the figure in the *Ping* box. It seemed a response to the diabolical constraints and canny moderation of Beckett's writing. In performance, it drives the musical culmination of my setting.

Rather than presenting the text through a single reading voice (too personally explicit) or a montage of voices (too congested with unmanageables), it appeared that the only way in which the attributes of Beckett's approach could be manifested in performance before an audi-

Fig. 15.2 *An instance in which the text projections for* Ping *have been distorted by optical filters*

ence was by means of *visual* presentation. I settled upon a subdivision of the text into what I considered its smallest viable modules.

Ping   murmurs only just almost never   one second   always the same   all known. Given rose only just   bare white body fixed   one yard   invisible   all known without within.   Ping   perhaps a nature   one second . . .

My wife, Karen, designed slides that were projected in combination with the modifying influence of prisms and coloured filters, and these allowed the text to be performed, to move in the mind without being heard.

The iconoclastic American critic, Peter Yates, wrote of a performance of *Ping* in Toronto that the experience was 'something like being seared under a broiler'. One wonders how Beckett would have responded to such an association. The indifference of the broiler to the broiled might have appealed. Surely Yates's reaction was appropriate to my intent.

I attempted to arrange a presentation of the completed piece in Paris

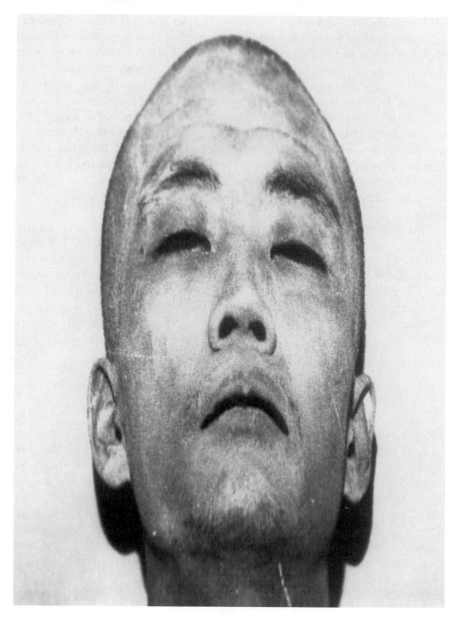

Fig. 15.3 *A close-up of Akaji Maro from the film for* Ping

while passing through on a planned trip to the Warsaw Autumn Festival
in September 1968, but the Festival was cancelled owing to the intensity
of political turmoil in Poland at that time. So I wrote to Beckett again in
December 1968 explaining that the film used to present the image of the
central figure in *Ping* 'was conceived and directed by me using an
excellent Japanese professional cameraman, Kazuro Kato. It is consider-
ably more austere than the production of your *Film*. . . . A figure [the
now notorious Butoh dancer Akaji Maro] in a white box stands motionless (with the exception of several rapid cuts related to "that much
memory almost never" in my mind) for the film's entire 22 minutes. The
camera perspective, however, changes constantly. Using a telephoto
zoom lens, I was able to move from a full body to a close-up of eyes, for
example, without a break'.

   This work was performed several times in Japan and toured in the
United States. It served, in fact, as the bridge which allowed my wife
and me to return to the American scene after a period of some seven
years abroad. The pattern of my interactions with Beckett's work
had also been set, in that each would involve an unanticipated and
genuinely radical response, an approach that I had not previously conceived of as practicable, and, in at least two instances, one that I never
repeated.

A *MERCIFUL COINCIDENCE* (1976) BY ROGER REYNOLDS WITH
             TEXT BY SAMUEL BECKETT

When I came from Japan to the University of California, San Diego, in
1969, I began at once to plan for the establishment of the Center for
Music Experiment. This 'organized research unit' of the University was
devoted to collaboration, and to exploring the experimental and scien-
tific aspects of music. It required us to assemble a group of energetic and
gifted young musicians as 'fellows' of the facility. Among them were
several singers who joined to form the Extended Vocal Techniques
Ensemble. As director of the Center, I overheard their daily rehearsals as
they perturbed the known. Their meddlings with accepted vocalization
included such procedures as ingressive sound production (drawing air
always inwards) rather than the normal egressive behaviour (outward
directed breath), Tibetan chant, Mongolian and Bulgarian folk techniques, and also exploration of the limits of modified forms of vocal
activity that were still perceivable as language. In the daytimes I began
to experiment with these gifted musicians, capable of and willing to
engage in a seemingly unlimited range of inflection. In the evenings I
read our daughter to sleep, trying to capture for each character in a story

an individual and vocally distinctive behaviour. She was a demanding critic, and stimulated in me both a surprising array of vocal gymnastics and a good deal of nocturnal reflection about vocal identity. In my mind and ear, then, was the notion of eccentric story-telling.

The Beckett text which I decided to use as a narrative source was taken from his philosophically experimental novel *Watt*, largely written during the Second World War. It shared with the later *Ping* a predilection for exhaustively exploring the effects of reformulation, the mutations of implication that can come from trying out varying orders of sets of words, ideas, circumstances. The narrator in *Watt* speaks of 'Thinking [. . .] of the possible relations between such series as these, the series of dogs, the series of men, the series of pictures, to mention only these series . . .'. Thus he implies that collections of things will be exhaustively placed in relationships to one another. Later in this passage, this comparative exercise is played out: 'If the fishwoman had pleased Watt, without Watt's pleasing the fishwoman, or if Watt had pleased the fishwoman, without the fishwoman's pleasing Watt, then what would have become of Watt, or of the fishwoman? Not that the fishwoman was a man's woman, for she was not.'

But the most arresting instantiation of interactive series occurs when Beckett posits a wry chorus: 'Three frogs croaking Krak!, Krek! and Krik!, at one, nine, seventeen, twenty-five, etc., and at one, six, eleven, sixteen, etc., and at one, four, seven, ten, etc., respectively'. Not content with spelling out the beginnings of the three numerical series that underlie the frogs' performance, he then consumes a page and a half with a literal rendering of the event. Part of it appears below:

```
Krak!   —     —     —     —     —     —     —
Krek!   —     —     —     —    Krek!   —     —
Krik!   —     —    Krik!   —     —    Krik!   —

Krak!   —     —     —     —     —     —     —
 —      —    Krek!   —     —     —     —    Krek!
 —    Krik!   —     —    Krik!   —     —    Krik!¹
```

It was this unique passage that seduced me, and an elaborate sonic rendering of it became a conceptual centrepiece of the resulting musical work, *A Merciful Coincidence*. The programme note for this composition observed that:

Growing out of a concern with the many spatial dimensions of language (metaphoric as well as sonic), the work's essential form is on quadraphonic tape. The live performance version [. . .] concentrates on the interactive pleas-

¹ See Samuel Beckett, *Watt* (New York: Grove Press, 1959), 137–8.

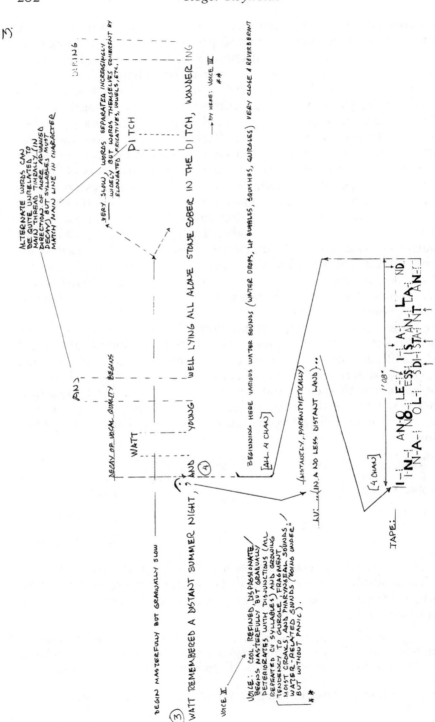

Fig. 15.4 Page 3 from the performance score for A Merciful Coincidence

ures of spontaneous response between the three vocalists. A key aspect of the compositional process was an effort to achieve vocal models ('voices') with distinctive (even peculiar) character, models attainable by all three performers yet idiosyncratically variable. 'Coincidence' is, naturally, not at all without design. [The reference in Beckett's text was 'And Watt pleased the fishwoman. This was a merciful coincidence, that they pleased each other.]'

The singers' alternating contributions to these model behaviours manifested, of course, a further more subtle reference to interactive series.

I conceived a nocturnal setting for *A Merciful Coincidence*, a vaguely miasmal swamp, bubbling, echoing with the occasional irritation of insects (their insistent whine moves around the audience by means of a quadraphonic speaker system), and demented birds (one hears, echoing in the distance, disquieting squawks). Each of the three performers is placed in a spatially distinct location; each has, as it were, a territory. And the performers, while striving to match my prescribed vocal ideals (e.g. 'creaky: maximum number of registral breaks'; 'ravaged, sexless croak', etc.), also had to depart radically from them in prescribed ways ('accumulating defect: breathless wheezing', or 'towards inflexibly rounded lips'). As with Beckett's maddening mundanities, my performers' vocal behaviours, though extreme, were always measured by a reference to the commonplace: anxious and drowsy, normal and pathological, human and non-human. *A Merciful Coincidence* is story-telling, but it offers a narrative that continually totters at the edge of the unintelligible.

My compositional interest included the extension and exploration of the particular acoustic character of individual words and of the ways in which they follow upon one another in speech, song, declamation, hysteria, reverie, and so on. The vocal characterizations I have mentioned earlier, it should be emphasized, were not reducible simply to the accents or manners of speech that an actor might adopt in a role, but involved the radical alteration of vocal production itself. And all of this was provoked by the uncompromising meanness of Beckett's players and their circumstance. The recursive atmosphere of his prose gives rise not only to frustration, but even to a certain urge on the reader's part to *retaliate* against the author's dogged persistence. Thirty-six minutes in length, *A Merciful Coincidence* employs a quadraphonic tape and three vocalists, three source-voices which constantly shift and blend ambiguously.

The text is simultaneously projected so as to enhance the distance between objective origins and subjective manifestations. The central (and 'natural') metaphor here, one that is extended in deliberately antic ways, arises from the 'voices' of non-human creatures: frogs, insects, birds.

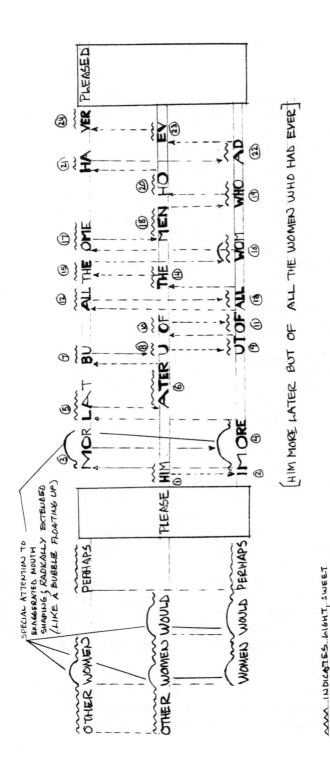

Fig. 15.5 *A portion of page 10 of the score for* A Merciful Coincidence

ODYSSEY (1989–93) BY ROGER REYNOLDS WITH TEXT BY SAMUEL BECKETT

The title *Odyssey* refers to a spiritual odyssey that I envisioned Samuel Beckett taking in his earlier life: the move away from Ireland, resettlement in Paris, and the finding of his creative position. Using three poems and one of the *Texts for Nothing*, my work traces a movement from:

> the recognition of a reciprocal ambiguity in human relationships— 'avec chacune c'est autre et c'est pareil'; through doubt of the self— 'que ferais-je sans ce monde'; and enquiry—'Mais qu'est-ce que je fais, j'essaie de me situer'; to a kind of credo—'je suis ce cours de sable qui glisse entre le galet et la dune'.

In this work, some seventy-seven minutes in length, my intention was to explore the unitary 'message' in Beckett's mind as manifested through a pair of distinctive pathways: French and English. Two bilingual speakers, one male, one female, recorded the parallel texts (Beckett, of course, produced both the French and the English versions). These readings were then computer processed so as to interweave without interfering with one another. Though one hears two texts spoken at once in performance, their words have been so extensively micro-adjusted in time that neither language obscures the virtually simultaneous presence of the other. The two texts coexist then, and, again with the help of computer processing, were made to move symmetrically in virtual space, reflecting the peregrinations of Beckett's questing mind.

Sixteen instrumentalists (four quartets, each a pair of pairs) and two vocalists also reflect upon and elaborate the images that the assembled text suggested to me. This occurs in a weave of live performance and computer-processed manipulations of vocal and instrumental materials. The latter frame and elaborate the more straightforward French and English readings. Algorithmic procedures and reference to certain mathematically chaotic phenomena (specifically the Hénon and the Lorentz attractors) were used in the formal design and methodological elaboration of musical materials. At every level, the piece attempts to respond to the suggestive pairs in the text that I put together from Beckett's work: the specific and the ambiguous, the self and the other, the mother and the tomb, the shingle and the dune....

It is normally my practice to plan out a musical work quite fully so that once the more flexible and intuitive process of actual composition begins, a great deal is already known about the scope, intent, shape, and content of the end-result. In conversation with Tom Driver, Beckett is reported to have questioned the relation between the chaotic nature of life itself and the orderliness of art: '"How could the mess be admitted, because it appears to be the very opposite of form and therefore destructive of the very thing that art holds itself to be?" But now we can keep it out no longer, because we have come into a time when "it invades our experience at every moment. It is there and it must be allowed in".[2]

He continues (p. 219):

What I am saying does not mean that there will henceforth be no form in art. It only means that there will be new form, and that this form will be of such a type that it admits the chaos and does not try to say that the chaos is really something else. The form and the chaos remain separate. The latter is not reduced to the former. That is why the form itself becomes a preoccupation, because it exists as a problem separate from the material it accommodates. To find a form that accommodates the mess, that is the task of the artist now.

This perspective is unassailable, and I decided to confront it in two ways. In shaping the whole of the composition, I invoked recent work on the mathematical description of chaos and the so-called 'self-similar' structures. I also entertained the thought that, in some if not all of the work's larger sections, I would proceed on *entirely* intuitive grounds. To make the personal significance of this decision clearer, I should explain that it involved proceeding in direct opposition to the entire evolved course of my compositional process—a course premissed upon lengthy and thorough examination of the reasons for and the implications of each formal commitment (it is an essentially *architectural* approach). In parts of *Odyssey*, on the contrary, I determined to act decisively on intuitive impulse alone, to welcome even the most improbable and inexplicable images into the composition. Naturally, these 'images' arose in consideration of Beckett's texts, and were, I now realize, not so distant from the murmurings that I described in the cases of *Ping* and *A Merciful Coincidence*, images that sprang up around Beckett's words and his ways with words.

Although I am by no means a linguist, I have a long-standing interest in the expressive dimensions of languages other than English: Japanese and French in particular. Considerable foreign experience is a factor, but one cannot in any case avoid an awareness of the diminishing viability of our longtime assumption that there exists an audience with a shared level of knowledge and cultural orientation. It is evident that some effort must be made to address this issue: we must seek ways to reach across linguistic and cultural divides through the special sorts of experience available in aesthetic contexts, particularly with the mediation of advanced technology. The origins of *Odyssey* are to be found in such

[2] Interview with Tom Driver, *Columbia University Forum* (Summer 1961), 21–5, reprinted in Lawrence Graver and Raymond Federman (eds.), *Samuel Beckett: The Critical Heritage* (London: Routledge and Kegan Paul, 1979), 219.

concerns. I wanted to write an indisputably bilingual work, to confront
this subject more deeply than montage could. For it, I chose three poems
and a prose text of Beckett's and parsed them line by line, so that it
would be possible to consider and monitor closely the degrees and
qualities of the similarities between English and French versions. Inden-
tation was used in order to suggest to the reader primary and secondary
implications.

The first poem:[3]

> they come
> different and the same

became in my treatment the section called *others*: (those that are external to the self, but whom one necessarily encounters). Its sexual undercurrent did not seem to me to dominate, completely, its implication.
Through this brief text, the device of paired alternatives is established,
and the fundamental dilemma of the simultaneous distinctiveness and
recessiveness of differences is posited.

The second poem:[4]

> what would I do without this world

is the origin of the second major part of my composition: *self*. Personal-
ized by the 'I', the voice here is an explorative one, conditional and
fatalistic. Death, or at least a diminished, 'convulsive' space, 'far from all
the living', is regretfully envisioned.

The prose section, the ninth of the *Texts for Nothing*, is the basis for
enquiry, the third and largest section of the whole. A series of *proposals*
is made (affirmation, assertion, observation, question, objection, realization), and each passes through a *response* (continuation, reconsidera-
tion, answer, objection, cry, conclusion) towards a *close* (which can
remain indecisive, develop or undergo transformation towards a new
proposal). This text is unexpected in the Dantesque affirmation it
reaches at the close: ('and see the beauties of the skies, and see the stars
again'). Another feature is the paired reference to origins (mother) and
ends (tomb).

The third poem:[5]

> my way is in the sand flowing
> between the shingle and the dune

describes the nature of the final section, *credo*. Beckett envisions peace
as the unencumbered state of 'a door that opens and shuts'. It was the

---

[3] See 'Poèmes 1937–1939', in Samuel Beckett, *Collected Poems 1930–1978* (London: John Calder, 1984), 41.
[4] See 'Six poèmes 1947–1949', ibid. 61.
[5] Ibid. 59.

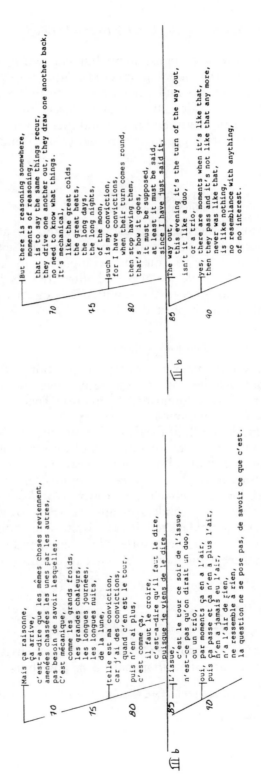

Fig. 15.6 *A passage from the parallel parsings of the French and English versions of* Texts for Nothing IX

images in this brief poem that were central for me in *Odyssey*. My associations were made between the shingle (specific words) and the dune (fluid meaning). My intention was to plumb the presumably unitary 'message' that existed in Beckett's creative mind, but was manifested through two distinctive though closely coordinated pathways, French and English. It seemed that an important intensification of the paired, male–female relationship of the first poem could be achieved by locating two bilingual speakers, so that—and this, of course, could only happen through the intercession of technology—the *same physical voice* (female in II and IV, male in III) could deliver the two texts simultaneously. The logical pathway was this: from one mind through two written languages to one executant who becomes a vessel for two spoken languages that reach a single auditor; it manifested a recurring cyclicity of the unitary and the multiple (each, reciprocally ambiguous). The process involved each executant rehearsing and recording the English text, section by section, while I functioned as a 'director', helping to shape and maintain the desired mood. When satisfactory English continuity was finalized, it was played back over headphones to the reader while the parallel French lines were produced in tandem, as though an elevated gloss.

When all of this material was fully coordinated and temporally interleaved, it was then spatialized by means of a computer. The text in each language appears to move in auditory space symmetrically, so that, for example, if the voice speaking English moves from the front centre into the distance on the right, the French speaking voice will move at the same time from the front centre into the distance on the left.

Since the overall work was to be musical in nature, including two vocalists, live instrumentalists and computer processed instrumental and vocal sounds stored on tape, the next step was to establish a formal scheme, or rather, more fundamentally, to establish the rationale for a formal scheme. In keeping with the inevitability of both sameness and disparity that Beckett's world of ideas invokes, I determined to appeal to recent developments in chaos theory as mentioned above. I adopted the Hénon attractor, a mathematical formula that models chaotic behaviour in an elegant, boomerang-shape.

Taking cross-sections of this provided a family of related, if irregularly proportioned, parts. Using them, I devised an overall plan of sectional durations that was directly indebted to chaos, both in its unexpected and in its deterministic aspects.

Just as the textual materials involve complementary alternatives (French–English, male–female, mother–tomb, etc.), there are paired relationships among the sixteen instrumentalists:

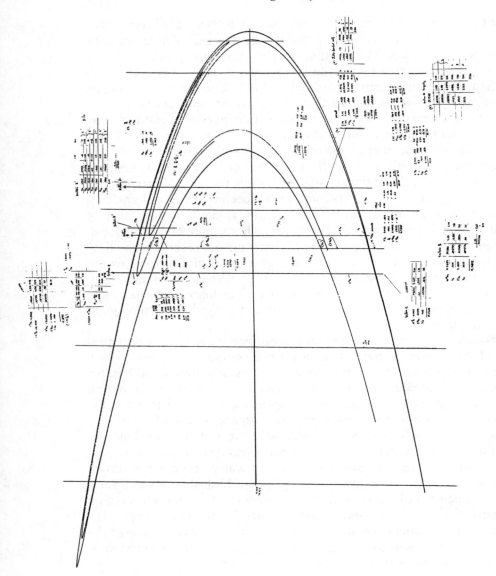

Fig. 15.7 *The Hénon Attractor with associated vertical cross-sections used in planning the form of Odyssey.*

(1)
flute   clarinet
oboe   bassoon
(2)
horn   trumpet
trombone   bass trombone
(3)
percussion 1   percussion 2   percussion 3
piano
(4)
violin 1   violin 2
cello   contrabass

Note that in the first there is only a relationship of instrumental principles (the oboe and bassoon are both double-reeds). In the second, there
are two instruments from the trombone family; in the third there is a
three-to-one relationship; only in the fourth are there two identical
instruments. These mutating distinctions in resources were exploited in
the composition in numerous ways.

Naturally, it is not possible, here, to undertake anything like a detailed
musical analysis of *Odyssey*. Rather, I have tried to suggest the many
ways as well as the different sorts of ways in which Beckett's texts
provoked reaction. Think of the three works I have discussed as involv-
ing 'virtual collaborations', which in fact they did. One immediately
realizes that in attempting to join with a creative visionary such as
Beckett, it is not for an instant thinkable to substitute one's own images
for his. After all, the exquisite reduction of his sauces results in a
concentration of substance and means that will brook no alteration. The
best that one can do, it is clear, is to give Beckett his own space. Thus,
in *Odyssey*, the presentation of the bilingual texts occurs in complete
darkness; only very slightly and very occasionally are they accompanied
in any way with other live or recorded materials.

Each time I have dealt with Beckett's work there has been a provocation, a resonance with other facets of my life as it was then being led,
and a response which reflected the emanations that I sensed from what
he had written. My contributions were not intended to elaborate, embel-
lish, or fill out his message, but rather to exist appropriately in its
vicinity. This is, perhaps, a curious pattern, or, perhaps, a curious
coincidence. His control has suggested my extremity.

16

Towards *Parole da Beckett*

Giacomo Manzoni
Translated from the Italian by Walter Redfern

At the start of the 1960s, there was much talk and writing about nuclear fall-out shelters. It was a very American vogue, and it seemed as if building oneself a fall-out shelter had become the distinguishing mark of the most well-to-do classes: it was *dernier cri*, and a proof that you had done so well in life that you could allow yourself not to fear even atomic war. These were crazy beliefs, of course, a pure and simple industrial and commercial opportunity, which nobody could really take seriously. It was in thinking about this phenomenon that the project of a theatre musical, *Atomtod* [*Atomdeath*], came about, with the intention of unmasking and denouncing this absurdity of present-day mankind. The stage was split, from a certain point in the development of the plot, into two sections: the external, which was to suggest an idea of desolation, linked with an encumbering mass of rubbish and rubble from an atomic explosion, as well as extending to piles of odd-shaped masses of a totally defenceless mankind; and some décors representing the interiors of atomic shelters, which we had seen being readied at the start of the performance. These were spaces thoroughly sealed against the outside world, in which small groups of hyper-privileged people enjoyed a security which turned out to be illusory: at the end they would be destroyed every bit as much as their fellow creatures who had remained outside, without any protection.

When I read, a little while after the first performance of *Atomtod* (at the Piccola Scala, 1965), some of Beckett's theatrical texts which I had not read before—in fact, at that time I scarcely ventured beyond *Godot* and some poems—I was struck by themes and settings which seemed to link up with the ideas both I and the author of the *Atomtod* text, Emilio Jona, had had. Between the setting of *Endgame* ('grey light'; 'curtains drawn'; 'covered with an old sheet, two ashbins'; 'Hanging near door, its face to wall, a picture', etc.), the 'den' of *Krapp's Last Tape*, and the setting we had devised for *Atomtod*, could be felt an affinity which bordered on identity to our eyes, but it was entirely unintended. The fact remains that with *Atomtod* I had started on a series of thoughts which discovered in general in Beckett's work an extraordinary integration and an enrichment of themes. There was then born the idea of a composition that might find in the works of this author their mainspring and their *raison d'être*. Reading further into Beckett I found myself before a very rich array of forms, impulses, possibilities: apart from the theatre, lyric poetry, novel, interior monologue, radio play, film. . . . My problem was what to do with this great profusion, how to find an acceptable musical solution. So was born a first, rather ambitious, project: the idea of a work which, making a montage of the most diverse Beckettian texts, would take account in the first place of the theatrical nature of the Beckettian *œuvre*, given that that seemed to me the essential (subsequently I felt less sure about this evaluation). And so the montage was sketched out substantially like a composition of visual type, yet without it being possible to speak of a straightforward theatre musical. Among working notes jotted down at the time—probably around 1965, as there is in my correspondence a letter from Beckett of December of that year in which he gives his consent to the project—I find the following thought:[1]

To understand the nature of this work, one needs to start not so much from the idea of musical theatre as from that of a cantata, an oratorio, or better still a sacred performance. The formal fragmentation of these pieces is carried here to extreme lengths, and very varied media are used, from the solo voice of a child to electronic tape, from an organ to an orchestra, from a reciting voice to an accompanied voice (and solo), and the real, proper theatre is finally suffused with the mime of 'Acte sans paroles', inserted into the general musical flux.

The stage is essential as the locus for sound happenings. Thus I imagine the child singing solo in the middle of the stage under a *certain* light; sometimes the stage will remain deserted and dark (or partly so), sometimes it will house the choir and the singers 'in concerto' (or else film screens with electronic tape).

   This formal/musical and visual fragmentation is pushed to the maximum degree according to shorter or longer arcs of tension, exhausted or else wiped out following a certain scheme. Parallel events can take place (after being first presented separately): for instance child + mime; or else: choir + film; or a silent mass + solo voice. The whole gets an obvious unity from a certain type of montage of the text. I am thinking of the use of true and proper orchestral 'monograms'; brief interventions by the tape; short and increasingly truncated phrases from the reciting voice; brief movements of the mimes (getting shorter and shorter); the whole intersecting and colliding and being superimposed, or vice versa.

---

[1] I keep the original form of the text as an aid to memory and in an unchecked form suitable for material meant for private consumption. All the same, I feel it might be useful to throw light on the intentions shaping that first choice of texts.

Is this a theatrical work? I wouldn't know. I would say that it is the realization of the possibilities of a 'pure' music carried right to the boundary with theatricality, at that moment when sound appeals for completion by an action which is nevertheless a function of the music itself, not of a third extraneous element: and so as oratorio and cantata, 'concerto' even, they are bordering on the scenic, to the extent to which the materiality of the performers requires it. *But these elements are not to be simplified*, making a game out of them. And in connection with allusions to the forms of cantata, oratorio, sacred performance, I still find amongst my notes of that period a feeble search for the formal working-out of some historical masterpieces, whose characteristics are clear from the viewpoint of the succession and the alternation of the ensembles and the durations: *Jephte* by Carissimi (historian; tenor; chorus; two sopranos, bass, etc.), Bach's B Minor Mass (chorus with orchestra; two sopranos-violin-bass continuo; chorus; soprano-violin-strings, etc.), *Dido and Aeneas* by Purcell (orchestra; soprano and chorus; soprano; soprano (recitative); chorus, etc.).

This research—which I have cited solely by way of an example of work-methods—was intended to create for the projected composition a formal frame, a reference-frame for the total structure; but it did not lead to very significant results, except the renewed pleasure of having spent a few hours with three magnificent products of the human intellect, and, on the other hand, the conception of the montage of 'musical visuality' or 'visualized music', which can be easily understood by looking at the project[2] set out at the end of these notes. From this conjunction there has still remained a tangible sign in some hypotheses of succession and alternation of the musical passages, for example:

speech
speech accompanied by orchestral music
recitative
sung
sung (solo), etc.
up to the point of joining with a succession which, embracing also the
    visual elements, corresponds to a large extent with the definitive
    version:

[2]   The project is obviously not complete in every detail. Apart from the frequent indications 'etc.', by which it is intended that the text continues on, normally on various lines, I point out that the column LIGHTS was abandoned half-way through, and that the wavy vertical lines indicating the duration of relevant episodes (sound or vision) are approximate, and at a certain point stop altogether. Furthermore, I have not carried forward a seventh column, DURATIONS, which, though also set up in advance, remained unused. On the other hand, it is possible to see how the vocal part (the first three columns) is linked together to a considerable extent, and is by now almost ready for the intervention of the music.

a reciter; loudspeaker
a chorus of women, sung, invisible
solo music
soloists + choir + reciter: spoken (invisible, + loudspeaker)
soprano, sung, invisible
two voices recited (with mimes on stage)
bass, sung: on stage, etc.

Further, the ensemble comprised 'a choir (divisible), 3–4 soloists, 2–3 reciters/actors, a mime (in reality perhaps two or more mimes), four sound-sources (loudspeakers), a children's chorus, a child, large orchestra'. It is easy to see—looking at the project in its complete form—that the one thing it is not about is a 'narrative' plot. The vocal contingent—solos, chorales, recited passages—intersect or overlap with the most diverse visual positions, through which I was aiming to give the most varied picture possible of the character of Beckett's theatre, even translating onto film a brief description taken from *How It Is* ('I see a crocus', etc.). The connection between the various elements—vocal, instrumental, visual, lighting—was probably of a purely reactive kind, sometimes accidental too: a vocal statement was answered by a visual datum in relation or in contrast with it; this would be followed in similar fashion by a vocal or orchestral element, and so was built up the great montage which I suppose could be programmed to last at least one hour. It stayed in my drawer for a long time, and seemed to have been forgotten for several years, almost certainly shelved to make room for other projects. (Between 1966 and 1969, some works which are very important to me were conceived: *Musica notturna* [*Night Music*], *Ombre* [*Shadows*, to the memory of Che Guevara], '*Insiemi*' ['*Sets*'].) But the work already done was slowly decanting, until it came back to the surface, though leading me in a different direction: it would serve as the basis for another composition, more compact and delimited, which was written between 1970 and the beginning of 1971: *Parole da Beckett* [*Words by Beckett*]. (The first performance took place in May 1971, directed by Bruno Maderna, in Rome).

How did this change of route come about? Probably, picking the project up again after a lapse of time, I found in it something that did not entirely convince me, and perhaps the main obstacle simply consisted in having allowed for a polyphony of musical and visual media which was in the end too rich, so that it damaged itself in the long run, in the huge complexity of the general structure; or else I realized—more or less consciously—that perhaps I was wreaking violence on Beckett's work, centrifuging it, so to speak, in a myriad of dispersed moments and aspects, and failing to seize the *climate* typical of this writer, his *psychological environment,* which demands concentration instead, immersion in a thematics which requires absorption, an undistracted listening, almost a meditation, across his words, on oneself: I believe it possible that I could have thought all this at the time, but I realize that I am making a completely hypothetical reconstruction.

The abandoned project did however prepare the ground for me to realize a composition of more limited dimensions and with less ambitious aims. It was a matter of stripping away, of selecting, of arranging the already existing text in a more compact way: indeed, that of *Parole da Beckett*[3] is taken in its entirety from the montage described earlier, as can easily be verified.[4] I sent the project to Beckett, asking him if he wanted to collaborate on it, but his reply, while very cordial, ruled out any such possibility, while still leaving me once again with full freedom of action. From that moment began the work on the musical structures, on the montage of diverse materials in terms of the poetical course of the text, on the preparation of the tape-recorded extracts, on the study for the spatialization of sound in accordance with the multiple acoustic sources. And one can perhaps discern here the intention to bring the variety of media used in the original project back to exclusively musical categories. It is true that the soloists are dropped, but the choir is subdivided into two groups (a chamber choir and a medium-sized choir), and the orchestra into three instrumental groups, which alternate, overlap, contrast (eight brass, seventeen stringed instruments, and a chamber group of twenty instruments); meanwhile, the presence of the tape becomes more and more substantial, as it handles choral material and a child's voice as well as the amplification and spatialization of the sound.[5]

There would be many other things to say, at this point, if I wished to go into the specific composition of the piece, ranging from the phonetic aspect—which is absolutely central—to the six distinct 'bodies' of the ensemble and the total formal structuring. But I think there is no reason to confront this in this article, and here ends the task I set myself: that of sketching out a journey which can be considered typical of the gestation of a particularly complex work, and which was likewise decisive in bringing into focus a theatrical work which was already beginning to emerge faintly from the background: the musical scenes *Per Massimiliano Robespierre* [*For Maximilian Robespierre*]. But that is another story altogether . . .

[3] Score, ed. by Ricordi, Milan, 1972. LP of the first performance in Rome, Fonit-Cetra, 1983.
[4] See Figure 16.1.
[5] For this aspect, see Figure 16.2.

SOLI (CANTO)	CORO	VOCI REC.	ORCHESTRA	AZIONE	LUCI
		voce masch., ampl. 'que ferais-je sans ce silence gouffre de murmures'	*attacca— informe— con amplif.*	*scena vuota— velluti neri*	*buio lentam. luce*
basso, cant. (in buca) 'puis les pas vers les vieilles lumières'	*donne, recit.; amplif.*'cantare troppo presto è un grave errore, ho scoperto. D'al=tra parte, può succedere di aspettare troppo'				
			musica sala— frastuono, sempre più f		
tutti, rec. ritmico (buca) 'vivas puellas mortui incurrunt boves— o subito subito prima che'	*recit. ritmico come* SOLI	*ritmico (amplif.) come* SOLI			
			silenzio		*lentam. buio*
sopr.—cantato lirico (buca) 'oh, ma questo sarà stato un giorno felice'		*voce masch., ampl.* 'ferais comme hier, comme aujourd'hui regardent' *ecc.*	*attacca, sfondo*		
		2 voci masch. 'Dovrebbe già essere qui. Non ha detto che verrà di sicuro. E se non viene? ecc.*		*due attori in scena—mimano le parti dei rec. ampl.*	*luce subito vivissima*
		Ha la barba il Signor G.?'	*vl. solo (buca)*	*exeunt*	*smorzare fino a un lieve barlume*
				cantante in scena, illuminato	
una voce (basso?) 'e a poco a poco vi prende una vera tristezza'	*parl., amplif.* 'uno sbandamento di sentieri e torrenti che scappano verso il mare'		*mus. più in rilievo—orch.*	*(film)* 'vedo un croco in un vaso in un cortiletto al	
		amplif. (un altop.) 'esco dal sonno e ci ritorno tra le due cose c'è tutto da fare, da sopportare da perdere da sbrigare da condurre a buon fine prima che il fango si riapra'		seminterrato uno zafferano il sole si arrampica lungo il muro una mano tiene al sole quel fiore giallo con una corda vedo la mano lunga immagine delle	*buio*
2 voci masch., invisibili ('conductus') 'può darsi che non sia ancora				ore il sole scompare il vaso ridiscende si posa a terra la mano scompare il muro scompare'	

[SOLI (CANTO)]	[CORO]	[VOCI REC.]	[ORCHESTRA]	[AZIONE]	[LUCI]
nient'affatto alla fine del mio viaggio'				*(segue film)*	
	bambini— amplif. 'Il giorne è ormai finito La notte si avvicina, L'ombra già ci porta L'ora vespertina'	*amplif.—(un altop.)* 'son così poco abituato al fatto che mi si chieda qualcosa' ecc.		*(uomo in scena* *esce)*	
		(a 3, mormorato) 'yes 'yes 'yes strange per= peace Dark= haps One ness A sha assu best' de' med' ecc. ecc. ecc. *voce masch.* 'Mio figlio dorme. Che dorma pure. Verrà la notte in cui anch'egli, non riuscendo a dormire, si metterà al suo tavolo di lavoro. Io sarò dimenticato'	*sfondo— rumore— amplificazione* *(alternata con recitazione + sfondo costante di amplificaz.?)*	*uomo in scena*	
voce femm. 'a meno che ti amino'	*masch. o misto* 'a meno che ti amino'	*voce masch.* 'un bel giorno, quando meno te lo aspetti, ritorna a galla. È questo che trovo meraviglioso'	*musica più elaborata* *(più confusa)*	*exit*	
	uomini (ritm., parlato, sprechg.) (invisibili) 'stanco di morire, stanco di poliziotti, il viso nel fango, la bocca aperta, il fango nella bocca, l'umanità riconquistata'				
uomo? donna? (invisibili) 'e il vetro terso sopra i tuoi occhi'			*dissolvenza del film*	*luce lentam., fino a essere molto cruda,*
		uno o pochi str.		

[SOLI (CANTO)]	[CORO]	[VOCI RECIT.]	[ORCHESTRA]	[AZIONE]	[LUCI]
	bambini recit. (amplif.) 'poi per miglia e miglia soltanto vento'	una voce (2? 3?) mormorato, soffiato, grave, faticoso (amplif.) 'questa terra clonica, perio= dicamente offuscata dal sonno è grassa, morta il resto gira a vuoto'	(sfondo)	scena vuota, con senso di profondità sconfinata	bianca
soprano (ampl.) 'perché il mio vegliare era una specie di sonno'	uomini, parlato [punteggiature al soprano]				
	un bambino 'Un cane andò in cucina E s'accostò al fornello Allora col coltello Il cuoco lo sgozzò Allora gli altri cani Scavarono una fossa E sulla terra smossa Scrissero con la coda Un cane andò . . .'		(nastro?)	un bambino in mezzo alla scena	
		voce masch., amplif. 'la natura ci ha dimenticato'		exit	
	parlato, amplif. 'non c'è più natura'				
	donne, invisibili [echi a voce masch. rec., vedi}	'niente emozioni, tutto è perduto il fondo è scoppia= to l'umidità' ecc. ecc.		proiezioni su più schermi	
	uomini parl., donne cant. (eco) 'non me ne intendo troppo di lacrime e di risa'				
		voce masch. 'c'è sempre la mia storia, naturalmente, quan=do tutto il resto viene a mancare'		un uomo in scena	
donna e uomo 'et vivrai le temps d'une porte qui s'ouvre et se re= ferme'				exit uomo e donna in scena	
		una voce (amplif.) 'non voler dire, non	quasi niente		

[SOLI (CANTO)]	[CORO]	[VOCI REC.]	[ORCHESTRA]	[AZIONE]	[LUCI]
voce femm., invisibile 'un altro giorno divino'		sapere quel che si vuol dire, non poter dire quel' *ecc.*			
	tutti gridato 'trovare ancora delle parole quando sono' *ecc.*	(come coro)	*inserti nel gridato*	*proiezioni di moltitudine*	
	recit. (amplif.) 'e la mente annullata nau =fraga nel vento'			'ATTOI SENZA PAROLE'	
		a 2 o 3, mormo= rato, amplif. 'straordinario come le matematiche vi aiutino a conoscervi: non passa quasi giorno senza un arricchimento del proprio sapere' *ecc.ecc.*			
		a 3, sfasati, rapido 'e quando per esempio dico preferire, o rimpiangere, non si deve credere che io' *ecc. ecc.*		*3 sulla scena?*	
basso, sprechst. amplif. 'stavo glà ammucchiandomi nella mia stasi da straccio, quando mi ricordai che era una cosa da non fare'					
			duetto dalla Vedova allegra		
		2 voci 1° 'a che somiglia questo posto? 2° Non si può de scriverlo. Non somiglia a niente. Non c'è niente [C'è un albero]'		*2 attori in scena*	
	tutti parl. (amplif.) 'dovessi mai ottenere che il fango s'aprisse sotto di me e poi si richiudesse'				

4

[SOLI]	[CORO]	[VOCI RECIT.]	[ORCHESTRA.]	[AZIONE]	[LUCI]
		una voce 'è questo che tro vo meraviglioso. La capacità di adattamento dell' uomo. Alle più diverse condizioni'		*recitante sulla scena*	
	recit.—amplif. 'tre volte venne l'uomo delle pompe funebri' *ecc. ecc.*				
basso = donne coro	*donne (cant.), invisi= bili* 'troppo tardi per rischiarare il cielo'				
bambino, urlato (amplif.) 'che ma =ledizione la mobilità'					
		voce masch., sus surrato—amplif. 'se potessi diventa= re sordo e cieco cre= do che riuscirei a tira re avanti fino a cent anni'		fine 'ATTOI'	
2 voci femm. (in= visibili) 'questo sarà stato un altro giorno felice' *voce masch. (in= frammezzata con orch.) (recit.)* 'e dietro le mie palpebre chiuse la piccola notte in cui delle macchie chiare nascono, fiammeggiano, si estinguono, ora vuota, ora popolata' *ecc.*			'melologo' con voce masch.	*cantante sulla scena*	
	donne, frusciato— amplif. (nessuna risposta)	*voce masch. (ampl.)* 'allora può cambiare		*attore in scena*	
		finire			
	(nessuna risposta)	potrei soffocare			
	(nessuna risposta)	inabissarmi il buio			
		non turbare più il silenzio			
	(nessuna risposta) tutti—uomini e donne 'urla	crepare			
		CREPARE			
		IO POTREI CREPARE			
	urla				
soprano, recit., rotto, sottovoce 'adesso cose talmente vecchie le sento le mormoro tali e quali pianissimo al fango'	urla' *donne (vocalizzi su solista)*	IO CREPERÒ			

[SOLI]	[CORO]	[VOCI RECIT.]	[ORCHESTRA]	[AZIONE]	[LUCI]
basso (cant.) 'pleurant celle qui crut m'aimer'	*donne {vocaliz =zi su solista}*	*una voce (cantic= chiando; amplif.)*			scena vuota, nuda, illuminazione fino alla fine
		'Then down a little way' *ecc. ecc. fino a:* 'My Lord!'			
		'My Lord!	sound of club let fall shuffling slippers, with halts. They die away. Long pause		
		Bob!	pause		
		Bob!	brief rude retort		
		Music!	*imploring*		
		Music	Pause. Rap of baton and statement with ele= ments already used or wellhead alone. Pause.		
		Again	Pause. Imploring		
		Again!	As before or only very slightly varied		
	tutti (amplif.) (deep sigh)				buio subito

CALA RAPIDAMENTE LA TELA

6

Page 1

SOLOISTS (SONG)

bass, sung (in pit): 'then the steps towards the lighted town'
everyone, rhythmic recitation (pit): 'vivas puellas mortui incurrrrrsant boves/oh subito subito ere she'
soprano, lyrical song (pit): 'this will have been another happy day'
a voice (bass?): 'and little by little . . . you begin to grieve'
two male voices, invisible ('conductus'): 'and perhaps my course is not yet fully run'

Page 1 cont.

CHOIR

women, recit., amplif: 'to sing too soon is fatal, I always find. On the other hand it is possible to leave it too late'
rhythmical recit: Like SOLOISTS
spoken, amplified: 'a rout of tracks and streams fleeing to the sea'

REC. VOICES

male voices, ampl: 'what would I do without this world faceless incurious'
rhythmical recit: Like SOLOISTS
male voices, ampl: 'would I do what I did yesterday and the day before peering out', etc.
two male voices: 'he should be here. He didn't say for sure he'd come. And if he doesn't come?'
'has he a beard, Mr. G?'
amplif. (loudspeaker): 'from sleep I come to sleep return between the two there is all all the doing suffering failing bungling achieving until the mud yawns again'

ORCHESTRA

strike up—shapeless—with amplif.
(pit)—hubbub, getting louder
silence
strike up, background
vl. solo (pit)
music more in prominence—
orch.

ACTION

empty stage—black velvet
2 actors on stage—they mime the parts of ampl. rec.
exeunt
singing on stage, illuminated
(film): 'I see a crocus in a pot in an area in a basement a saffron the sun creeps up the wall a hand keeps it in the sun this yellow flower with a string I see the hand long image hours long the sun goes the pot goes down lights on the ground the hand goes the wall goes.'

LIGHTS

darkness, slowly light
slowly darkness
sudden dazzling light
extinguish down to a light glimmer
darkness

Page 2

SOLOISTS (SONG)
'and perhaps my course is not yet fully run'
voice of a woman: 'unless they love you'
man? woman? (invisible): 'and the glass unmisted above your eyes'

CHOIR
children—amplif.: 'now the day is over I Night is drawing nigh. I
   Shadows of the evening I Steal across the sky'
male or mixed: 'unless they love you'
men (rhythmical, spoken, Sprechgesang); (invisible): 'tired of dying, tired of policemen, the face in the mud, the mouth open, the
   mud in the mouth, abating humanity regained'

REC. VOICES
amplif.—(loudspeaker): 'I am so little used to being asked anything'
(3, murmured):

'yes	'yes	'yes
strange	per-	peace
Dark-	haps	One
ness	A sha	assu
best'	de'	med'
etc.	etc.	etc.

male voices: 'My son is sleeping. Let him sleep. The night will
   come when he too, unable to sleep, will get up and go to his
   desk. I shall be forgotten'
male voices: 'Another heavenly day. It will come back, that is what
   I find so wonderful, all comes back'

ORCHESTRA
background—noise—amplification
(alternating with recitation + constant background of amplification?)
more elaborate music
(more confused)
one or a few instruments

ACTION
(follows film)
(a man on stage)
(he leaves)
a man on stage
exit
fading of the film

LIGHTS
light slowly, eventually very harsh

Page 3

SOLOISTS (SONG)
Soprano (amplif.): 'for my waking was a kind of sleeping'
woman and man: 'and live the space of a door that opens and shuts'

CHOIR
children recit. (amplif.): 'then for miles only wind'
men, spoken (punctuations to the soprano)
a child: 'a dog came in the kitchen I And stole a crust of bread I The cook up with a ladle I And beat him till he was dead I Then all the dogs came running I And dug the dog a tomb I And wrote upon the tombstone I For the eyes of dogs to come I A dog came in the kitchen . . .'
spoken, amplif.: 'there's no more nature'
women, invisible: (echoes to male rec. voices: see next column)
men speaking, women singing (echo): 'tears and laughter, they are so much Gaelic to me'.

RECIT. VOICES
a voice (2? 3?), murmured, whispered, grave, weary (amplif.): 'this clonic earth see-saw she is blurred in sleep she is fact half dead the rest is free wheeling'
male voice, amplif.: 'nature has forgotten us'
'no emotion all is lost the bottom burst the wet', etc.
male voice: 'there is my story of course, when all else fails'
a voice (amplif.): 'not to want to say, not to know what you want to say, not to be able to say what' etc.

ORCHESTRA
(background)
(tape?)
almost nothing

ACTION
empty stage, with a sense of bottomless depths
a child in middle of stage
exit
projections on more screens
a man on stage
exit
man and woman on stage

LIGHTS
white

Page 4

SOLOISTS (SONG)
woman's voice, invisible: 'another heavenly day'
bass, speaking, amplif: 'I was already settling in my raglimp stasis
  when I remembered it wasn't done'

CHOIR
all shouting: 'find more words'
recit. (amplif.): 'and the mind annulled wrecked in wind'
all speaking (amplif.): 'were it the signal for the mud to open
  under me and then close again'

REC. VOICES
(like the choir)
2 or 3, murmured, amplif.: 'extraordinary how mathematics help
  you to know yourself'
'not a day goes by . . . without some addition to one's knowledge'
3, out of phase, quickly: 'and when I talk of preferring, for example, or regretting, it must not be supposed that I . . .'
2 voices: 1: 'What is it like?' 2: 'It's indescribable. It's like nothing.
  There's nothing. [There's a tree]'

ORCHESTRA
inserts in the shouting
duet from The Merry Widow

ACTION
projections of multitude
'ACTS WITHOUT WORDS'
3 on stage?
2 actors on stage

Page 5

SOLOISTS
bass = women, choir
child, shrieking (amplif.): 'What a curse, mobility'
2 women's voices (invisible): 'This will have been another happy day'
male voice (interwoven with orchestra) (recit.): 'behind my closed
  lids the little night and its little lights, faint at first, then flaming
  and extinguished, now ravening, now fed'
soprano, recit., broken, in an undertone: 'in the present things so
  ancient hear them murmur them as they come barely audible to
  the mud'

Page 5 cont.

CHOIR
recit.—amplif.: 'thrice he came | the undertaker's man'
women (singing), invisible: 'too late to brighten the sky'
women, babbling—amplif. (no response)
(no response)
(no response)
(no response)
all—men and women
'shout
shout
shout'
women (vocalizations with soloist)

RECIT. VOICES
a voice: 'that is what I find so wonderful. The way man adapts
   himself. To changing conditions'
male voices, whispering, amplif.: 'if I could go deaf and dumb I
   think I might pant on to be a hundred'
male voices (amplif.): 'so things may change | end I may | choke
   sink | the dark | trouble the | peace no more | the silence | die |
   DIE | I MAY DIE | I SHALL DIE

ORCHESTRA
speech accompanied by orchestra music, with male voices

ACTION
reciters on stage
end of 'ACTS'
singer on stage
actor on stage

Page 6

SOLOISTS
bass (singing): 'mourning her who thought she loved me'

CHOIR
women (vocalizations with soloist)
all (amplif.): (deep sigh)

RECIT. VOICES
a voice (humming: amplif.): 'Then down a little way' *etc.,*
                              up to 'My Lord!'
                              'My Lord!

Page 6 cont.

Bob!
Bob!
Music!
Music
Again
Again!'

ORCHESTRA
sound of club
let fall
shuffling
slippers, with
halts. They
die away.
Long pause
pause
brief rude
retort
imploring
Pause. Rap of
baton and
statement
with ele-
ments already
used or
wellhead
alone. Pause.
Pause.
Imploring
As before or
only very
slightly varied
LIGHTS
empty stage, bare, illumination till the end
sudden darkness
CURTAIN RAPIDLY FALLS

che farei senza questo silenzio dove si spengono i bisbigli

stanco di morire

farei come ieri come oggi guardando dal mio oblò se non sono solo a errare a girare lontano da ogni vita in uno spazio spasmodico senza voce tra le voci chiuse con me

non voler dire non sapere quel che si vuol dire non poter dire quel che si crede di voler dire e sempre dire o quasi ecco quel che bisogna non perdere di vista nell'ardore della stesura

vivas puellas mortui incurrrrrsant boves

niente emozione tutto è perduto il fondo è scoppiato l'umidità il trascinio l'abrasione gli amplessi le generazioni un vecchio sacco da carbone cinquanta chili, benissimo, tutto andato le scatole l'apriscatole un apriscatole senza scatole mi è stato risparmiato, scatole senza apriscatole stavolta nella vita questo non mi sarebbe capitato

puis les pas vers les vieilles lumières

un altro giorno divino

Mio figlio dorme. Che dorma pure. Verrà la notte in cui anch'egli, non riuscendo a dormire, si metterà al suo tavolo di lavoro. Io sarò dimenticato

a meno che ti amino

stanco di morire stanco di poliziotti il viso nel fango la bocca aperta il fango nella bocca la sete che si perde l'umanità riconquistata

morire

questa terra clonica/periodicamente offuscata dal sonno/è grassa mezzo morta il resto gira a vuoto

esco dal sonno e ci ritorno tra le due cose c'è tutto da fare da sopportare da perdere da sbrigare da condurre a buon fine prima che la melma si riapra

Un cane andò in cucina/e si accostò al fornello./Allora col coltello/il cuoco lo sgozzò./Ciò visto gli altri cani/scavarono una fossa/e sulla terra smossa scrissero con la coda:/Un cane andò in cucina...

Dovrebbe già essere qui./Non ha detto che verrà di sicuro./E se non viene?/Torneremo domani./E magari dopodomani./Forse/E così di seguito./Insomma.../Fino a quando non verrà./Sei spietato./Siamo già venuti ieri./Ah no! Non esagerare, adesso!/Cosa abbiamo fatto ieri?/...Ha detto sabato. Mi pare./...Ma quale sabato? E poi, è sabato oggi? Non sarà poi domenica? O lunedì? O venerdì?/Non è possibile.

e la mente annullata/naufraga nel vento

piangendo quella che ha creduto di amarmi adesso cose talmente vecchie le sento le mormoro tali e quali pianissimo al fango

e può darsi che non sia ancora alla fine del mio viaggio

se potessi diventare sordo e muto credo che riuscirei a tirare avanti fino ai cent'anni

bisbigli
non passa quasi giorno
sempre la mia storia
questo sarà stato
mi si chieda qualcosa
...sapere cosa sia
stasi da straccio
nascono...
si estinguono... spazzature di santi
si aprisse sotto di me

allora può cambiare, finire, potrei soffocare, inabissarmi, non insozzare più, il fango, il buio, non turbare più, il silenzio, crepare, CREPARE, IO POTREI CREPARE, IO CREPERO

anche questo è stato un altro giorno felice

Fig. 16.1 *Montage of texts from Manzoni's* Parole da Beckett

what would I do without this world faceless incurious

tired of dying

would I do what I did yesterday and the day before peering out of my deadlight looking for another wandering like me eddying far from all the living in a convulsive space among the voices voiceless

not to want to say, not to know what you want to say, not to be able to say what you think you want to say, and never to stop saying, or hardly ever, that is the thing to keep in mind, even in the heat of composition

vivas puellas mortui incurrrrsant boves

no emotion all is lost the bottom burst the wet the dragging the rubbing the hugging the ages old coal-sack five stone six stone that hangs together all gone the tins the opener an opener and no tins I'm spared that this time tins and no opener I won't have had that in my life this time

then the steps towards the lighted town

another happy day

My son is sleeping. Let him sleep. The night will come when he too, unable to sleep, will get up and go his desk. I shall be forgotten

unless they love you

tired of dying tired of policemen

the face in the mud the mouth open the mud in the mouth thirst abating humanity regained

dying

this clonic earth/see-saw she is blurred in sleep/she is fact half dead the rest is free wheeling

from sleep I come to sleep return between the two there is all all the doing suffering failing bungling achieving until the mud yawns again

A dog came in the kitchen/And stole a crust of bread./The cook up with a ladle/And beat him till he was dead./Then all the dogs came running/And dug the dog a tomb/And wrote upon the tombstone/For the eyes of dogs to come:/A dog came in the kitchen...

He should be here./He didn't say for sure he'd come./And if he doesn't come?/We'll come back tomorrow./Possibly./And so on./The point is-/Until he comes./You're merciless./We came here yesterday./Ah no, there you're mistaken./What did we do yesterday?/...He said Saturday. I Think./...But what Saturday? And is it Saturday? Is it not rather Sunday? Or Monday? Or Friday?'

and the mind annulled/wrecked in wind

mourning the first and last to love me

in the present things so ancient hear them murmur them as they come barely audible to the mud

and perhaps my course is not yet fully run

if I could go deaf and dumb I think I might pant on to be a hundred.

the murmurs
not a day goes by
my story of course
this will have been
when I am asked something
to know what
my raglimp stasis
then flaming and extinguished
as fire by filth and martyrs
to open under me

so things may change end I may choke sink the dark trouble the peace no more the silence die DIE I MAY DIE I SHALL DIE

this will have been another happy day

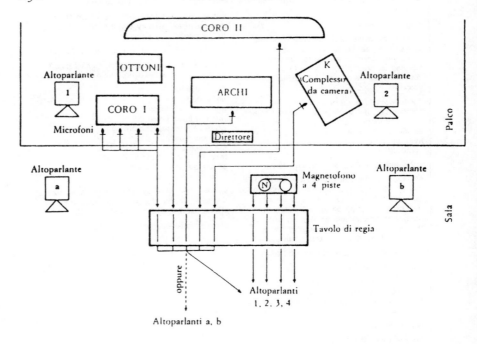

Fig. 16.2 *Layout of choirs and instrumental groups and plan of magnetic tape and amplification system for Manzoni's* Parole da Beckett

17

Songs Within Words: the Programme *TXMS* and the Performance of *Ping* on the Piano

CLARENCE BARLOW

It was in early 1971 that I first treated music as an abstract art. My compositions previous to this show an abundance of permutatory and probabilistic mechanisms, but their methods of application and the resultant sounds were invariably and obviously a product of my cultural background, a phenomenon even more evident in my recent work. In 1971, however, a passing need to purge my methods of personal traits drove me to a closer awareness of the role of cultural roots within the act of composing.

In my eyes, the work of John Cage, then meaningful to me, sought to circumvent musical tradition by generating unpredictable sounds through multiple and complex operations. These he entrusted nonetheless to musicians, without whose cultural specialization the intended work could neither be realized nor performed.

I sought the reverse—a compositional mechanism plus sound generator neither entailing the need for a musician nor thereby precluding the 'musical'. Research soon indicated a familiar household object as an appropriate sound machine of well-balanced lay accessibility and potential musical yield: in Pidgin terms, if I am correct, a 'Big-Black-Box-He-Got-White-Black-Teeth-All-Time-You-Fight-Him-He-Cry-Out'.

I refer of course to the Piano, which, as I wrote later, simply 'possesses fifty-two white and thirty-six black keys, which on being pressed can engender sounds, soft or loud, depending on the force used. They can furthermore be pressed singly or severally at once. The sounds resulting can be made to cease at any time, shortly after they commence or after being allowed to die away over a relatively long period. Of the two pedals visible at the bottom, the more effective one on the right permits sounds played in succession to continue sounding together.'[1] None of the terms used in this description necessitates musical knowledge.

For my compositional tool, I sought generally available pre-structured material, such as a catalogue or telephone book or (plainer and more

---

[1] From programme of a concert on 2 Feb. 1985 in America House, Cologne (Cologne Society for New Music), 7. Translated from the German by the author.

practical) a text, plus a simple means of translating this into sound. The result was *Textmusic for Piano*, a composition described in the same programme note (p. 7) as 'consisting solely of the instructions listed below; the extreme simplicity of these instructions was geared towards a reduction of the amount of musical knowledge necessarily pre-supposable in the potential realizer and therewith of links to the body of tradition'.

TEXTMUSIC FOR PIANO (4 APRIL 1971)

Take a text consisting of a number of words, phrases or sentences. Prepare the keys of the piano in the following way: A key somewhere in the middle of the keyboard is marked with the first letter of the chosen text. The next keys of the same colour, alternating to left or right (or vice versa) are treated with the succeeding letters in the text; if a certain letter occurs a second time, it should be dropped, and instead the next letter which has not yet occurred taken, until every letter of the text is represented on the keyboard. This procedure is then repeated with the keys of the other colour; and then yet a third time, without taking the colour of the keys into consideration. The text can now be 'played' according to the three key-colour-systems, and one can:

* 1. play the letters singly, or together as syllables, words, phrases (in their order of appearance in the text) or even an entire sentence: in all cases, the sound should be repeated as often as the number of syllables it contains.*

* 2. change the position of the right pedal (between depressed and released), the loudness (between loud and soft), and the length of the sound (between short and long) at best only at change of syllable, and the key-colour at best only at change of word.*[2]

This was better said than done: to this day, not a single non-musician has volunteered to realize and/or perform a version of *Textmusic*. Curiosity and the lack of choice prompted me to do this myself: declaring the above set of instructions as the Text in question, I realized a twenty-minute piece now known as *Version 1* and performed it in a concert at Cologne Music Academy on 4 March 1972. Particularly satisfying to me during its realization was my being permitted to indulge in two addictions at once—language and music—orthography and syntax of the former being rendered audible on the tonal-rhythmic and formal plane. The three key-colour-modes (black, white, mixed) yielded music penta-

---

[2] *Textmusic for Piano* (Cologne: Feedback Studio [FB7305]), 1973.

tonic, diatonic, and chromatic, not a popular choice in those days of the late avant-garde. Herbert Henck's performance at the Darmstadt Summer Course of 1972 triggered an intense, mainly negative public reaction, which lasted as long again as the piece itself. However, according to Rudolf Frisius, who reviewed this concert: '*Textmusic* [. . .] generates an unusual state of suspension between seemingly consonant and seemingly dissonant intervals, between apparent periodicity in the foreground and an unobtrusive change in the general movement, [. . .] yielding a consistent and novel sound, even though no unconventional piano techniques were resorted to.'[3]

During the autumn of 1971, I was able to formulate the realization processes involved in the making of *Version 1* as a Fortran computer programme named *TXMS*,[4] input being transferred to punched cards from a set of forms filled in by a prospective realizer: see Figure 17.1, where probability is shown as a function of time. Of the fourteen versions following, six were made in 1972–3 with this programme, two of them (Nos. 4 and 8) by myself, and the other four (Nos. 2, 3, 5, and 6) by various colleagues. The text material used here ranged from a newspaper leading article on the then rampant Vietnam War, through a 1930s song text in Cologne dialect by a popular songwriter of that city, through Schwitter's *An Anna Blum*, to Beckett's *Murphy* and *Ping* (with an excerpt from de Sade's *La Nouvelle Justine* inserted in the middle of the last-named). The fifteen versions of *Textmusic* range in duration from two minutes (No. 10, 1974) to just under four hours, this being No. 6,[5] on *Ping*, realized by Richard Toop in 1973 and first performed only nine years later by Thomas Silvestri in Walter Zimmermann's *Studio Beginner*, Cologne.

Subsequent performances of *Textmusic* 6 by Silvestri in various European cities and by Mats Persson in Stockholm, and James Clapperton in The Hague, revealed an interesting pattern of public behaviour: no matter how many people were initially seated in the auditorium, there were almost invariably six left at the end. During a Beckett festival in Frankfurt's Theater Am Turm in the early 1980s, all but twenty of a 200-strong audience stormed out thunderously after an endurance of just about five minutes.

It is not unusual for people well schooled in one of the arts to be totally at a loss in another. Audiences for contemporary theatre and those for contemporary music form no exception. The highly specialized nature of the arts to which they respectively adhere make these groups

---

[3] Rudolf Frisius, 'Ein musikalisches Forum verliert sein Format', *Neue Musikzeitung* (Oct./Nov. 1972), 3. Translated from the German by the author.
[4] Published in 1973 in Cologne by Feedback Studio (FB7318).
[5] Published in 1973 in Cologne by Feedback Studio (FB7305F).

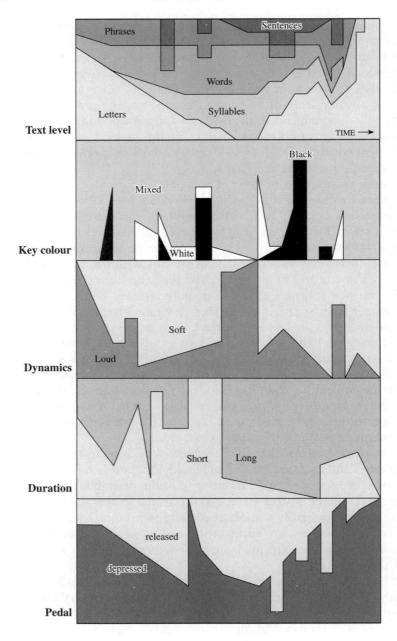

Fig. 17.1 TXMS *parameter form filled out for* Textmusic 6

more often than not immiscible, similarities of language and music (outlined below) notwithstanding. Never did I experience the Theater Am Turm phenomenon related above in a purely musical context; yet it came as no surprise, and therefore was of no immediate consequence to myself. An audience's cultural background, coupled with the performance venue—whether in a theatre, concert hall, or art gallery, in a large, medium-sized, or small city—shapes the reception offered to a given work in a more or less predictable way. More cross-cultural events would probably help to remove the barriers between the arts. At a performance of *Textmusic 6* at a Beckett Festival in The Hague in 1992, the audience (apart from some troublemakers at the rear who soon left) was more patient, though initially far smaller.

Written language exhibits in its orthographic hierarchy (letters, syllables, words, phrases, sentences) and syntactic form (modular recurrence) a structure intrinsically musical, permitting its viable transfer to that domain. *Textmusic* owes its existence to this.

Version 6 is a sensitive piece of music, passing in its long course almost unnoticeably from one constellation (e.g. slow, soft, single notes) to another (e.g. fast, virtuosic passages or a mixture of all possibilities). However, as in the other versions, it owes a large part of its basic character to the chosen text (here, *Ping*), providing an instance of unusually concentrated prose bearing a strong resemblance in its inner structure to music itself. (*Justine*'s brief appearance is not significant and will not be treated here.)

On a simple level, a comparison between a traditional piece of music and one of prose shows the former to consist of notes often grouped into chords, and the latter of letters mainly grouped into words. In music, a stream of single successive notes can also show a degree of such mutual cohesion as to coalesce, as it were, into a note-group or a broken chord. In any case, the level on which both music and prose start to be meaningful is the 'event' in time, which here means notes, chords, and words. However, the first significant difference to be seen here is in the vocabulary, which tends to be more limited in music than in prose.

Take the well-known melody of Ravel's *Bolero*, for instance: its first part contains 101 notes, of which only nine are different, showing an exhaustivity of less than 9 per cent. In the second part, this value more than doubles, to 19 per cent. Here, there are eighty-eight notes, of which seventeen differ. Going back in history to Mozart's *Musical Dice Game*, well exemplifying the typical music of that time, we find sixty-five notes, chords and trills combined in various ways to form 1,203 events in all, an exhaustivity of 5.4 per cent.

To take an example from this century: the first part of Stravinsky's *Danse Sacrale* from *The Rite of Spring* (rehearsal numbers 142–8) forms a succession of fifty-nine chords and twenty-three interspersed bass notes drawing on a repertoire of twelve and two, respectively, the overall exhaustivity being 17 per cent. Proceeding similarly in the final part (numbers 195–200) the value obtained is 16 per cent. Rather more recently: Conlon Nancarrow's *Study No. 7* exhibits an exhaustivity of 33 per cent. An increase in the number of events examined in each case would indeed further lower the percentage.

By way of contrast, Tom Johnson's *Chord Catalogue* is 100 per cent exhaustive, because not one of the chords therein occurs twice: all seventy-eight two-note, 286 three-note, 715 four-note, 1,287 five-note (etc.) chords possible in one octave are played once each, as is to be expected from the title. But works of this nature are bound to be the exception; I have deliberately restricted my observations here to music of a less self-conscious nature.

In comparably non-experimental prose, the vocabulary tends to be somewhat richer—four random excerpts of roughly 1,000 words each taken from transcripts of lectures held in English by scholars of different origins showed percentage values of 47 per cent, 45 per cent, 43 per cent, and 38 per cent for the French, English, German, and Palestinian lecturers respectively.

Not so in Beckett's *Ping*, where a text of 962 words draws on a vocabulary of only 123 (13 per cent). His 1,103-word text *Imagination Dead Imagine*, published in the same collection, uses significantly more—37 per cent—though this value, too, lies more in the range of traditional musical usage.

In *Textmusic 6*, single words of the Beckett text keep returning as melodies and chords, giving the whole an enormous homogeneity familiar in the original. Take, for instance, the word *light*, which occurs thirty-two times: it is rendered in the 'mixed' or chromatic key-colour mode as the hauntingly beautiful:

Fig. 17.2

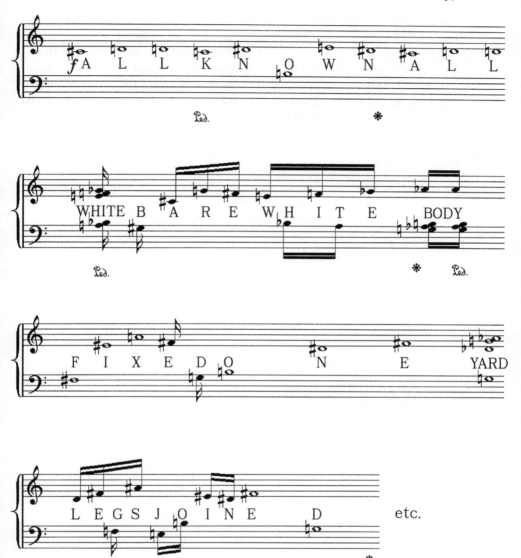

Fig. 17.3 *The first minute of* Textmusic 6 *(shown here with* Ping*)*

sometimes in sequence and sometimes as a chord, sometimes fleeting, sometimes lingering. Compare these notes with those for the most frequent word *white* (ninety-one times) as seen in the beginning of the piece, shown in Figure 17.3, where there is an ascending chromatic scale for the letters in italics and a descending one for those underlined.

Textmusic 6 is a sort of slow-motion rendition of *Ping*, in which Beckett's characteristic syntax, despite licence in matters such as tempo, is faithfully adhered to. Further, this syntax is a valuable musical ingredient in the piece. Finally, the emotions evoked by the music can be seen to bear a viable relation to those engendered by the original text.

18

Between Word and Silence: *Bing*[1]

JEAN-YVES BOSSEUR
Translated from the French by Mary Bryden

How can we initiate a musical process in relation to a text by Samuel Beckett without taking away its nakedness, and violating its essential purity? How can we undertake a temporal project which is likely to place word and sound on equal terms? How can we conceive a musical thought which does not just tack itself onto the literary discourse, but which can melt into it? These are just a few of the questions I pondered when I first considered working on a text by Samuel Beckett. In fact, I did not wish to set to music a pre-existent text, but rather to inflect it in a musical or even operatic direction—preferably with Beckett's cooperation—while somehow bringing out its inherent musicality. In fact Beckett's writing already seemed musical to me, each text having its own rhythm, and that is why I wasn't the slightest bit surprised when he told me, during our first meeting, that he dreaded the domination by music of a spoken word which in itself represented an attempt to interweave these two modes of expression.

Among the various texts suitable for such a project, Beckett suggested *Bing*, no doubt because it contains a very particular exploration of the concepts of repetition and variation, with words and expressions coming back repeatedly, internally arranged in seventy 'sentences' stripped of all punctuation. I could discern an opening of sorts for a musical interpretation of the verbal placements within the whole, and decided to take the text on board as if its music were already formulated, and to react to it as I had in the past with regard to works by Schumann, Monteverdi, or Satie.

But the difficulty remained of transferring a text whose display and timing were designed for reading in a book to the time and space of a stage performance. *Bing* is in effect a kind of proliferating narrative, not a theatrical work.

---

[1] This is a translated and modified version of Jean-Yves Bosseur's article, 'Entre Parole et silence: *Bing*', which appeared in *Revue d'esthétique* (special number on Beckett, 1986), 261–4.

I had originally envisaged a choral score; the choir would be positioned at different heights, under spotlights which would illuminate only their faces. The successive textual elements would be shared out amongst them in a manner which would be both discontinuous and linear; even if the voices did not superimpose on each other, I wanted there to emerge an impression of a polyphony of voices and faces, with a large portion given over to silence. The words would never be sung, but a few muffled sounds would be heard here and there; the vocal register would hover between murmuring and speaking. However, Beckett seemed a little put off by the idea of so many people being on the stage, and suggested that the vocal contingent should be reduced to six participants at most.

I therefore started by inscribing the text within a score designed for six speaking voices, sharing the rhythms between word and silence, never compromising their intelligibility, but simply extending their musical potentiality, taking infinite care not to force the text into an alien rhetoric of composition, and to remain close to it without seeking to invest it with too much of myself.

Each 'sentence' is allocated to one or several voices, and linked to a play of spotlights, as subtle as possible in accordance with various forms of counterpoint and imitation, the common denominator still being the concentration upon relative durations and time-modulations; the words occur within sequences marked out by lighting changes, which 'articulate' them rhythmically.

When I felt sufficiently suffused with the text, and increasingly fascinated as its elements kept returning higgledy-piggledy to my mind, I undertook to compose an instrumental structure (for piano, clarinet, cello, trombone, accordion) which was organically linked to the seventy 'sentences' and to the distribution of the words in time. For this structure, I cut down the musical resources as drastically as possible, and chose a relatively flexible notation method for the sequences. This experience served to strip bare my musical writing, filtering out the systems I had hitherto used, and according an active role to silence in the process of composition. I intended the music to be free of dramatic tension and psychological effects: a flow of isolated chords and sound events, with minute variations of tone and intensity which, without intruding, would underlie the text just sufficiently to lend it musical colouring. As if selecting available objects within a given space, I first chose a group of chords, and then subjected them throughout the composition to gradual transformations and alterations of perspective. I was trying, without seeking a one-to-one correspondence, to respond to a minimal base of semantic elements making up Beckett's text, and to work towards what he himself termed 'ontological reduction'. Whatever attempt there is to fuse word and music must be attributed to the general direction set by Beckett: traces which progressively fade into blankness; elements of meaning which eventually reduce to fragments circling in a void, like converging atoms; an atmosphere of finality which emerges and then irreversibly sets in.

I tried to ensure that the three temporal discourses I was using (sound, word, and light) followed relatively autonomous courses. At first, I had considered instigating a vocabulary of vocal events which would intervene to disturb the contributions of both the instrumentalists and the choir members. These vocal phenomena—only just perceptible—would include sounds emitted through closed lips, breaths, tongue-clickings, lip-smackings, and mutterings; this would provide possibilities for transition from voice to instrument. In the end, I cut these out, so that nothing would interfere with the essential restraint of the text, and so that the vocal emission would remain focused upon a rigorous enunciation of the words.

I had also imagined that I could play upon the relationship between hearing the text at a remove, and hearing it direct: most of it would be pre-recorded, but there could be a play of time-lapses between the words broadcast over the loudspeaker and those which would be delivered live. I envisaged, too, that some superimposing effects could be achieved, and that I would then take up again a group of key words, making a kind of whispered interior monologue which would mix from time to time with the spoken sentences. My conversations with Beckett quickly persuaded me to give up this idea, and to aim for a greater simplicity, which would lend the project all the more intensity.

Following our first meeting, we decided that there would only be a transfer from vocal to instrumental at the moment when the two phonemes *bing* and *hop* occurred. According to Beckett, the 'bings' sprinkled throughout the text are like signals which aim to prompt a question, a change of mind, a brainwave, an interior light; they are like a tic, a nervous reflex, a shock, the image of a begging eye (that of a woman, probably), a memory.

It was desirable to isolate these 'bings' which imply that silence is dead and that an impulse is gathering pace; in order to bring them into prominence, we would contrive a period of suspense before each of their appearances.

The first time it intervened, the 'bing' would be simultaneously played and pronounced, so that it could be identified in relation to the title. Instrumentally, the 'bings' would be rendered each time by a cello pizzicato.

The 'hops' indicate a change of angle, or of the degree of orientation in space, the text suggesting a fixed stare which never takes in either

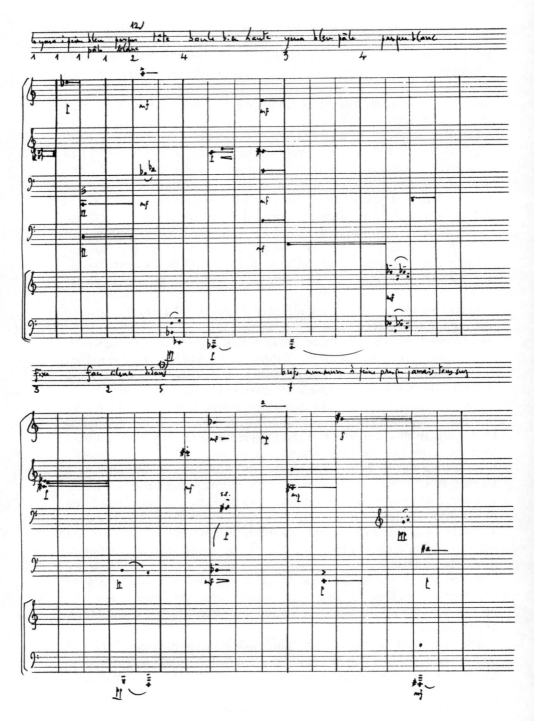

Fig. 18.1 *Part of the manuscript score of* Bing

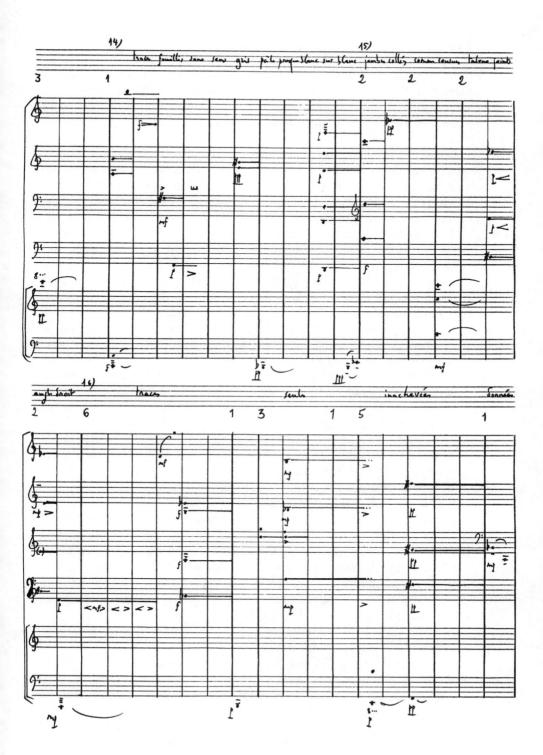

floor or ceiling. Whereas the 'bings' would suggest more of a movement at right angles, the 'hops' would prescribe a diagonal movement, which in fact changes nothing, since the four surfaces of the space suggested are identical. Each 'hop' would be translated into a trombone glissando.

Beckett suggested that a seventh person, standing apart from the others, but illuminated like them, should be added to the six voices who were to share the reading of the text. This person would somehow give meaning to the vocal group, since the impression would be given that the other voices were all sounding inside his head. He would wear a mask, and would be the first to appear and the last to disappear. Moreover, while in general the lighting was to remain low (a white light), this person would be rather more brightly lit than the others. It would be necessary to tone down any differences between the faces, to neutralize them; a similar uniformity was to be sought in the case of the vocal tones. These would be just comprehensible, 'marginally alive'. Certain key words would emerge from the darkness. The voices would all be pre-recorded. All wearing the same head-covering, the six people who had previously recorded the text would keep their eyes closed. However, as soon as the trombone glissandi corresponding to the 'hop' phoneme sounded, one member of the vocal group would suddenly open his or her eyes. The six participants would be arranged in a row, very close to one another. At the edge of each person's spotlight, another would be just visible, like a shadow. The words would be clearly distinguished but were to be articulated with increasing difficulty, as if brokenly, and there was to be a gradual but noticeable slowing-down of the vocal delivery until it became a mere murmur. The loudspeakers broadcasting the text would be placed at the four corners of the stage.

In the course of a further meeting, the nature of the sextet's contributions in relation to the pre-recorded text became clear; upon hearing their own voice over the loudspeaker, each person was to tighten his or her lips for the duration of the word or phrase, and this would resemble a shudder. Sometimes, a silence in the text could allow the light to concentrate upon the silent face. Every so often, the six participants could mumble barely audible sounds.

A beam of very pale, tentative light, as if emanating from an eye, would fall upon some point in space.

The isolated, masked person would give the signal by raising a finger, and then dropping it onto a percussive instrument; at the moment when his hand was near his face, he would have his eyes wide open, only to reclose them and remain head bowed as soon as his hand dropped. He would go through this procedure three times, with his hand raised and held in the air, as if his memory were momentarily failing him; as soon as his hand reached the light, a fairly long period of silence would ensue; then, at the click of his finger, the process would recommence.

Finally, he would resume his original position for about five seconds, while the light began to fade and the text came to an end, by itself.

This is the form in which *Bing* was presented at the Maison de Culture in Grenoble, on 15 May 1981, with set design by Patrick Brunel, the cooperation of seven amateur actors, and the participation of the group 'Intervalles'.

The most delicate problem in this production was to ensure that the complexity of the lighting arrangements did not distract from the basic sparsity of the text, and that the changes in lighting, indicated with the precision of musical notation, as well as the splitting-up of the phrases across the six voices, should shed any mechanical association and assume a certain directness and simplicity.

Following the performance, I discussed these difficulties with Beckett, who seemed to share my fears, and suggested, under the circumstances, a much clearer solution: one which might constitute a second version of this 'musicalized' interpretation of *Bing*.

The text would be pre-recorded by a solo voice (at that point, Beckett had in mind Roger Blin). When Beckett read it to me, I realized that his reading contained the elusive qualities of purity and of a kind of ingenuousness, but he never allowed me to record his voice. The voicer would be mixed in with the musicians, who would be positioned very closely together. The lighting, concentrated upon the space occupied by the performers, would be blue-grey, and would then gradually lose all trace of colour as it turned pure white and intensified slightly. This would be an alternative route towards total blankness. The text implies, in effect, that the eyes should progressively lose their colour, and the walls their marks and traces, so as to culminate in whiteness.

Punctuated with a few meetings with Beckett, this work on *Bing* represented for me an experience of gradual erasure. Within this dynamic of reduction, the creative act becomes a process which is not simply simulating complexity by means of formal devices, but is, rather, living that complexity from within.

19

Working with Beckett Texts

Melanie Daiken

I could talk of my childhood and theatre and the early days, when my father and mother, Leslie and Lilyan Daiken, visited Paris time and again for Sam's new productions. My father had been part of the Trinity College group—Leventhal, McCarthy, Beckett—of the Dublin literary circle of the 1930s. Sam insisted on financing their trips: such was his generosity to his friends. 'Sam is a saint,' said my mother. When my father died suddenly at the age of 52, in 1964, I made a long summer visit to Ireland, travelling our old verdant haunts of Wicklow, Bray, Dun Laoghaire, and cycling round the whole of Dublin in a fervent attempt to imbibe my father's spirit, to imbue myself with his character, to immerse myself in the childhood playground of his *Circular Road*.[1] Once, I lost my route at Windy Arbours: it turned out to be a mental asylum and I wrenched myself away. I read all the books that Sam had presented to my parents, and so Sam and my father and Ireland became engrained in my soul for ever. Later, teaching at Goldsmiths' College, I was asked by its Head of Music, Stanley Glasser, to write a piece for a summer concert. It seemed natural to want to work with 'Echo's Bones', from the *Poems in English*. It started life as *Band Music*, and later I gave it the ironic name *Gems of Erin*.

There were thirteen short movements for woodwind, brass, piano, and percussion, and yet *Gems of Erin* had no singer. For, with or without this protagonist, musical syntax can evoke verbal language through a number of correspondences and at a spectrum of levels. From wide concept to tiny intuition, from an overriding mood to the nuance of a shudder—(Bluebeard's 'shadow of a sigh', as in Bartók's *Bluebeard's Castle*)—from global atmosphere to local scapes, from ideas to images, from colour to the stress and pulse of words, music can exaggerate, heighten, magnify, double, triple, or quadruple the sensation of a thought by a sort of creative amplifying. And, all the while, it can avoid the limitations of a 'reading in/with music' that Boulez rightly

---

[1] This was the title of a radio play by my father. First broadcast by the BBC in 1959, it contained autobiographical material about his life in Dublin.

dismisses as restrictive, talking about his work *Pli selon pli*.[2] See how Fauré deftly conveys with rhythmic patterns the double concept of rocking cradles, rocking vessels, as well as the 'diminishing port' in *Les Berceaux*.

Melody can imitate dialects; harmony can pinpoint emotions; counterpoint can support or negate by the cleverest musical psychology, creating lateral thinking, spinning several trains of thought at once. In opera, especially with one's own libretto, music and text become truly one, grafted together, interacting with little links and episodes and longer interludes, with the composer controlling the subtlest detail of stage action, costumes, lighting, and scenic design. Schoenberg knew the fun of it in *Die glückliche Hand*, and Wagner above all knew the temptation and the power of *der Gesamtkunstwerk*. I remember Sam directing the San Quentin players in *Fin de partie* at the Riverside Studios not long before his death—and what care was in his ballet of directions. Much of Beckett's work is music itself: *Waiting for Godot* is operatic repartee; *Lessness* creates development through miniscule block forms like Messiaen's *Neumes rythmiques*; *Not I* is an elaborated rondeau. Thus, for much of Beckett's work, the addition of music could be redundant, spurious, a liberty. But read the stanzas of 'Echo's Bones', of *Quatre poèmes*, of 'Saint-Lô'—and dare to adorn them as I have done with their own secret music as a snapdragon envelops a bee, to present them with a mirror of themselves, in homage to the dear man, to understand them, to enter and express the space between their utterances.

GEMS OF ERIN (1975): FOR WOODWIND, BRASS, PIANO, AND PERCUSSION

The 'Introduction' of *Gems of Erin* is concerned with the general metre of the poetic lines. Thus eight heavy downbeats per phrase correspond to eight heavy downbeats per stanza. A leitmotiv is presented in two of its manifestations—*inflessibile* for the vulture 'dragging his hunger', *dolce* for the life waiting to be created. The two merge in the third mocking stanza.

'Exeo' traces the inflections of the words with an effect of massed bugles as the poet tears himself out of the Portobello Nursing Home and plunges off between *creatures* (navvies on the Grand Canal, an ancient cripple scuttling, children 'acting the maggot' in a ganzy-field, a bevy of

---

[2] See Pierre Boulez, translated by F. Aprahamian, with recording of *Pli selon pli* (CBS 72770), BBC Symphony Orchestra conducted by Pierre Boulez, 1969: 'It strikes me as too restrictive to limit oneself to a kind of "reading in/with music"; from the point of view of simple understanding, this will never replace a reading without music, which remains the best way of being informed as to the contents of a poem.'

heroes after 'a pint of nepenthe', their hurley over and done). These are coloured by short episodes of woodwind and percussion and vivid, vitriolic *scapes* (of fetid wind, sullen mountains, doomed Liffey, a spew of sewers, that country, that everlasting city) done in cadenza explosions on the piano, with split seconds of lyricism on the saxophone. The 'bleeding meat' of a hoarding hurls forth an existentialist slogan, and to end the number the band struggle into feverish *stretto* to express the surreal.

In 'World', *parlante* horn serves to convey zeugmas of the earthy—'give us a wipe for the love of Jesus'; the spiritual—'veronica mundi | veronica munda'; the crazy—'heart in marmalade | smoke more fruit' and the compassionate—'the old heart the old heart | breaking outside congress'. 'Dawn' is an abstraction, a concept, a flash of Death. Death was in the poet's mind: his own mother's. Flute and vibes personify the radiant and benign, while double bass and horn render a single protest. 'Dusk' is all atmosphere and idea-painting. *Lied*-style is chosen for the classic beauty of 'she royal hulk'; little slurred cadences create the image of 'a scroll, folded'; *aus der Ferne* is the 'thin K'in music of the bawd'. 'Bicycle', a wind quintet, works with sound moving spatially, following the motion of 'tires bleeding' on a scenic cycle jaunt around the outer precincts of Dublin city. Within cliché phrases as lyric as Burns's songs—('all the livelong way', 'with the green of the larches', 'breasting the swell', 'shed a tear')—past and present lose their dimensions. 'Happy Land' is a collage, leaping savagely from literal to metaphorical, from rudeness to reverence, from hymn-tune-become-jive to one famous Dublin ditty (that of 'Molly Malone'). A Schumann adagio is torn to pieces. In 'Ireland', there are no word-rhythms in the music, but merely symbols: a debauched anthem does for England's grandeur, a well-tried folk-tune for the classic prayer of the expatriate Irishman drowned in nostalgia. I changed the sequence of this poem and the next so as to set up the beginnings of musical panic and the encroaching end.

In 'This Clonic Earth', the slow centrepiece of the cycle, the poet watches the mountain Croagh Patrick giving birth to spring. Warm brass utterances express the writhing verdure, an Edith Piaf song on pitched percussion and piano provides the background. It is a rich fairytale, a proud lullaby of the maudlin and the sublime. 'Ska', a Jamaican reggae-variant (and, in particular, the 1960s song 'Up Orange Street', by Prince Buster [Campbell]) uses genre to create a mood of vandalism, decay, and eros; 'plush hymens on your eyeballs' swoops out from Joyce's *Ulysses*. This number is hell-bent, and, within its blaring chorale, sanity jousts with doom.

'Malacoda' is about the aura of the ceremony of Death's day and the rituals of the hearse. Reeds intone the words, while a Purcell flute tune

Fig. 19.1

soars and sinks in a skitter of *enlèvement* and *abaissement* towards 'Redeem', a glassy number, a cutting of eternity. My imagination lighted on the image of a wind pelting across a snowy cemetery at Hither Green, with a nether train whining miles away down a field of fresh-dug earth and thin poplars. A forest of diminutive embellished chapels beckoned beyond, sweet bowers for new voyages. A woodwind race across furrows of hornpipes, brass leer. In the 'Conclusion', five beats of 5/4 in the music correspond to the poem's iambic pentameter; a five-line stanza equals a five-bar section. Ruthless is the staggered brass of the 'vulture' theme, the vortex of *piano moto perpetuo*, the asylum's 'muffled revels', the eternal ceilidh tune.

Gems of Erin was performed at Goldsmiths' College and at the Royal Academy of Music in 1986 (See Figure 19.1).

QUATRE POÈMES (1995): FOR CLARINET, VIOLA, AND PIANO

Much later, the Kegelstatt Trio invited me to write a piece for their concert at St John's Smith Square. I thought of sketches for clarinet and voice that I had made years earlier—along with some settings for girls' choir. All were Beckett texts, still unfinished. I saw that I could enlarge them into a study of Dieppe, with its shingle-shores, its summer rain, the engulfing wave, a fairground ditty. I could speak in my music of Mathieu in Sartre's *L'Âge de raison*, of *L'Étranger* by Camus, of some of the pain of existentialism and of some of the fortitude of the Resistance. *Quatre poèmes* were again to be 'songs without words'; but Ben Payne, the viola player, had the idea that I should read each poem before its setting, and at the first performance I felt it worked well. Thus the format became reading, instrumental presentation, and commentary, not unlike Boulez's approach to the form of 'Le Marteau sans maître'.

In the first poem, 'dry', the viola 'speaks' in octaves for resonance and the clarinet echoes, following the exact rhythm of the words. The commentary that follows is a limpid song-melody on B♭ clarinet, accompanied by viola 'drones' and the soft footsteps of the piano, each phrase inflecting differently towards a null end. In the second poem, 'lyrical', the viola 'sings' the exact motion of Verlaine's rain falling gently on the rooftops of Paris in 'Ariettes oubliées'. A mournful commentary reaches a dark core. The third setting lunges straight into stormy seas: annunciation of the poem, commentary, and cadence are welded into threefold phrases for bass clarinet, marked *appassionato*, *ruvido-parlando*, and *calmo, claro*. The range of the piano is huge, all of it at a stroke—seething yellow foam uncovers pellucid stranded turquoise rockpools. A visit to Cornwall with some friends, the Murails, opened up vistas of the

Fig. 19.2 *Quatre poèmes*

melting-glowering evening sun on Tintagel's coastline, of fairy-tale
rocks out of Wagner's *Der Fliegende Höllander*, jutting mauve out of
the sea, of lush Trelissick gardens shining with dew where river and sea
collide, coincide. The caustic finale—'I would like my love to die'—takes
a children's jingle as its source-idea. The E♭ clarinet, doubled by piano,
chants the text in a sing-song manner, softening somewhat at the inscru-
table end. In a cruel coda, a song of the Resistance—'La Route est
dure'—is twisted into rhetoric by biting blackest clarinet 'in a tin-whistle
style' (see Figure 19.2).

EUSEBIUS (1968–)

However, my most important encounter with Sam Beckett—and thus
Eusebius was born!—was during my studies in Paris from 1966 to 1968.
I remember our first walk down the avenue of statues at Port Royal
towards a restaurant that served us smoked salmon and Muscadet.

(Long had I mooched alone round the Port Royal area, Gare d'Austerlitz, and the Jardin des Plantes, watching the Spanish people and the Moors on their way back to Spain and Tunisia, past the 'Bullier' student restaurant with my Romanian friends, past the Cinématique, the Schola Cantorum, pink in the scalding sun, the little stone fountain, gardens scattered with scanty yellow leaves . . .). We talked about music: I had sent him Haydn's F minor variations and the Schubert late Impromptus, of which he was very fond. Then we would meet from time to time in his apartment in the Boulevard Saint Jacques, overlooking the walls of the 'Prison de la Santé', with its bleeding rags and vomissaries out of Messiaen's *Poèmes pour Mi*. I had sent my libretto to Sam at Ussy-sur-Marne, and he had read it and wanted to talk it through. He liked it, and gave me many ideas and suggestions. I worked on the opera, among other projects, during my studies with Messiaen, and submitted Act I for my second-year Composition Concours at the Conservatoire in March 1968. With very good luck, I had managed to find an excellent tenor, Zwinglio Faustini, from the Brazilian House, and a bass, Bill Mount, from the 'Fondation des États-Unis' of the Cité Universitaire, for my Eusebius and Florestan. I remember making photocopies of chunks of the score in Metro stations as far away as Les Invalides and La Bastille, because they were open at night. I organized the performance with two pianos of Act I in front of Messiaen and Nadia Boulanger, and the jury of the Conservatoire. That summer, May 1968, the student riots started, and the Conservatoire soon dispersed into chaos, along with the Sorbonne. I returned to England from Dieppe to Newhaven much disturbed. The opera *Eusebius* is still 'work-in-progress' and its secrets must await its première.

20

A Note: *Dead Calm*

EARL KIM

Samuel Beckett has been central to my development as a composer. Most of my works which include the voice are based on his texts, taken from various sources—novels, poems, and plays. I identify closely with the beauty and virtuosity of his language in which every detail is reduced to its maximum—only essentials remain.

The following musical example, *Dead Calm* (over page), is a setting of a portion of Addenda (1) of *Watt* which was suggestive of palindromes and silences. It is a part of a larger work entitled *Exercises en Route* which includes excerpts from *Malone Dies*, *Krapp's Last Tape*, and *The Unnamable*.

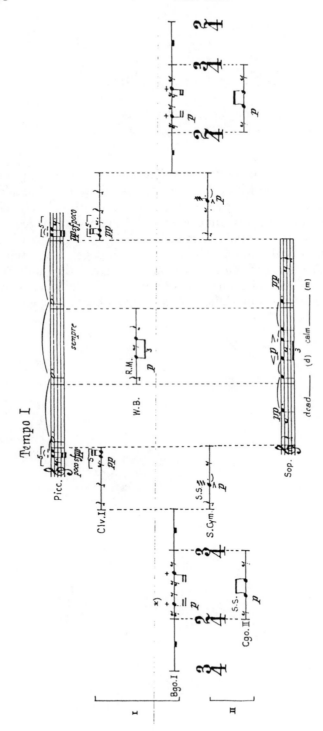

Fig. 20.1 *Page 2 of* Dead Calm. *Reproduced by kind permission of Theodore Presser Company*

Select Bibliography

Books

The following books contain passages which are useful and relevant to the topic of Beckett and music.

BERNOLD, ANDRÉ, *L'Amitié de Beckett* (Paris: Hermann, 1992).

BRATER, ENOCH, *The Drama in the Text* (New York: Oxford University Press, 1994).

COPELAND, HANNAH C., *Art and the Artist in the Works of Samuel Beckett* (The Hague: Mouton, 1975).

FLETCHER, JOHN, and SPURLING, JOHN, *Beckett: A Study of His Plays* (London: Eyre Methuen, 1978, 2nd edn.).

GLASS, PHILIP, *Music by Philip Glass*, ed. Robert T. Jones (New York: Dungaven Music Publishers, 1987).

GONTARSKI, S. E., *The Intent of Undoing in Samuel Beckett's Dramatic Texts* (Bloomington: Indiana University Press, 1985).

HESSING, KEES, *Beckett on Tape: Productions of Samuel Beckett's Work on Film, Video and Audio* (Leiden: Leiden Academic Press, 1992).

KALB, JONATHAN, *Beckett in Performance* (Cambridge: Cambridge University Press, 1989).

KNOWLSON, JAMES, *Damned to Fame: The Life of Samuel Beckett* (London: Bloomsbury, 1996).

MERCIER, VIVIAN, *Beckett/Beckett* (New York: Oxford University Press, 1977).

OSMOND-SMITH, DAVID, *Playing on Words: A Guide to Luciano Berio's Sinfonia* (London: Royal Musical Association, 1985).

WEBB, EUGENE, *The Plays of Samuel Beckett* (Seattle: University of Washington Press, 1972).

——*Samuel Beckett: A Study of His Novels* (Seattle: University of Washington Press, 1973).

WHITELAW, BILLIE, *Billie Whitelaw . . . Who He?* (London: Hodder & Stoughton, 1995).

ZILLIACUS, CLAS, *Beckett and Broadcasting* (Abo: Abo Akademi, 1976).

ZIMMERMAN, WALTER (ed.), *Morton Feldman Essays* (Kerpen: Beginner Press, 1985).

Chapters in Books

ACHESON, JAMES, 'Beckett Re-Joycing: *Words and Music*', in Phyllis Carey and Ed Jewinski, (eds.), *Re: Joyce'n Beckett* (New York: Fordham University Press, 1992), 50–60.

MIHALOVICI, MARCEL, 'My Collaboration with Samuel Beckett', in *Beckett at Sixty: A Festshrift* (London: Calder & Boyars, 1967), 20–2. (Reprinted in

French as 'Ma Collaboration avec Samuel Beckett', *Adam International Review*, 25/337–9 (1970), 65–7.)

Articles

AMIRKHANIAN, CHARLES, 'Pâte de *Pas de Voix*', *Perspectives of New Music*, 26/2 (Summer 1988), 32–43.

BERNOLD, ANDRÉ, 'Cupio dissolvi: note sur Beckett musicien', *Détail*, 3–4 (Winter 1991), 24–34.

CATANZARO, MARY, 'Musical Form and Beckett's *Lessness*', *Notes on Modern Irish Literature*, 4 (1992), 45–51.

DUX, PIERRE, 'De la musique avant toute chose', *Revue d'esthétique*, special number on Beckett (1986), 271–3.

FOURNIER, EDITH, '*Sans*: cantate et fugue pour un refuge', *Lettres nouvelles* (Sept./Oct. 1970), 149–60. (Reprinted as 'Samuel Beckett mathématicien et poète', *Critique*, 46/519–520 (Aug./Sept. 1990), 660–9.)

FROST, EVERETT, 'Fundamental Sounds: Recording Samuel Beckett's Radio Plays', *Theatre Journal*, 43/3 (Oct. 1991), 361–76.

GABURO, KENNETH, 'The Music in Samuel Beckett's *Play*', *Review of Contemporary Fiction*, 7/2 (Summer 1987), 76–84.

GAVARD-PERRET, JEAN-PAUL, 'A bout de souffle, ou le silence en plus', *Les Temps modernes*, 584 (Sept./Oct. 1995), 186–201.

GRIM, WILLIAM E., 'The Developing Variation in Samuel Beckett's *Molloy*, *Romance Studies*, 11 (Winter 1987), 47–52.

GRINDEA, MIRON, 'Involved with Music' (editorial), *Adam International Review*, 25 (1970), 337–9. (Theme of issue: 'Four Writers and Music: Bernard Shaw, André Gide, Samuel Beckett, David Gascoyne'.)

LEES, HEATH: '*Watt*: Music, Tuning, and Tonality', *Journal of Beckett Studies*, 9 (1984), 5–24. (Reprinted in S. E. Gontarski (ed.), *The Beckett Studies Reader* (Gainesville, Fla: University Press of Florida, 1993), 167–85.)

LONSDALE, MICHAEL, 'Un précurseur du théâtre musical' (Interview with Raymonde Temkine), *Revue d'esthétique*, special number on Beckett (1986), 255–9.

MEYER-THOSS, Gottfried, *Facetten des Transluziden*, *Musik-Konzepte*, 48–9, special number on Morton Feldman (May 1986).

PARK, ERIC, 'Fundamental Sounds: Music in Samuel Beckett's *Murphy* and *Watt*', *Modern Fiction Studies*, 21/2 (Summer 1975), 157–71.

SENNEFF, SUSAN FIELD, 'Song and Music in Samuel Beckett's *Watt*', *Modern Fiction Studies*, 10/2 (Summer 1964), 137–50.

SKEMPTON, HOWARD, 'Beckett as Librettist', *Music and Musicians*, 25/9 (May 1977), 5–6.

VOUILLOUX, BERNARD, 'Tentative de description d'une écriture sérielle: sur une séquence de *Watt*', *Poétique*, 91 (Sept. 1992), 259–72.

WAI-ON, HO, 'Music for Sotoba Komachi and Journey', *Contemporary Theatre Review*, 1/2 (1994), 162–83.

WARRILOW, DAVID, 'La Musique, pas le sens' (Interview with Valérie Lumbroso), *Revue d'esthétique*, special number on Beckett (1986), 251–3.

WORTH, KATHARINE, 'Journal de *Cascando*' (trans. from English by Bernard Turle), *Revue d'esthétique*, special number on Beckett (1986), 267–8.

ZURBRUGG, NICHOLAS, 'Interview with Philip Glass', *Review of Contemporary Fiction*, 7/2 (Summer 1987), 101–7.

Music

In the constantly changing field of musical composition and publishing, a comprehensive listing would be unattainable. The selective listing given below normally contains the basic information of composer's name, title of work, date of work, and the Beckett text or texts to which it relates (if the latter is not clear from the title of the work).

AMIRKHANIAN, CHARLES, *Pas de Voix* (1987) (prompted by Beckett's writing).

BARLOW, CLARENCE, *Textmusic for Piano 6* (1973) (*Ping*).

BARRETT, RICHARD, *Fictions* (11-part cycle, written during the 1980s, and relating to a wide range of Beckett texts).

——*Invention 6* (1982) (*Company*).

——*Coïgitum* (1983–5) (*All Strange Away*).

——*Ne songe plus à fuir* (1985–6) (*Molloy*).

BARRY, GERALD, *Lessness* (1972) (now withdrawn).

——*All the Dead Voices* (1974–5) (*Waiting for Godot*) (now withdrawn).

BECKETT, JOHN, *Act without Words I* (1956) (now withdrawn).

——*Words and Music* (1962) (now withdrawn).

BERIO, LUCIANO, *Sinfonia* (1968) (*The Unnamable*).

BOSSEUR, JEAN-YVES, *Bing* (1980–1).

BUSSOTTI, SYLVANO, *Winnie dello sguardo* (1978) (*Happy Days*).

CHRISTIANSEN, HENNING, *3 Beckett-sange* (1976) (poems).

CROWDER, HENRY, *From the Only Poet to a Shining Whore* (1930) (poem) (published in Henry Crowder, *Henry-Music*, The Hours Press, 1930).

CSAPÓ, GYULA, *Krapp's Last Tape* (1982).

DAIKEN, MELANIE, *Gems of Erin* (1975) (poems).

——*Quatre poèmes* (1995).

DODGE, CHARLES, *Cascando* (1978).

FELDMAN, MORTON, *Elemental Procedures* (1976) (Beckett quotations).

——*Neither* (1977).

——*For Samuel Beckett* (1987) (instrumental ensemble piece to celebrate Beckett).

——*Words and Music* (1987).

FORTNER, WOLFGANG, *That Time* (1977).

GIACOMETTI, ANTONIO, *Reliqua* (1982) ('Mirlitonnades').

GLASS, PHILIP, *Play* (1965).

——*Cascando* (1975).

——*The Lost Ones* (1975).

GLASS, PHILIP, *Mercier and Camier* (1979).

——*Company* (1984).

GNAZZO, ANTHONY, *Ping* (1975).

HAUBENSTOCK-RAMATI, ROMAN, *Credentials: Or, 'Think, Think, Lucky'* (1961).

——*Play* (1967).

HESPOS, HANS-JOACHIM, *Blackout* (1972) (dedicated to Samuel Beckett).

HOLLIGER, HEINZ, *Come and Go* (1977).

——*Not I* (1979–80).

——*What Where* (1988).

HOPKINS, BILL, *Musique de l'indifférence* (1965) (ballet after Beckett's poem of same name).

——*Sensation* (1965) (poems).

——*En attendant* (1976–7) (*En attendant Godot*).

JANSSEN, GUUS, *Zonder* (1986) (*Lessness*).

KIM, EARL, *Exercises en Route* (1961–70) (*Malone Dies, Krapp's Last Tape, The Unnamable*).

——*. . . Dead Calm . . .* (1961) (Addenda in *Watt*).

——*They Are Far Out* (1966) (*Malone Dies*).

——*Gooseberries, She Said* (1967) (*Krapp's Last Tape*).

—— *. . . Rattling On . . .* (1970) (*The Unnamable*).

——*Narratives* (1973–6) (various texts).

——*Earthlight* (1973).

——*Footfalls* (1981).

——*Now and Then* (1981) (various texts).

KRAFT, WILLIAM, *Cascando* (1988).

KURTÁG, GYÖRGY, *What is the Word?* (1990).

McINTOSH, MICHAEL, *Watt* (see Reading University entry below) .

MAIGUASHCA, MESIAS, *Lindgren* (1976) (*Krapp's Last Tape*).

MANZONI, GIACOMO, *Parole da Beckett* (1971) (various texts).

MARSH, ROGER, *Bits and Scraps* (1979) (*How It Is*).

MIHALOVICI, MARCEL, *Krapp, ou la dernière bande* (1960–1) (*Krapp's Last Tape*).

——*Cascando* (1963).

——*Fifth Symphony with Soprano* (1966–9) (poem).

OSBORNE, WILLIAM, *Hamm* (1981) (*Endgame*).

—— *Winnie* (1983) (*Happy Days*).

—— *Words and Music* (1983).

——*Etude* (1986) (*Rockaby*).

RANDS, BERNARD, *Memo 2* (1973) (*Not I*).

REYNOLDS, ROGER, *Ping* (1968).

——*A Merciful Coincidence* (1976) (*Watt*).

——*Odyssey* (1989–93) (poems; *Texts for Nothing IX*).

RHYS, PAUL, *Not I* (1995) (commissioned by Annenberg/Beckett Fellowship, Reading University, and premièred at Reading University on 9 Dec. 1995; recording held in Reading University Library).

RIJNVOS, RICHARD, *Radio I* (1991) (*Rough for Radio I*).

SEARLE, HUMPHREY, *Words and Music* (1973).
——*Cascando* (1984).
STEENHUISEN, PAUL, *Between Lips and Lips There Are Cities* (1993) (Beckett quotations).
TARICCO, GIORGIO, *Elegia II* (1991) ('Echo's Bones').
TURNAGE, MARK-ANTHONY, *Your Rockaby* (1993–4) (*Rockaby*).
WAI-ON, HO, *Journey* (1991) (various texts).
WILKINSON, MARC, *Voices* (1958–9) (*Waiting for Godot*).

Items of Musical Interest in Beckett Collection, Reading University Library (accession number given where appropriate)

Sound: Cassette recording of Morton Feldman's *Neither* (MS 3327).
Cassette recording of Paul Rhys's *Not I*.
Master copies of production recordings, made at the University of London Audio-Visual Centre, of *Words and Music* (1973), and *Cascando* (1984), with music by Humphrey Searle.
Scores: Crowder, Henry, *From the Only Poet to a Shining Whore* (MS 3055). Photocopy of sheet music (3 leaves), The Hours Press.
FELDMAN, MORTON, *Neither* (349.139). Universal Edition, hardbound, presented to Reading University by Samuel Beckett.
FORTNER, WOLFGANG, *That Time* (349.138). Schott, hardbound, signed with a dedication to Samuel Beckett (1977) by the composer, and presented to Reading University by Samuel Beckett.
HAUBENSTOCK-RAMATI, ROMAN, *Credentials, or 'Think, Think, Lucky'*. Universal Edition.
HESPOS, HANS-JOACHIM, *Blackout*. Edition Modern, hardbound, signed by the composer, dedicated to Samuel Beckett, and presented to Reading University by Samuel Beckett.
McINTOSH, MICHAEL, *Watt* (MS 3324) (Opera with libretto by Donald Riley Grose).
MIHALOVICI, MARCEL, *Krapp* (MS 1227/7/10/2). Original manuscript notebook of the French, English, and German texts, with vocal score. Front cover bears the signature of the composer, with a note that the notebook is being donated to Reading University Library.
WILKINSON, MARC, *Voices* (MS 3205). Universal Edition, softback.
Other: FELDMAN, MORTON, *Neither*:
MS 3076: Photocopy of Beckett's typescript of *Neither*, with the note 'Feldman text' at the head of the page, in Beckett's hand.
MS 3033: Folder containing material relating to *Neither*, including reviews and correspondence.

Index

Note: Italics are used for titles of texts by Beckett. Where a Beckett text, and a composer's setting of that text, have an identical title, that title is indexed only where the original Beckett text is under discussion. Composers are indexed under their own names.